HUNGRY

CRYSTAL RENN

with Marjorie Ingall

SIMON & SCHUSTER

New York   London   Toronto   Sydney

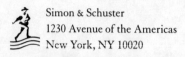 Simon & Schuster
1230 Avenue of the Americas
New York, NY 10020

First Simon & Schuster hardcover edition September 2009

SIMON & SCHUSTER and colophon are registered trademarks
of Simon & Schuster, Inc.

For information about special discounts for bulk purchases,
please contact Simon & Schuster Special Sales at
1-866-506-1949 or business@simonandschuster.com.

The Simon & Schuster Speakers Bureau can bring authors
to your live event. For more information or to book an event
contact the Simon & Schuster Speakers Bureau at
1-866-248-3049 or visit our website at www.simonspeakers.com.

Designed by Helene Berinsky

Manufactured in the United States of America

10   9   8   7   6   5   4   3   2   1

Library of Congress Cataloging-in-Publication Data
Renn, Crystal.
   Hungry / Crystal Renn with Marjorie Ingall.
      p.   cm.
   Includes bibliographical references.
   1. Renn, Crystal.   2. Models (Persons)—United States—Biography.
3. Overweight women.   I. Ingall, Marjorie.   II. Title.
   HD8039.M772U569   2009
   746.9'2092—dc22
   [B]   2009022748
   ISBN 978-1-4391-0123-0

To Mom, for her endless love, patience, and support.
No daughter could ask for more.

CONTENTS

HUNGRY

INTRODUCTION

This is a story about two pictures.

The first is a photograph of the supermodel Gisele. Taken by the photographer Steven Meisel, it appeared in *Vogue* in 2000. Gisele is in a clingy white gown, posing in a studio against a seamless gray backdrop. Her skin is golden and gleaming. Her hair is windblown, as if she's been surprised by a breeze from an open window just out of view. Her hands, her eyes, the curve of her back—everything is graceful and expressive. She's mesmerizing.

I was fourteen years old when I saw that picture. It was the first time I'd ever leafed through a copy of *Vogue*. I'd never cared about any fashion magazine; I'd looked at that one only because a man I'll call The Scout had handed me a copy. He was working for a major modeling agency—let's just call it The Agency—in New York. His job was to troll the back roads of America, visiting junior high schools and suburban malls, in a ceaseless quest for the next top model.

I had never met anyone like The Scout before. He was urbane and kind, smooth-talking yet sincere. I was dazzled by his shirt. Tailored to perfection, it was probably more expensive than my entire wardrobe. When he opened *Vogue* to Gisele's picture, he knew exactly what he was doing. He was planting a fantasy. In the few seconds it took me to absorb all of Gisele's beauty and allure, I'd constructed a new idea of female perfection. It was Gisele.

That's when the Scout said, "This could be you."

And even though I was only fourteen and weighed sixty pounds more than Gisele and had all the sophistication of a girl from Clinton, Mississippi, population twenty-three thousand, I believed The Scout.

The second photograph is from 2007. It shows the naked back of a curvy woman, her dark hair curling into tendrils at the nape of her neck. Her body is half draped in rich red fabric. She's gazing off into the distance, lit from the side in a soft northern light. She looks like a Greek goddess or an Old Master painting—a Vermeer, a Titian. There's an eye-catching weightiness to her. As she leans slightly to her right, two modest folds of flesh collect at her waist. (If you were a snarky sort, you might call this lush abundance "back fat.") The picture was taken by photographer Ruven Afanador for the Breast Cancer Research Foundation. It was a public service ad, designed to look timeless but also of the moment. The objective was to show beauty and strength, to offer hope of a healthy future for all women. It ran in every major women's magazine, from *Vogue* to *O* to *Bon Appétit* to *Prevention*. The woman in that photograph is me.

Hungry is the story of how I got from the first photograph to the second.

A straight line may well be the shortest distance between two points, but for me, the journey from the first picture to the second crossed continents and set the numbers on my bathroom scale spinning backward and then forward like a time-lapse sequence in a 1930s black-and-white melodrama. The interim was a time of triumphs and humiliations, a jagged line of drastic weight loss and brushes with fame and success and failure and emaciation and eating disorders, until I finally said: Enough.

I started to eat. I stopped churning mindless circles on an elliptical cross-trainer for seven or eight hours a day, my arms and legs jerking like a marionette's. I stopped obsessing about chewing a single stick of sugar-free gum. I got heavier. I put on pounds by the dozen and leap frogged dress sizes—from 00 to 12. But I honestly didn't mind the weight gain and the loss of my matchstick limbs. I made a choice to stop starving.

Here's the strange part: Call it crazy or ironic or simply perfect justice, but when I stopped starving myself, my career took off. That was when I shot five international editions of *Vogue* and the covers of international editions of *Harper's Bazaar* and *Elle*. That was when I starred in Dolce & Gabbana's ad campaign. That was when I worked the runway as the final model in Jean Paul Gaultier's prêt-à-porter show in a gauzy, breathtaking, form-fitting fairy-tale dress covered in an explosion of tissue-paper-thin silk flowers. That was when I appeared on *The Oprah Winfrey Show*. That was when I became the highest-paid plus-size model in America. That was when I became a favorite model of the man who took that amazing picture of Gisele in 2000: the great Steven Meisel. And I did it all at the weight my body wanted to be.

I was hardly alone in my descent into weight obsession and madness. Five to ten million Americans have eating disorders. A 2005 study found that over half of all teenage girls and nearly a third of teenage boys use unhealthy methods to try to be thin, such as skipping meals, fasting, smoking cigarettes for the express purpose of losing weight, vomiting, and taking laxatives. Even women without clinical disorders spend a heartbreaking amount of time obsessing about their weight, hating their bodies, and thinking that if they were only thinner, their lives would be richer, fuller, happier.

I'm the embodiment of the truth that it doesn't have to be that way. You can learn to love the size you're supposed to be. I had to lose seventy pounds (along with lumps of hair, muscle mass, the ability to concentrate, and any sense of joy) before finding my sanity. I regained the weight and, in the process, became an infinitely more successful model. My self-acceptance led to a return of the intellectual curiosity I'd had as a child, before I got on the weight-loss express. It led to a better career. It led to romance. I'm proof that life doesn't have to wait until you're skinny.

HUNGRY

1

WE ARE FAMILY

find it! I find it!"

Like an ecstatic little pinball, I ricocheted around our Miami backyard in search of Easter eggs. Striped ones! Sparkly ones! Color-washed ones in the blues and greens and purples of Monet's water lilies! I'd triumphantly seize an egg hidden in a glazed stoneware flowerpot or in the crook of the sea grape bush and shriek with joy, plunging it into my already overflowing basket. There seemed to be an endless supply: Eggs were behind the bayberry bushes, nestled in the fronds of the staghorn ferns that filled our terra-cotta planters, peeking out from under the birds-of-paradise in the flower beds. My mom and grandma, giggling, replenished them as quickly as I could scoop them up. I was oblivious to their sneaky helpfulness. I was three years old, and all I knew was that there was an infinite supply of glittery prizes. When I was exhausted, I sat in Mom's lap in the cool grass, carefully sorting my piles of jelly beans, marshmallow Peeps, bright foil-covered eggs, and chocolate bunnies.

I loved Easter. But then I loved being in the backyard all year 'round. To me, it was a fairyland even when it wasn't teeming with gold and silver eggs. We had our own pool surrounded by feathery fishtail palms, pink-flowered bougainvillea trees, and hanging orchids. When I was two, Grandma held me in the water and taught me to breathe through a straw. I was a water baby, enrolled in swim classes at the University of Miami at twenty-six months. I loved splashing in the water with Grandma or just playing in the yard by myself. I had tea parties with imaginary friends, scattered Pogs (brightly painted little discs every kid seemed to collect in the halcyon days of the early nineties) in the grass, chased dragonflies, and caught tiny green frogs. I had my own wooden swing set—I'd always try to swing high enough to see the ocean only a few miles away.

If you'd seen me swinging into the sky, making tiny bouquets for the fairies out of bougainvillea blossoms or lying on my back watching the clouds, you'd never have thought: When that girl is fourteen, she's going to hate her body so much, she'll nearly kill herself to change it.

Back then I was blissfully happy. Mom and Grandma created a world for me—filled with books, songs, games, and egg hunts—in which I felt serene and secure, the center of the universe. I enjoyed being with them, but I also enjoyed my solitude. When I was small, I never felt the absence of my "real" mother.

I knew Mom wasn't actually my mother; she was my grandmother. I knew Grandma wasn't actually my grandmother; she was my great-grandmother. But I called them Mom and Grandma because that was who they were to me.

My birth mother—we'll call her Lana—was a teenager. She was the fourth of Mom's six kids. Let's just say she was absent for much of my childhood. I'm not comfortable going into Lana's story. It's not my story. Her demons were different from mine.

My story is this: Lana dropped me off at her mother's when I was three months old. I was a preemie, and tiny. No one knew who my father was. I was quite sick with a bronchial infection. I couldn't turn over. My head was totally flat in the back from spending all my time lying in a crib, staring up. I had major intestinal problems. My motor skills were terrible. "You were like a little vegetable," Mom says now.

Lana had told Mom she was going away for a few days, but weeks passed and she didn't come back. That may sound sad, but it was a blessing, because that's how I became Mom and Grandma's little girl. They'd talked it over and decided that when Lana returned, they'd ask her if they could have custody of me. But since Lana was flat-out gone, Mom got an adoption lawyer, went to court, and became my legal mother. I was three months old. She'd already raised her six kids to adulthood and wasn't expecting to have a seventh at her age, but when the need arose, she stepped up. She was my North Star—she was how I learned to navigate the world. Sparkling, steady, and always there, she gave me room to soar and to make my own mistakes. To me, she'll always be Mom.

At first Mom spent a lot of time with me at the pediatrician and at the physical therapist. She did all kinds of exercises with me; putting me on my belly so I'd develop muscles in my neck, bicycling my legs, dangling toys above me so I'd reach for them. Eventually, my motor skills developed. I gained weight, and my head lost its flatness.

Mom was always matter-of-fact about who Lana was; she never lied to me. And she never gave me more information than I could handle. When I was little, she said simply, "Your mother couldn't raise you because she was too young when you were born, and I was so happy when you came to live with me." For a few years, that was all I needed to know. Mom was Mom, and Lana was a very young woman who occasionally visited, shifted uncomfortably on the living room couch, then disappeared again for months.

I know now how much Mom grieved about Lana's absence. But when I was little, she never shared her agony with me. She created a beautiful life for us, surrounding me with comfort and glamour. Mom loved ornate things. She drove a pink Cadillac, a testament to her prowess as one of Mary Kay's top saleswomen. A brand-new pink Caddy appeared in our driveway every couple of years. The walls in our home were covered with big oil paintings in carved, gilded frames—no insipid pastel seascapes or *Miami Vice*–meets-nail-salon posters for her. The house was full of gold-leaf house-plants, a huge lamp shaped like a heron, sinuous Egyptian art, intricately filigreed antiques about which I invented colorful ghost stories and secret histories. That chest was smuggled out of Russia by the fur-clad daughter of a czar; this bureau belonged to a noble-woman in a powdered wig in some ancient French court.

Mom had come a long way from her childhood as a self-described hillbilly from Tennessee. She'd lived in a succession of southern cit-ies as her dad, a chemical engineer, moved from job to job. When she was in her late teens, the family settled in Connecticut, where Mom got married too young and had two kids. After her divorce, she up and moved to Florida "because it was warm and because it wasn't Connecticut." To support her children, she worked in a fancy beauty salon as a receptionist, modeled for the showrooms of the Miami International Merchandise Mart, and wound up performing in dolphin shows at the Miami Seaquarium. "I'd never even swum underwater or touched a dolphin," she told me, "but I've always been a don't-put-me-in-an-office kind of girl!" She was beautiful, and the Seaquarium folks could tell she was smart. She learned fast, developed a real rapport with the dolphins, and became one of the attraction's most popular performers. "They built me an underwa-ter tank with an air hose," she recalls, "and I was photographed un-derwater, swimming with Carolina Snowball, the only albino porpoise in captivity, for *National Geographic*."

That *National Geographic* shoot must've gone *really* well: Mom wound up marrying the underwater cameraman. She quickly joined him in his business; her intellectual curiosity and innate smarts helped her pick up both still and motion picture underwater photography skills. Together they shot the underwater footage for such shows as *Wild Kingdom* and *American Sportsman,* as well as for a Frank Sinatra movie called *The Lady in Cement* (in which Frank goes hunting for one of the many treasure-filled Spanish galleons sunk off the coast of Florida in 1791; during one dive, he finds a beautiful woman at the bottom of the sea, her feet encased in cement. A mystery ensues. It always does). Mom and the cameraman had four more kids, but that marriage was as ill fated as her first. Mom desperately wanted it to work. She had six kids to support. But after twelve years of ugliness, even Mom's kids were begging her to dump the guy, and eventually, she did.

That was when she got into selling Mary Kay. Our fleet of pink Caddies was proof of how good she was at her job. She supported not just her own children but other family members off and on as well. When her mother, Frances, was diagnosed with breast cancer, Mom moved Frances in with her.

Four years after her second divorce, Mom got married a third time. You can probably predict how this story ends. That marriage dissolved, too. "Now it's three strikes, I'm out," she told me, stroking my hair. "But I couldn't be happier with the life I have." That life wasn't always easy, taking care of her own children, her mother, and then the grandchild who was foisted on her, but she lived it with such grace.

Sometimes I played in her home office as she did inventory and made phone calls, listening as she worked her sales magic. I quickly learned to mimic her sweet ultra-southern phone manner. *"Hiiiiiiiiii!"* I'd trill in a high-pitched Tennessee-tinged baby voice. Mom was peaches and cream on her telephone sales calls. She would turn her accent on and off like a faucet. As part of her sales pitch, it was astonishingly effective. She always seemed to know exactly what her clients yearned for. Did a particular customer want to be younger, entice her distracted husband, feel more glamorous, take time out of a dreary day to feel treasured and pampered? Mom could zero in on her customer's secret desires and make the act of shopping feel like therapy. "Mary Kay is like an honorary degree in psychology," she told me modestly. Mom always understood that beauty makes people feel good. I don't think it's coincidence that I, too, grew up to be someone who sold the fantasy of beauty. It wasn't until much later that I learned how beauty could be a double-edged sword.

Grandma loved pretty things as much as Mom did. She collected Asian and Egyptian art, and she relished the beauty of words. She'd studied at Columbia and Rutgers, spoke several languages, and would read to me for hours. All that said, she was a little intimidating. Before her illness, she'd been a teacher for highly gifted children with emotional and developmental issues. By the time I came along, her cancer was in remission, she had a ton of energy, and I became her next big educational project. While Mom sold Velocity moisturizers and Facial Highlighting Pens, Grandma turned her considerable focus on turning me into a well-read, well-socialized young lady.

Grandma was like Mary Poppins—from the books, not the movies. She was brisk and efficient, very stern, with the tiniest hint of twinkle. She always wore skirts and dresses; she didn't own a pair of jeans. Her huge collection of white gloves—Mom laughed that she kept wearing them long after everyone else stopped—were a staple in my dress-up trunk. From infancy on, Grandma had me working on eye-hand coordination, diction, music appreciation, good manners, and most of all, literacy. Just like Mary Poppins's, her lessons took. By the time I was four, I was reading on my own. At seven, I devoured *Charlotte's Web,* poring over it again and again, making myself weep melodramatically at the loving, unconventional family Wilbur found in the barnyard. When I cast the book as a movie in my head, Grandma played Mrs. Arable. I was Wilbur. Mom was Charlotte, weaving together many lives and saving mine.

In third grade, I read *Romeo and Juliet* and *Hamlet.* (I'd heard people talking about Shakespeare being an important writer, so I thought I'd get a jump on reading him.) I finished both plays, though I wouldn't say I fully understood them. Still, I was steely in my determination to power through. I hated to give up. Once I was done, I decided I could leave Shakespeare alone until high school, when I'd probably know more words like "gibber" and "bodkin."

Even before I could read, I was full of questions. Mom tells a story about when I was maybe fifteen months old and starting to put sentences together. She and I were driving to the supermarket.

"Trees are big," I announced from my car seat in the back. "There are green trees and trees with flowers."

"That's right, honey," Mom said absently, turning the wheel.

"There are big trees and little trees."

"There sure are," Mom answered.

"Who makes trees?"

"God makes trees."

"Who is God?" I asked.

Mom, gulping, explained that God was a force that set the universe in motion, creating all life on earth and allowing people to make choices. The answer didn't satisfy me.

"That's not who!" I said. "Who is? Who is?" My voice started to rise in pitch and urgency. "That's not who! That's not who!" I wailed.

Distressed and frustrated, Mom pulled over. She turned around to look at me over the back of the driver's seat. "I don't understand what you're asking or what you want me to say," she told me gently.

Through my tears, I looked into her eyes and replied, "I don't have the words to tell you, Mom!"

Mom loves telling this story to anyone who'll listen, as an example of how my teeny mind worked and as an illustration of how challenging it was for her to deal with my ontological dilemmas. I wish I could remember what was causing me such agita! I know only that I had huge questions about the universe from a ridiculously early age, and twenty-two years later, I'm still trying to find answers.

Another time, when I was three or four, we were driving past the cemetery on the way back from ballet. (Because of her concern about my early, stunted physical development, Mom kept me in a constant stream of muscle-building activities such as gymnastics, softball, and dance.) "Who is in the ground there?" I'd ask. "How do they get there? What is dead? How do you know they are dead? Is it like asleep? Where do the souls go? What is heaven? Are there stairs? Does each dead person have a star?" Once again, my existential anxiety was rearing its head. Mom finally stopped driving by the cemetery. She'd drive ten minutes out of her way to get back from ballet because she'd run out of metaphysical answers for me! Still, I kept on asking questions. Then and now, whether I'm struggling with epistemology or a decision to buy a pair of Ann Demeulemeester boots, I'm obsessive and single-minded.

Mom and Grandma respected my questions about the nature of being. They were churchgoers with a strong faith in God. I loved the ritual of dressing for church—and the suspense about which of Grandma's many kooky vintage hats she would wear—as well as the pageantry, the shiny wood of the pews, the pretty hymns. We didn't go every week, more like once a month, but I was never a kid who whined about having to go. Mom let me bring my Pogs, and I'd quietly sort and study them in the pews during the boring parts.

Once, when I was five, an unfamiliar woman approached Mom

after the service. "Excuse me," she said. "Have you ever thought about getting your daughter into modeling?" She proferred a card.

Mom, ever polite, took it. "No, thank you," she said sweetly, turning to continue her conversation with Mrs. Canella from down the street.

"Are you sure?" the woman interrupted insistently. "We're always looking for great child models."

"Quite sure," Mom said with finality and a smile. And then, in her inimitable way that brooked no further argument, she changed the subject. "I declare, I just love your hat. Wherever did you find it?"

Mom never made a big deal about my looks. Thanks to her experience doing floor modeling at the Miami International Merchandise Mart, she wasn't seduced by some abstract notion of modeling as an inherently thrilling, self-esteem-boosting profession. Unlike some moms of kids who model, she didn't have churned-up, unexamined desires to have her child crowned the fairest of them all. Her sense of self wasn't tied up in my being perceived as beautiful.

I knew Mom loved me. I knew she thought I should dress nicely, comb my hair, and display good manners. But she never rhapsodized about my prettiness in front of me. I was unaware that other people thought the way I looked was anything special. I knew I was the tallest kid in kindergarten; I knew that even though my early development had been stunted, I'd caught up fast under Mom and Grandma's ministrations. My pediatrician told Mom he thought I'd grow to be six feet tall. (Alas, if only he'd been right. My agency would be beyond thrilled if I were three inches taller!) I knew that sometimes the other moms cooed about my long, curly brown hair, wide-set dark eyes, and olive skin. I knew I didn't look anything like Mom, with her clear green eyes and pale skin. But those were observations, not value judgments that were central to my identity. My looks never really meant anything to me.

I was a happy kid, despite my tendency to dwell on the mysteries of the universe. I was not a wide-eyed Keane painting or a deadpan little character from a Tim Burton movie. I had a wild imagination and roving gangs of imaginary friends. I had a white-canopied fairy-tale bed, my own small TV on a white wicker stand, and plenty of input into how I wanted my bedroom decorated. At five, I chose a leopard-print comforter (my love of animal prints has stayed with me to this very day) that I adorned with a huge menagerie of stuffed animals. I was indulged but not spoiled. I loved to play dress-up. I had a trunk full of vintage slips, one of Mom's red nightgowns I kept "liberating" from her dresser, a selection of Grandma's old-fashioned hats. My favorite was a truly hideous veiled turquoise number from the 1950s. The myriad aunts, uncles, and cousins who came to visit always admired my imaginatively lunatic outfits.

But even when I was very young, my obsessive streak was evident. Exhibit A: my unending questions about the nature of existence. Exhibit B: my need to amass an inhuman number of Pogs. I also collected snow globes, Beanie Babies, bottle caps, stamps, and a menagerie of Tamagotchis that all went dark and died (I filled a drawer with their tiny electronic corpses). I went through a yo-yo phase during which I got yo-yo books from the library and practiced for hours. My yo-yo finger developed a blister, which sounds like a euphemism but isn't.

Many years later, I read that anorexia is often correlated with obsessive-compulsive disorder. (The connection between anorexia and OCD is much stronger than any connection with bulimia or binge eating.) Thanks to my own purely anecdotal experience, I believe there's a link. My collecting obsessions bordered on mania and were vital to me; I had extraordinary discipline about them for as long as my engagement lasted. Any article you read about anorexia (and believe me, I've read most of them) talks about how it's tied to issues of control and achievement. In my own experience, these fierce drives all came together.

Some armchair psychologists might also suggest that a yearning for my birth mother or the grief at being rejected by her were what detonated my future problems with anorexia. Those people would be wrong. My problems derived from a perfect storm of factors, but none of them triggered by my childhood.

This isn't to say I wasn't troubled by my relationship with Lana. By the time I was five, I was dwelling on the mathematical problem of how this woman I barely knew could be simultaneously my mother and not my mother. Mom was my mother. Lana was the person whose body had made me. What did the word "mother" really mean, anyway? I wasn't sad, precisely, but I was confused.

Mom was hyperalert when Lana came over. Sometimes Lana was exuberant and huggy. Other times she was monosyllabic and hollow-eyed. She never stayed long. At some point—Mom and I aren't sure when—Lana came back to Miami, sought help for some of her troubles, and moved into a trailer park across town.

One day when I was five and a half, Mom sat me down in the living room and told me we were going to visit Lana.

"There's going to be a baby there," she told me. "Lana had a baby. You have a half sister."

My mind reeled. I had a sister? Some of my friends had sisters. Would she live with me? Would we get a bunk bed? Could I give her a bottle? Would I have to share my toys? Would she be smelly when she pooped?

"Lana has a husband now," Mom went on. "His name is Trip." I studied her face for clues about what I was supposed to feel. I looked to the kitchen doorway, where Grandma leaned against the doorjamb, one eyebrow raised. I sensed that she wasn't happy. Was she mad at Lana or at Mom for telling me about Lana? I liked to please; I wanted to make the right face. Should I try to look excited or serious?

Mom buckled me into my car seat, and Mom and I pulled out

of the driveway. From inside the screen door, Grandma watched us go.

We drove to the other side of Miami. The tidy flower-bed-surrounded ranches of our neighborhood gave way to hulking warehouses and crumbling housing developments. We pulled into a trailer park. Tacked-up plywood covered the windows of several rusting old trailers. Stained, cracked concrete slabs with crabgrass poking through the jagged scars marked the spots where long-gone trailers had once stood. Mom held my hand as we made our way through the LEGO-like maze of blocky structures. There stood Lana, holding open a door, her eyes clear and shining. A chubby, burbling ten-month-old baby was on her hip.

Mom and Lana made small talk as I sat on the floor, playing with the baby. We stacked blocks. Or rather, I stacked them and the baby knocked them over. The baby found this hilarious, and I loved hearing her laugh. The baby's name was Angelica. She had huge blue eyes. They were heavily lashed, like my eyes and Lana's, and she had our arching brows.

A man was there, too. That was Trip. He was very tall, with broad shoulders and salt-and-pepper hair. His face was ruddy and rugged, with a fine network of burst capillaries across his nose and cheeks. I wasn't terribly interested in him, or in Lana, for that matter. I viewed my birth mother the way I did my piano teacher or my pediatrician—as someone you have to see because someone else decrees it. But I hoped I'd get to see the baby again.

We stayed for a half hour or so, then Mom stood up, rubbing her hands briskly. "Time to go, honey," she said to me. I kissed Angelica goodbye and rubbed her nose with mine. She giggled. I was proud that I was so good at making her laugh. I kissed Lana with the same sense of duty I always did, then somberly stuck out my hand to shake Trip's. He took my little hand in his big one, amusement in his eyes.

As we drove home, my thoughts raced. "Is the baby going to live with us?" I asked Mom. "No, hon," she replied.

That meant the baby was going to stay with Lana and Trip. Mom had chosen me, but she wasn't going to choose this baby. If the baby was my half sister, was Lana my half mother? I wasn't distressed, just baffled. I twisted various queries over and over in my head like a Rubik's cube, but ultimately, I chalked everything up to the mysteries of adult behavior. It wasn't until I got a bit older that I needed solid answers.

In 1992, when I was six, everything else took a backseat to the forces of nature. Hurricane Andrew came to Miami. As the very serious TV newsmen droned on about Dvornak numbers and circulation centers, I followed Mom around the house while she moved the porch furniture into the garage, took down the hanging plants, closed all the shutters, and checked the batteries in our emergency-preparedness kit. I helped by self-importantly wheeling my bike into the garage. Some of our neighbors fled the city for higher ground, but Grandma, ever deadpan and ever amused, thought they were being great big drama queens. The sky darkened. At eight, my bedtime, the windows were starting to rattle.

Mom crouched down to my level and told me with great enthusiasm that Grandma and I were going to have a sleepover. She moved us into the back bedroom, the guest room, because she thought it was the safest in the house. It had only one window, and there were no trees nearby that could fall on it. Grandma got the daybed. Mom piled up a bunch of blankets on the floor for me. This was an adventure. "You can play Princess and the Pea!" she told me. She pretended to slip a pea under the bottom blanket. Thrilled, I cuddled up with my toy guinea pig, innovatively named Guinea. Grandma read me two chapters of *The Cricket in Times Square,* and I fell asleep as I always did, repeatedly rubbing one spot on Guinea's flank with my thumb.

Overnight, Hurricane Andrew blasted South Florida. It was the second most powerful hurricane of the twentieth century, a Category 5 storm with peak gusts of at least 169 miles an hour.

Though Mom had sealed off every other room in the house, she'd forgotten to cover the air conditioning unit in the guest room wall. The rest of the house was cooled by central air, but this one small outpost still had a window unit, and the driving rains poured though it. Grandma and I slept through it all. When Mom came in to check on us at around five A.M., she found me, still in my nest on the floor, curled in an inch and a half of water.

The South Coast was devastated. At least sixty-five people died— probably more, since it was impossible to account for all the migrant workers in the area. The hurricane cost around $27 billion in damages. A quarter of the trees in the Everglades were destroyed. Fortunately, except for some serious damage to our roof, we were all fine. No one in our extended family was hurt or killed. But we were without electricity for three months, and all of our neighbors came by to get water from our pool to flush their toilets.

Years later, when I was glued to the news footage of Hurricane Katrina, I felt as if history were repeating itself. I remembered the government's slow response to Andrew as I watched all the disaster footage while sitting next to Mom on the couch. Back then Dade County's emergency management director exclaimed on national TV, "Where in the hell is the cavalry on this one? They keep saying we're going to get supplies. For God's sake, where are they?" President George Herbert Walker Bush did send in relief after that. But a decade later, Katrina was even more devastating than Andrew, and the younger President Bush's response made his father's reactions look timely and generous.

As Miami (as well as the the rest of Florida and Louisiana) picked itself up, dusted itself off, and started to rebuild, I went back to work, too. I was in first grade at the local public school, which I loved. Until third grade, school was a cinch for me. I loved the feeling of a perfectly sharpened pencil and the sight of a clean notebook page. I loved our class trips to the school library. I felt warmly toward all books, as if they were friends. I didn't make much distinction between Corduroy, my stuffed bear, and *Corduroy,* the book: They were equally real, warm-blooded, and loving to me.

I loved school supplies. This was nearly my downfall. A few months after the hurricane, Mom happened to take me to Get Smart, an educational supply store that sold accessories for teachers. The moment we walked in the door, I saw the clouds part and heard the angels sing. I was surrounded by enticing "Good job!" stickers, colored chalks, rubber stamps, hole punchers, plastic pots of glitter. It was straight-A-student paradise. I was hypnotized. I couldn't restrain myself. When Mom's back was turned, I grabbed two big handfuls of erasers with smiley faces and stuffed them into my pockets. Unfortunately, I forgot to take them out that night. When Mom decided to do laundry, she came into my room, picked up the hamper, took it to the washing machine, and promptly found a hundred or so erasers in my pants. The next day she took me back to the store and made me give back the erasers and apologize to the owner. I was mortified. That was my last brush with theft.

However, it made Grandma take notice. From her experience in teaching very bright kids with learning differences, Grandma had figured out that I had attention deficit and hyperactivity disorder. I didn't fit the stereotype of kids with attention issues—I was never disruptive, loud, or fidgety. But Grandma felt that those erasers could be an indication of a problem with impulse control that had the potential to get worse. And she worried about my distractibility. She knew I could be a laser beam when I wanted to be. She also knew that my brain was perpetually whirring and my attention could dart about like a hummingbird.

I'd get so distracted by a butterfly passing the classroom window that I'd stop hearing the teacher's voice. I perpetually had a million ideas going at once. If a teacher didn't engage me completely, forget it. She might as well have been one of the adults droning in a *Peanuts* cartoon. And when I was bored or distracted, I was a dithery mess. I was always exhausted at the end of the day; the sheer effort of staying on task or, conversely, letting go of a task I was obsessed with required Herculean strength for me.

So in the spring of 1993, Mom and Grandma took me to a neurologist who agreed with Grandma's ADHD diagnosis. He put me on the lowest dose of Ritalin. The change was unbelievable. I could focus on my schoolwork instead of daydreaming about what would have happened in *Matilda* if one of her parents had been nice. When I was supposed to be doing math, I could keep all my attention on sums instead of simultaneously wondering who was inside the sarcophagus at the Bass Museum, how long it would have taken him or her to decompose, and what he or she might have looked like as her eyeballs were disintegrating. (I liked pondering decomposition. Maybe I did have a little bit of Tim Burton inside me.) Ritalin helped me compartmentalize and to stop the interference in my brain. It made life easier, and I think it made me less obsessive in general.

We were in a good place, Mom, Grandma, and I. When I think of that time, I think of coming home from school to delicious smells. My great-grandmother was an unbelievable cook—she made all kinds of veggies and meats, stuffings and desserts. She made artichokes with special dips; when I was a baby, I was already able to pull the leaves from an artichoke one by one and scrape off the flesh with my teeth. Mom's friends always thought it was hilarious when she served me an artichoke on a china plate while I was still in a high chair. I was never the kid who wouldn't eat lima beans or recoiled in horror at okra—I loved everything.

My favorite after-school snack was cream cheese and marmalade on raisin bread, which seemed sort of elegant and English to me.

Grandma was supposedly descended from English nobility on one side—perhaps that was where her proper posture and diction came from. Eating marmalade and scones and cucumber sandwiches made me feel like a character in a children's book. Grandma was supposedly part Cherokee on the other side (hmm, maybe that's why I was olive-skinned when everyone else in my family was so pale), but she didn't seem to know anything about Cherokee food. I'd read in a children's book about the Trail of Tears, when the Cherokees ate raccoons and squirrels, so I decided not to ask her to explore that part of our heritage, at least not at lunchtime.

Mom was a fine cook, too, if less adventurous than Grandma. She loved to bake, and she was great at it. Her specialty was an angel food cake with royal icing. When I was small, I thought it looked like a beautiful castle. With the golden glaze dripping down the sides, it seemed like something a princess would have after her four-and-twenty-blackbird pie. I'd start salivating, Pavlov-style, the minute she took that special pan out of the cupboard. My other favorite dessert of hers was a lot less pretty, but it sure tasted fine. It was pecans, canned cherries, cake batter, and buttloads of butter all dumped in a pan; and it went by the appetizing name of dump cake. It had to be the unhealthiest thing you could eat, but oh my, it was a jumble of paradise in a Pyrex dish. I loved to help her make it. In the mornings, even on school days, Mom would make croissants with jam or blueberry muffins. I liked mine split in half with a slab of butter in the middle, then put back together like a sandwich. She always made sure I had fruit in the mornings before school. She was a big "It's the most important meal of the day!" person, a one-woman public service campaign.

My favorite errand was going to Gardner's, one of the oldest and fanciest gourmet shops in Miami, which had an amazing bakery. Mom let me pick out whatever I wanted. We'd get their perfect croissants, and she'd serve them for Sunday breakfast. She'd split one in half for me and put a pat of butter between the sides, and I'd nibble and peel off the flaky exterior until I was left with a wad of butter-saturated dough. Another favorite treat was Gardner's key lime cake, a round, pretty delight made with fresh key lime juice, so it was moist and tart and sugary all at once. I also loved the black-and-white half-moon cookies, even though I only liked the vanilla side. Gardner's was the only place I knew that carried them. When I first moved to New York and discovered that black-and-white cookies were sold at almost every deli on almost every corner, I knew I'd found the place I was destined to live.

Of course, when I first moved to New York, I wasn't eating at all. That would pretty much make me Tantalus in the ancient Greek myth. You remember him—the guy they named "tantalizing" after. Punished by the gods, he was condemned to spend eternity standing in a pool of fresh water under a branch dripping with fruit. Whenever he bent down to drink, the water would recede; whenever he reached up to pluck a fruit, the branch would rise out of his grasp. To belabor a metaphor, those damn black-and-white cookies were my punishment from the gods of anorexia. Sitting in their plate-glass windows and waxed-paper nests, they taunted me with their untouchable sweetness every time I walked by on my way to a casting.

But that was later. When I was a child, food held no terrors for me, only pleasures. I loved the rituals of mealtime. We always had nice dinners on china plates; Mom thought it was uncivilized to eat standing in front of the fridge or on the run. It was all about the southern sit-down, socialize, don't-be-a-heathen meal. Occasionally, we'd go to fancy restaurants. I was always proud to step out with my glamorous mom and dignified grandma. We dressed for dinner. Grandma wore one of her dainty hats; my slender and graceful mom wore one of her many brightly colored suits; and I wore a dress with a sash or a skirt and round-collared blouse. I wasn't the fidgety kid desperately swinging her legs under the table, blowing the paper off her straw into the head of the person in another booth, or whinily ordering plain pasta with butter or chicken nuggets in an elegant *boite*. I knew how to behave, and I ate what Grandma and Mom ate. I tried to keep my culinary adventurousness under wraps at school, though. No one else ate marmalade or artichokes. For lunch, I had Mom make me peanut butter and jelly every day. Peanut butter was awesome, don't get me wrong, but I was also becoming increasingly aware of how mean kids could be. I didn't want to give anyone any fuel for teasing me, especially since I didn't have a conventional family like other kids.

When I was seven, everything changed. Grandma died.

There was no warning. There was no slow decline. On April 1, 1993, she said, "I have a stomachache." She never complained, so the fact that she mentioned feeling ill was uncharacteristic. It must have hurt a lot. Concerned, Mom asked her, "Do you want to go to the doctor?" In her perpetually amused, clipped tone, Grandma brushed the suggestion off.

I wasn't worried. I knew Grandma had been sick before I was born, but her breast cancer had been in remission for as long as I'd known her. And my attention was elsewhere. Mom had told me that morning that we were going to stay in a hotel for a few days while the house was being tented for termites. I loved hotels. I was thinking about Eloise at the Plaza and about room service. Mom drove me to school and dropped Grandma at the hotel.

My uncle Donnie, Mom's brother, picked me up at school that afternoon. I loved him but was surprised to see him—Mom or Grandma always picked me up. Was there a problem with the termite people? "Grandma's in the hospital," Uncle Donnie told me gently. Mom was with her.

Uncle Donnie and I played Go Fish and Old Maid and War in the hotel room. It was April Fool's Day. I'd thought of a prank to play on Mom—I'd gotten my art teacher to give me some white crepe paper, and I was going to wrap up my arm and tell Mom I'd broken it at recess.

Uncle Donnie and I ate dinner together in front of the hotel room's TV. Somehow room service wasn't as much fun as I'd hoped, even though my ice-cream sundae had come with an assortment of little glass bowls of candy and sauces to dump on top.

Mom came at bedtime to tuck me in. She had shadows of exhaustion and fear under her eyes. She kissed me, straightened the covers around me, and brushed aside my questions about Grandma. "She's very sick," Mom said. "The cancer has moved into her bones and her liver."

"Will she get better?" I asked.

"We can pray, honey," Mom answered. She went back to the hospital.

The next afternoon after school, Mom walked into the hotel room. Donnie and I were playing cards on the bed. I took one look at her face and I knew.

"She never woke up," Mom said. "I never got to say goodbye."

I cried, but Mom didn't. I never, ever saw her cry. Perhaps after everything she'd experienced in her marriages, and after everything Lana had done, she didn't have tears left.

A few nights after Grandma died, she appeared in my room. It was late at night; moonlight danced across my bed. She was sitting in lotus position, which was pretty astonishing, since she'd been old and stiff and rotund in life, not exactly a nimble yogini. She was glowing as if backlit, and she gave me a smile. I knew she was telling me she was all right and that Mom and I would be, too.

Perhaps Grandma's death was what lit a tiny spark of longing in me. I wanted more family. I wanted to see Baby Angelica again. Only a couple of weeks after Grandma's death, Mom told me that Lana had given birth to another girl. "Can we see her?" I asked.

"Now's not a good time, sweetie," Mom answered. Shortly after that, Lana and her new family moved to Mississippi. I wondered what the new baby looked like and if I'd ever get to meet her.

I often thought about Angelica's life with her new sister. Was it hard to be a big sister? Did Angelica and her baby share a room? Did the whole family still live in that same trailer but in another state? Did they pull the trailer from Florida to Mississippi, and if so, did Angelica ride in the car or in the trailer? Did she remember me at all? And now the hint of a new question: Did Lana ever wish she had three daughters instead of two?

Mom kept me too busy to dwell on such questions. Grandma was gone, but Mom was determined to follow her educational and physical development program for me. I had to keep taking piano, and Mom continued to search out athletic pursuits that might engage me. She never forgot that I'd lagged behind my peers in muscular development as a baby, and she wanted to make sure my coordination continued to improve.

So when I was in third grade, she enrolled me in a martial arts class. I was immediately smitten. By age eleven, I was a brown belt in Chinese Kenpo. I danced with a fan, spun with the bo staff, swung the three-section staff. While other girls dreamed of majorette batons, I was whirling nunchakus—two sticks connected at the ends by a chain—in perfect arcs. I imagined myself a ninja, doing upside-down flips off walls and engaging in covert assassination-type activities. (I wasn't exactly sure who I would assassinate, but I was ready for the assignment.) The sensei's studio felt like home to me. Sensei could be a little scary; when the boys didn't listen, he'd shoot at them with a loaded BB gun. But he didn't shoot at girls.

The nunchakus were my favorite weapon. In fourth or fifth grade, I was ranked first in Florida in nunchakus in my age group— I won a six-foot trophy that towered over me. I studied other weapons, too: metal whip, fan, double fan, bo staff, sword, throwing stars.

(Geeky boys always get excited when I tell them I studied the throwing stars. I think it taps in to some primal anime or *Star Trek*kian longing.)

Mom came to every exhibition and match. As I practiced at home, she gave me the blessing of her full attention, letting me jabber on about why the *sansetsukon* was made of maple instead of teak and why I was frustrated by my inability to execute a loud crisp *crack* when I snapped my fan during a wushu dance. "Well, that is just fascinating!" she'd say. I sincerely doubt any of it was even mildly fascinating, but she made me feel, as she always did, that my passions were worthwhile. "I cannot *believe* you remember all those steps!" she'd exclaim, shaking her head. "You are just so graceful!"

I would beam and work harder.

Martial arts held my interest in a way nothing else had. I enjoyed both the discipline and the performance. I loved feeling all eyes on me during my katas—dances with martial arts. I knew I was good. I loved the feeling of control and mastery over my body. The adrenaline I felt was a bit like what I would experience years later during runway shows: Both were about showing beauty and strength in motion. When I was ten, my desire for control wasn't yet the monster it would become when I was sixteen and anorexic.

Kenpo was what I needed. It was a release from grief after Grandma's death. It was a locus for my tendency to obsess. I discovered just how competitive I could be. I loved the sweat, the movement, the combination of strength and grace. I felt completely in touch with my body, confident in what it could accomplish. Years later, in the depths of my sickness, I found it hard to believe I ever could have trusted and loved my body that way.

Lana, who hadn't come to Grandma's funeral, began to visit now and then from Mississippi, looking healthy and happy. I played with Angelica and her new sister, Brianna. We never had any warning about when they'd show up, and they never stayed as long as I wanted. I started to imagine myself as a stepsister in a folktale. Lana wasn't the wicked stepmother, but she was the master who had all the control. I couldn't ask her to come, and I couldn't make her stay. I didn't want her to take me with her when she and her daughters left, but I felt a stone in the pit of my stomach when I watched the car drive away.

One day when I was nine or so, Mom and I were driving home from school when she suggested casually that I might want to talk to a clinical psychologist. "That's a person who is an expert in feelings," she said. "Grandma always thought that one day you'd have some sad or angry emotions that you'd want to discuss with someone outside the family."

I don't remember much about the first appointment. I recall feeling that Debra, the lady in the leather chair, was trying to pull sentences out of me. She was fishing. I had to clamp my mouth shut to keep the quicksilver words from escaping. I wrapped my arms around my knees and stared at the coffee table, at the soothingly patterned box of Kleenex I didn't need. "Sometimes it takes a while for the emotions to come out," Debra murmured afterward to Mom as I waited impatiently by the door.

After the second session, I decided it was okay to tell Debra that I was a little confused about who my family was. She taught me the word "biological." We talked about how it was okay to feel seemingly contradictory feelings—love and loss, attraction and anger— at the same time. Suddenly, something clicked. I sailed out of the office into the waiting room, where Mom was sitting with a magazine. I planted myself in front of her, put my fists on my hips, and announced, "I've got this all figured out! Lana is my biological mom, and *you* are my real mom, and that's the way it is. I'm finished. I'm all done." I was delighted with this solution. If Lana was not in fact my real mother, I had nothing to be tormented about. If Angelica and Brianna were Lana's daughters, they were not my real relatives.

They were just people we saw every few months. They were nothing to be confused about. QED.

Since I was very good at talking myself into things—five years later, I effortlessly talked myself into starving—I was satisfied with my solution. I had a gift for compartmentalizing. I shoved my confusion about Lana and her family to the dark shadowy corners of my consciousness for several months.

Mom continued to make sure I knew I was loved. Every Friday night, we rented a movie at Blockbuster and watched it while we ate microwave popcorn. It was our ritual. I'd put my head in Mom's lap, and when the movie ended, she'd run her nails along my back, up and down, up and down, until I fell asleep. Mom was never a big fan of TV, but on Saturday mornings, she let me watch *Sailor Moon,* my favorite cartoon. The protagonist is an ordinary schoolgirl who discovers she has hidden powers.

When I grew up, I decided, I'd become an astronomer, as familiar with space and the planets as Sailor Moon was. I papered the walls of my room with posters of the solar system, stars, and asteroids. I drew pictures of the planets and imagined discovering a new one. Then again, maybe I'd go to Yale and become a lawyer. (I'd seen a movie in which someone smart went to Yale. I looked up America's best law schools on the Internet, and Yale's name kept coming up). I'd fight injustice like Sailor Moon, but with a briefcase instead of a talking cat and thigh-high red boots. Maybe I'd be an astronomer *and* a lawyer.

Thoughts about the family I didn't really know kept intruding on my fantasies. I thought about defending Lana in a court of law, or wearing a stylized sailor suit and tossing my blond superhero locks as I rescued Angelica and Brianna from a burning house.

The psychologist told Mom that I was idealizing Lana and my siblings because of their absence. Well, duh. I remember sitting in

Debra's office wailing, "I want to live with both Mom *and* Lana!" Of course, that was impossible.

In distress, I started to act out more. I'd promise to take out the trash, then fail to do it. I hung out with kids in my class who were less than stellar students, who laughed too loudly and didn't do their homework. Mom didn't yell at me. She always treated me like a rational person, asking me to talk about my feelings. Maybe because she'd already raised six kids, she was unshockable.

My teachers were not as patient. By fourth grade, I was openly rolling my eyes at any authority figure I thought was stupid. I started to talk back in class. I still got A's, but I was developing a swagger my mom didn't like. So when I was in fifth grade, she took me out of public school and put me into an evangelical Christian academy. That was a mistake.

I immediately disliked the school's emphasis on the many ways one could go to hell. I didn't like hearing about the vast numbers of sinners who were destined to go Down There for being, well, not like the teachers at the school. A partial list of the doomed included Jews, Muslims, atheists, people who read the book that was sweeping the country about a Satanist named Harry Potter, Hindus, people who listened to Marilyn Manson, people who wore short shorts, people who watched the Disney movie *The Sorcerer's Apprentice,* people who had premarital sex, people who committed adultery, and trick-or-treaters. All were headed for the screaming agony in the fiery flames. Mom had taught me to be respectful to everyone, but at the evangelical Christian school, respect was reserved for true believers.

The question about God I'd had as a tiny child still concerned me. I hoped the school could help me clarify my beliefs. I wondered about God's intercession in human history. Did I believe in a personal God, a God who was an anthropomorphic white-bearded guy on a big throne, or a God who was simply a force or influence on human behavior? I didn't know, but my teachers were confident they had all the answers. If someone suffered, it was because he or she was bad. "But what if he or she isn't bad?" I asked. Well then, God had a plan we couldn't understand.

The messages I got from my teachers didn't enhance my vision of a loving, forgiving God. Mom and Grandma had faith, but they also had tolerance. At my school, these two attributes seemed mutually contradictory. My sixth-grade teacher in particular seemed to enjoy delivering spittle-flecked fire-and-brimstone tirades. Once she went around the classroom asking each kid, "What is your personal hell?" She put her hands on our desks, leaned forward, and looked expectantly into our faces. The boys reveled in devising hideous tortures for the sinners—limbs being slowly pulled off by horses and chains, bodies being burned alive, people being made to eat grenades. That night I couldn't sleep. My brain burned with all the horrors I'd just heard described in loving, luscious, lurid David Cronenbergian detail. Was *I* going to hell for wishing my classmates would be more understanding toward other people's beliefs?

The rules of the school grated on me more and more. Though Miami could get awfully hot, we weren't allowed to wear shorts that came up higher than our fingertips when our arms were by our sides. (Some teachers were more vigilant than others. The cool girls rolled their shorts up and down all day depending on the teacher.) We weren't allowed to wear any makeup, not even lip gloss. If you wanted to use ChapStick, you had to be careful to get the kind that didn't have the slightest tint.

I didn't want to be a shorts-rolling girl. I wanted to be judged for my mind, not my legs. But I was also interested in clothes and the messages they could convey. So I wore huge JNCOs, super-wide, super-baggy jeans that were popular then. Some of them had leg openings as wide as fifty inches—I could have smuggled an entire family of Harry Potter–carrying Jewish Hindu satanists under my hems. I was always the last kid to finish the mile run in gym class, even though I was acing martial arts competitions and was in amazing physical condition from all my Kenpo practice. I suspect I was slowed down by wind drag on my giant pants. I was all air resistance and bad attitude.

I wore my JNCOs with black Vans, like a skater, though I did not skate. I favored long-sleeved black and green velvet shirts, even in 90-degree heat. I wore tons of silver rings and let my hair fall in a curtain that hid my face. Sometimes I wore eyeliner, even though I was sent to the girls' room repeatedly to wash it off. Rumors would swirl that I was a Satanist or a witch. But I wanted to express myself through fashion even then. Clothing can mark you as a member of the tribe, or it can set you apart.

On Fridays after school, I'd put on black nail polish. On Sunday nights, I'd take it off. I was rebellious, but I wasn't an idiot; I didn't want to be sent home to get nail polish remover. I filled my room with candles so I'd look deep and spiritual. But I kept my posters of planets all over my walls. I didn't want to grow up to be a bassist in a Joy Division cover band or to own a mall-based chain of occult stores selling gold-plated pentagrams. I still wanted to be an astronomer.

Mom was patient through my Goth phase. She was always great at picking her battles, deciding when to lay down the law and what to let slide. From day one, Grandma had always told Mom, "Never make a decision for Crysti." (They both called me Crysti. Mom still does; she's grandfathered in on the nickname front. To everyone else, I'm Crystal, and anyone who calls me Crysti goes to hell with the trick-or-treaters.) Grandma had maintained that I was the type of person who needed to make her own way. For that reason, Mom always gave me choices: Do you want to wear this outfit or this one? Should we go to the playground or the pool? She tried to make me feel that I had agency and power even when I didn't. That was anti-thetical to the philosophy of the evangelical Christian academy. We weren't supposed to decide for ourselves. We were good or bad. We were saved or we weren't.

The academy was where I discovered eating disorders. In sixth grade, I made a friend named Cara who was obsessed with her weight. She ate only SnackWell's cookies. I'd never heard of "fat-free cookies" before. At my house, we ate real cake, not these artifi-cial-tasting, cloyingly sweet, crumbly lumps. When you ate my mom's angel food cake or Gardner's key lime cake, you knew you'd had *dessert*. But when you ate one of these cookies, you were hungry again the moment you'd wiped the crumbs from your lips. Cara al-ternated between the vanilla cream sandwich cookies and the choco-late mint cookie cakes. They were all she ate during the school day and whenever I went to her house after school.

Cara's house was huge. Her parents were professionals in high-powered careers, and she felt a ton of pressure to live up to their expectations. She felt that she could never please them. If she got an A-, they asked her why she hadn't gotten an A. But there was one thing she was great at: puking. She had a gift. She and I saw a TV show in which a flight attendant made herself throw up so she could stay thin enough to fly, and Cara got the hang of it immediately.

By sixth grade, most of the girls had learned to talk loudly about how fat and disgusting they were. It was just what you did. It was how you bonded. Many years later, I read a book by an anthropolo-gist named Mimi Nichter called *Fat Talk: What Girls and Their Par-ents Say About Dieting* (Harvard University Press, 2001). In it, Nichter coins the term "fat talk"—the conversation in which one girl says, "I'm so fat!" and another girl rushes to say, "No! You're so skinny! *I'm* so fat!" It's almost a ritual. Nichter says it serves a social purpose. When we engage in fat talk, we're actually soothing each other. We complain about weight as a way to build solidarity with other girls, to ask for reassurance without looking desperate, and to get compliments without having to beg. It's a game like Tag or Duck, Duck, Goose—everyone knows the rules, but none of us remembers learning them.

I refused to engage in fat talk. Whenever a classmate wailed, "Oh, I shouldn't be eating this!" while spooning ice cream into her mouth or plunging her fork into a slice of birthday cake, I'd say brusquely, "Then don't." I didn't understand why these girls were wailing. What was the point in bemoaning what they were doing, but doing it anyway?

Two years later, I'd make their eating behaviors look healthy. But I didn't know that then.

I escaped from the strictures of school into music. I listened to the Smashing Pumpkins, Nirvana, Bush. I listened to GWAR, a hard-core-thrash-punk sci-fi band, even though I didn't like the sound. It just seemed rebellious and raunchy but in a totally safe way. I felt supercool, pretending to like a band whose albums included *Phallus in Wonderland* and whose lead singer was arrested for performing in the South while wearing a "Cuttlefish of Cthulhu" prosthetic penis.

Mom wouldn't let me bring home records with parental advisory stickers; I had to borrow them from my pothead neighbor in secrecy. Scandal! A kid in my class heard from his friend that I'd listened to a Marilyn Manson record, and he informed me that he was sorry I was going to hell. After a long pause, he asked if he could borrow the album.

Once he'd listened to Marilyn Manson, he learned that he *liked* Marilyn Manson. So did a lot of my classmates. The CD made the rounds of fifth and sixth grade; everyone wanted to listen to my neighbor's copy because they sure as heck weren't allowed to buy it themselves.

Then some moron got caught passing it to his friend in the cafeteria. Both boys immediately ratted me out. I was plucked from another table at the caf, marched to the office, and accused of foisting ungodly music on the innocent ears of my classmates.

I got detention. I had to "write lines" like Bart Simpson at the blackboard:

I will not listen to ungodly music.

I will not listen to ungodly music.

I will not listen to ungodly music.

I will not listen to ungodly music.

I will not listen to ungodly music.

One hundred times. I gritted my teeth and kept writing. It wasn't even my album! I consoled myself that at least I hadn't gotten the other punishment: standing in the corner for forty-five minutes with your nose nestled in the angle where the walls met. If you coughed or sneezed, you had to start your time over.

My sixth-grade year had only one highlight: Lana called out of the blue to say that Trip had a meeting in New York City, and did Mom and I want to come? I sure did. I suspect Mom was more ambivalent. But she saw how desperately I wanted to go, so she acceded.

We stayed at Trip's boss's house on the Jersey Shore, a short walk from the beach. While Trip had his meeting, we took a train into the city, went on a tour of Rockefeller Center, and rode a red double-decker bus. The next day we all took a boat tour of New York Harbor, saw the Statue of Liberty, and took the subway to Coney Island, where a bird pooped on Lana. Lana screamed and cursed, but the rest of us laughed, and finally, Lana laughed, too. In the evenings, back in Jersey, we built sand castles on the beach and ate cotton candy on the boardwalk.

There was so much to do, there wasn't any time for awkwardness. Lana and Trip were affectionate with each other. My half sisters treated me like a visiting rock star. When it was time to come home, I got very quiet. I wanted to stay with Lana and my sisters. And Mom knew it.

When we got home, I started an ever quickening drumbeat of "Can we move in with Lana?" I wanted Mom to come, too. I wasn't happy at the hellfire school. I wanted to have a big family. I imagined Mississippi as a paradise banked in hollyhocks and myrtle trees. I appealed to Mom's love of nature. In Miami, our lawn was a science project requiring constant maintenance, and even then the grass was always scratchy. I bet in Mississippi, there'd be infinite rolling, soft, downy green waves. She could have a new garden. She could educate herself about different soil! A change of scenery would be good for both of us. I was relentless.

I could see I was starting to sway Mom. She knew the academy's repressive environment wasn't good for me. And she had concerns about the public high schools in Miami, which were widely regarded as god-awful. The simple fact was this: Miami was a wonderful place for a little girl to grow up, but it wasn't so wonderful for a bigger girl. There were drugs everywhere; there were guns and sex and sleaze. The city in the '80s and early '90s was corrupt. Alex Daoud, the mayor of Miami Beach for much of my childhood, was convicted of bribery. He called Miami "a nonplace populated by rootless people." And I'm sure Mom lived with the perpetual memory of her own daughter's rootless teen years, which must have been a pretty powerful cautionary tale.

But Clinton, Mississippi, was a low-key college town. The public high school was supposed to be good. Lana seemed to have her life in order: a husband with a good job, sweet little girls, and a home of her own, one that wasn't on axles. Her problems seemed to be behind her.

"Okay," Mom said. "We'll give it a try." I'm sure there were behind-the-scenes machinations I wasn't privy to. I don't know whether Lana was thrilled or grudging about this plan. All I knew was: We were in.

I willingly gave up my friends, my sensei, my piano for the privilege of living with Lana. But Mom gave up far more—her home, her primacy as head of the household, her business.

And she did it all for me.

2

ODD GIRL OUT

So when I was twelve, a few months after our successful New York trip, we packed up and moved to Mississippi. I imagined heart-to-hearts with Lana, fishing excursions with Trip, giggly pig piles on a quilt-covered bed with my half sisters, all of us sharing a bowl of popcorn in front of a Disney movie.

It didn't happen exactly that way.

Mom sold our beautiful house in Miami and let go of her Mary Kay. To this day, it's hard for me to wrap my brain around that level of *Giving Tree* generosity. She sacrificed so much for me.

Mississippi isn't what most northerners imagine; a humid, languorous southern landscape of drooping wisteria and Spanish moss, heavy with the scent of gardenia and magnolia. That's the low country; that's not Clinton. Clinton is strip malls and sharp-edged pine trees, crawfish shacks and shooting ranges, tract houses and cookie-cutter developments. It's the Payday loan store and the Wal-Mart and the Froghead Grill. You know it's southern because people say "*in*-surance," with the accent on the first syllable, and because you can't buy beer on Sundays. People talk about Yankees and don't mean the baseball team. The N-word is used liberally. People say "bless her heart" when they mean "fuck her."

Clinton began its life as a trading post on the Old Natchez Trace. It was founded in the early 1800s by Walter Leake, a Mississippi senator and the state's third governor. Like the rest of the state, it was battered by the Civil War and the postwar occupation by Union troops. Gradually, it settled into what it is today: a quiet, not wealthy southern town with a small college campus and generations of long-time residents, both white and black.

Trip had made a good life for his family there. He sold PVC conduit to telecom and utility companies, and though he made money, he was perpetually on the road. The family lived on a quiet cul-de-sac that poked like a broken finger out of a winding suburban street. The house abutted the tip of a lake shaped like a wizard's cap, fringed with pussy willows and Scots pine. It had a faux-brick facade and white vinyl siding. It wasn't fancy, but it was beautiful to me.

That was the outside. The interior was another story. It was chaos.

As Mom and I stepped inside for the first time, holding our suitcases, I heard her sharp intake of breath and felt her stiffen beside me. Piles of clothes and crusty dishes were everywhere. Appliances were broken. Ratty toys, old magazines, and tilting stacks of videotapes littered the floor. The furniture was draped in rumpled, faded sheets. This was a country house—not in the Hamptons sense but in the Spears sense. As in "I don't put my baby in a car seat because I'm country."

Mom and I were determined to make it work. My fantasy of bunking with my half sisters quickly fell by the wayside; they already shared a room, and there was no way a third body could fit in there. Instead, I moved into a tiny alcove down the hall that jutted out of the side of the house like a zit. It had one window that overlooked the neighbor's live oak tree. I filled my room with the stuffed animals I'd brought from Miami, a disco ball, and the collection of brightly colored ritual candles I hoped were magic. I had a small TV and a stereo. I rehung my astronomy posters and draped my star-covered blanket over my new bed.

Mom moved into the garage and spent twenty thousand dollars fixing it up. It looked like a miniature version of our Miami house, elegant but homey. It became my refuge. Mom quickly found a job as a store manager at Chico's, an upscale clothing chain that sold drapey tunics, patterned cotton-flax jackets, and wide-legged linen pants that made everyone look like a middle-aged Gestalt therapist in Berkeley. If it felt to Mom like a step down after owning her own business, she never complained.

I didn't know what was wrong with Lana. Her bedroom door was often closed. She ricocheted between absence and hovering, sweetness and fury. I was perpetually on edge, never sure which version I'd wake up to. Trip was gone most of the time, selling conduit.

We arrived two weeks before the school year started, and I didn't know a soul. Clinton Junior High was an elongated brick block with a parking strip of asphalt in front. Its only architectural feature was a looming rectangular overhang at the front door held up by concrete poles. When it was raining, you'd wait there for your parents to pick you up.

On the first day of school, I watched and listened. When Mom drove up at three-twenty, I told her, "I'm gonna be on student council."

"Honey, it may be hard for you to get elected," Mom said gently. "These other kids have lived here all their lives. No one knows you."

"I can do it," I told her.

I still wanted to go to Yale for undergrad and law school. I'd given up on the *Sailor Moon* career plan, focusing instead on a more mature vision of as yet undefined advocacy and social justice work. Student government seemed like the clear first step. Mom explained that campaigning involved asking one's fellow citizens what they wanted and assuring them that I'd fight for their needs. She said I'd need to show the kids how I'd work for them, but I'd also have to learn not to alienate the school administration. I knew I could win a seat. I spent the first week of school learning the names of as many students, teachers, and administrators as I could. I figured out what the cliques were and who had the power. I made buttons and gave speeches. I campaigned like a dervish. And I won.

I immediately put a suggestion box (a Tupperware container with a slit cut in the top) in my homeroom. After the first few weeks of school, I stopped checking it. The kids asked for things like "no school on Fridays" and "fire Mr. Jenkins." At thirteen, I lacked the power to have the water in all the fountains replaced by Mr. Pibb. We did run some canned-food drives, sell magazines to raise money for the school, and put up streamers for school dances. But that was not why I had entered public service. It was a bit of a blow.

My constituency consisted of around nine hundred kids, seventh and eighth graders, almost equally divided between white and black. Surreally, no one looked like me. In Miami, my long, thick, wavy black hair hadn't stood out. But Clinton was a festival of blond: white blond, honey blond, golden blond, platinum blond, ash blond, caramel blond. Almost immediately, I acquired the nickname Pocahontas. It was affectionate but not. "You sure don't look American, Pocahontas," one kid informed me with zero irony.

The queen of this entire domain was Madysson Middleton. Kids in every social bracket feared and worshipped her. She was tiny— half her height was hair, and half her weight was teeth. She wore her cotton-candy, soft-swirl froth of bright blond hair in sproingy, hot-rollered barrel curls down her back. When she wore a French braid, other girls copied her for the next few days. She was That

Girl, everything the other seventh- and eighth-graders of Clinton wanted to be—tanned and petite and enthralling. She knew her power. She started spider-legs mascara, the hottest trend in junior high. The trick was to get the cheapest mascara you could, pile it on so heavily that the weight of your own lashes made it hard to keep your eyes open, and keep adding coats until your lashes clumped into medieval-looking spikes. If it flaked off so that your cheeks were dusted with black specks, all the better. I wore black makeup, too, but Madysson took it to the next level. You could hear her voice float out over everyone's heads in the lunchroom: "Oh my word, I'm fixin' to go kill myself if they don't have chicken nuggets today!"

It took me a while to get used to her as an exemplar of beauty. In Miami, the popular girls had been Cuban and Spanish, with coffee-colored skin and dark hair. To me, that was how a pretty girl was supposed to look, not like a little pink fluffy-haired newborn guinea pig. But within the first few weeks of school, I could see how commanding Madysson was. She set the fashion trends: Timberlands, flared Mudd jeans, Joe's Crab Shack T-shirts. After she wore a Joe's shirt, they started cropping up all over school like mushrooms after a rain. Wearing one connoted worldliness, since there were Joe's Crab Shacks in Tennessee, Louisiana, Alabama, and Florida, but there weren't any in Mississippi.

I studied Madysson as if she were a fetal pig in formaldehyde, a science project. She wasn't beautiful, but she made everyone believe she was. What was the source of her power? It had to be her confidence, her unshakable belief in her own fierceness. I respected her ability to sell herself as if she were gorgeous. Too bad I didn't apply that lesson to my own life for another four years. I had to become emaciated and sick and lose my hair by the handful before I internalized what I should have learned from Madysson Middleton.

Junior high is the laws of physics in action. Popularity is both wave and particle. If Madysson talked to a girl at the lockers, instantly, that girl became powerful, too. Another girl would be invisible until a rumor started—no one knew how—that she gave blow jobs in trucks. The gossip would arc through the school, and then that girl was isolated.

Back then I thought my best strategy for making it through junior high was to keep a low profile. I didn't try to compete in the cuteness sweepstakes. How could I? I didn't fit in any of CJH's slots. I didn't look like a white girl or a black girl. I was on student council, but I wasn't in any cliques. I was an outlier, the way I'd be later as a plus model doing high fashion.

Trouble found me even though I wasn't looking for it. In seventh and eighth grades, there was a schoolwide vogue for telling people off. It was a big event. A group of ten or so kids would plan an attack, grouping together and approaching the chosen victim in the school courtyard to berate him or her for some manufactured, meaningless offense. They'd hurl words until the person burst into tears. It was performance art. One day a few weeks into the school year, I wound up on the list. As the gang approached, led by a frizzy-haired, gap-toothed girl, I kept talking to my fellow council members. The yell-mob surrounded me and started heckling me, accusing me of some made-up sin: cheating on a test, spreading lies about a popular kid, wearing stupid pants—I forget what they said, and it doesn't matter. I simply pretended they were invisible. I could feel the heat of their bodies, their spit as they yelled at me. I tuned out their words, pretending I was underwater. When it was clear they were going to get no response at all, they retreated.

Relief. I had won. My prize was respect.

Later that afternoon, between class periods, the frizzy-haired girl was waiting at my locker. I steeled myself for a confrontation. Instead, she grinned at me. "That was pretty cool," she said. "You didn't even flinch."

And just like that, we were friends.

Her name was Tina. She was the only Mexican kid at CJS and the only other person whose hair looked like mine. Her parents were strict, but she constantly evaded them. I admired her toughness. She sometimes went to parties thrown by high school kids, where she drank beer. I never drank; I was too afraid to lose control. But I liked having a friend who did. It made me feel daring and brave by association.

Tina looked out for me. She became my best friend.

It was through Tina that I met Joey Harrison. After begging me nearly every weekend, Tina got me to go to a party with her in late November 1998. Joey and I slow-danced, and I was a goner. He had dark hair swept back off his forehead; a sweet, slow smile; and downy cheeks. We had the most innocent bubblegum romance. I held his hand, and we pecked each other on the cheek. He was my first love.

Joey and I dated off and on until the summer before ninth grade. It took us that long to kiss on the lips, with tongue. Which was perhaps a mistake, since a few days later, he deputized his best friend, Tim, to break up with me; Joey didn't even have the guts to do it in person. Tim called me on the phone and said, "Hey, Joey had a dream. God came to him and said you guys aren't supposed to be together."

I was devastated, but who could argue with divine intervention? Maybe Joey was afraid of commitment; maybe he thought I was a terrible kisser. I was stricken. I felt like I'd made myself vulnerable and gotten nothing back. I already had trust issues, but this magnified them.

But back then, in the middle of seventh grade, I was starting to feel a little more socially secure. As a sort of sociology experiment, I decided to see if I could get more popular. Market myself better. Raise my stats. Popularity was currency, after all. With my usual single-minded focus, I determined that being a cheerleader was the fast track to the A-list. So student council fell by the wayside. At the end of eighth grade, I tried out for cheerleading and made the squad.

Eighth grade became My Year of Cheer. Thanks to martial arts, I'd always been flexible and athletic. Now I immersed myself in pom-pom-tastic gymnastics. Back handsprings were nearly my downfall—at five-seven, I was taller than anyone else, and the ground seemed awfully far away. Coach and I spent hours on the trampoline. I hurtled backward unsuccessfully, landing on my neck and back on the rough elasticized fabric over and over again. I couldn't commit to the move; I was chickening out in midair every time. I didn't feel secure throwing myself into the unknown, the unseen, not only backward but also upside down. As I said: Trust issues. Finally, I refused to do any more. Coach excused me from back-handspring duty, and routines were rechoreographed around my tragic nonspringy disability.

I was spending hours at practice. I barely saw Lana during the week. Mom picked me up after cheerleading, and we often had dinner together. By the time I got home after hours of jumping, flipping, tumbling, and pyramid-building, I was exhausted. I did my homework and went right to bed. On weekends, when Lana and I did see each other, our relationship was tense. Her eyes would narrow as she studied me. "Are you doing drugs?" she'd ask. "Do you cheat in school? Are you having sex? You can tell me." I assured her that I wasn't doing any of those things. She rolled her eyes. Did she think I was lying? Or was she inwardly sneering at me for being a Goody Two-shoes? I couldn't tell. Anyway, she didn't seem that interested in what was going on in my life. Weekends were when Trip was home from work, and she'd lie on the couch watching movies with him.

I was annoyed at myself for craving Lana's attention and approval. Toughen up, I told myself. I felt aeons older than Angelica and Brianna. I wanted to prove I was a grown-up. In the late spring of 1999, I told Mom, "I want to go off Ritalin. I don't need it anymore."

I'd been on the medication for almost three years. Now that school was about learning rather than fire-and-brimstone sermons, I was sure I could focus. I was learning complicated cheers—that was proof of my powers of concentration, wasn't it? And most of my classes were interesting enough.

But I had an additional motive for going off my meds. In Clinton, unlike in Miami, there was a real stigma attached to taking ADHD drugs. School policy wouldn't allow me to keep the pills in my backpack or locker; I had to take them in the school office, with the nurse watching like a hawk. I felt as though I were being judged, as though the administration felt that any kid who needed brain medicine was apt to come into school in a black trench coat with a bag of firearms. Or maybe the school was worried that if we were allowed to have prescription medicine in our backpacks, we might sell it. By ninth grade, after all, some kids I knew at other schools were selling their Ritalin and Adderall: Girls who wanted to lose weight were the big market.

Later, I'd learn that some professional models also relied on the drugs to keep their weight down. When I was a professional model, I would have swallowed strychnine if someone had told me it could make me skinnier. I would wish desperately to be back on Ritalin, because it might have a skinny-making effect, even though it hadn't when I'd been on it before. By then I was too afraid to ask for a prescription, because I knew any qualified medical professional would take one look at me and recognize my eating disorder.

When I was just a normal eighth grade girl, I wanted to go off the drugs. Mom halfheartedly tried to convince me to stay on them, but by now she knew that when I wanted to do something, I was unstoppable. I tapered off the meds. I continued to get A's but started to become more impatient with teachers and more annoyed at Lana for not seeming to care about me. Was I more short-tempered because I'd gone off Ritalin or because I was thirteen? Who can say?

Things started getting worse at home. Lana whipsawed between benign neglect and controlling behavior. After months of disinterest in my school activities, she wanted to check my homework. She wanted me to account for all my time on the weekends, even though she herself disappeared for hours. When she tried to tell me what to do, I'd be simultaneously angry and grateful that she was engaging me at all. "I have a mother, and she's not you!" I'd snarl at her. "I'm just trying to be nice by including you in my life!"

I could see that Mom was unsure how to handle these confrontations. Lana often exploded at her, too, accusing her of turning me against her and alluding cryptically to sins that Mom had supposedly committed many years earlier.

Inevitably, the troubles with Lana came to a head. One weekend a few months into the school year, Mom was in Florida, visiting family. As part of my sullen teen routine, I'd refused to go with her; I'd announced my intention to stay home and read deep books and think deep thoughts. I was trying to stay out of Lana's line of vision as much as possible, so on Sunday morning, I decided to take a break from being deep and go to a friend's house to shoot hoops. I told Lana where I was going, but I guess she forgot; maybe she hadn't heard. As my pal and I played H-O-R-S-E in his driveway, I saw Lana's van screech around the corner. She was wearing the sweatpants she'd been sleeping in for days. Her eyes were red. My little sisters sat stiffly in the backseat. There was a look on her face I knew too well.

"Get in the car," she hissed.

I was mortified. "I told you I was going to play basketball," I said, trying to keep my voice level.

She started screaming. "You did not! I had no idea where you were! You said you'd be at the house! I don't know what you think you're doing, playing with boys! Did you go inside his house? You're forbidden to go into boys' houses!"

With an apologetic look at my friend, I got in the car. I was scared to drive with Lana but more scared to let other kids see her this way. She drove wildly back to the house, calling me selfish and irresponsible. She screeched to a halt in the driveway, then stormed into my room and yanked out the Nintendo, tossing it onto the living room couch. Then she grabbed my TV. "You have *nothing* for a month!"

"Fine," I said flatly. I wouldn't give her the satisfaction of a reaction. After she slammed the door, I sat on the floor of my closet, hugged my pillow, and cried.

The next morning, my electronics were on the kitchen counter. Lana said, "Take them." No further mention was made of being grounded or toyless. Life with Lana could give a girl whiplash.

A week or so later, the end came. It was five in the afternoon. Mom was in her room. Lana was standing at the stove, reheating some pasta for dinner. I wordlessly opened the cabinet above her head and reached for a Rice Krispies treat. "You can't have that," she snapped. "We're eating soon." I replied, "You can't control me!" and grabbed the little electric-blue package and left, slamming the screen door behind me. I ate my Rice Krispies treat in the backyard.

When I came back, it was clear that Lana had been stewing. She picked up the pot of spaghetti with marinara sauce and threw it at me. My first reaction was: Thank God it's lukewarm. Then Lana slapped me hard and pushed me against the wall next to the coat hooks. Rough stucco scraped my back. I broke free of her grasp and darted into the garage, screaming, "Lana's gone crazy!" Mom ran to put her body between us. Lana shoved her.

I ran back into the kitchen and grabbed a carving knife. I could hear Lana raging at Mom. I yanked the cordless phone from its cradle, dialed 911, and left the phone on the counter. I ran back to the garage. Waving the knife at Lana, who had Mom backed against the wall, I said, "I will slit your throat if you hurt her."

I ran to our next-door neighbor's house and banged on the front door with my open palm. What must they have thought when they opened the door to see a girl with spaghetti in her hair, her white tank top completely spattered in red, holding a butcher knife? I felt Mom's cool hand on my shoulder. "I'm just fine, honey," she said softly. Behind us, Lana sped off in her van. We could hear the sirens approaching.

The police car pulled up, lights flashing. Two blank-faced cops got out. One, with his hand resting casually on his nightstick, asked, "Is everything okay here?"

In her best Mary Kay voice, Mom answered, "Oh, there's no problem, Officers!" She explained that there'd been a misunderstanding. They drove away after giving us and the neighbors a hard look. When the cop car was gone, Mom turned to me. "We're leaving."

We stayed at a hotel for a few days and then moved into our own place. I didn't see or speak to Lana for two years.

Mom and I lived in a two-bedroom apartment in a complex off the highway. It was sterile and charmless, with wall-to-wall beige carpeting and white walls. But the complex had a pool, and it was quiet. I felt safe. While I was at school, Mom got our stuff moved from Lana's house. My sisters came over once. I think Mom picked them up for a visit. That was also the only time I saw them for two years.

All I wanted to do was go to school and hang out with Mom. But after a few weeks' recovery time, Mom sought a distraction for me— and perhaps a little break for herself—by enrolling me in charm school. I was too numb to resist. Mom had been to charm school and had faith in its civilizing powers, as most Southern ladies do. She believed in it the way she believed in God. Charm was everything. Her success with Mary Kay had been testament to her powers of enchantment. She could talk to anyone from a homeless person to the president of the United States. She'd been a showroom model, a job that required poise. And she felt I needed comportment.

My instructor, Miss Vivian, was a firm believer in the dictum "The higher the hair, the closer to God." Like the Olympia Dukakis character in *Steel Magnolias,* she believed that the only thing separating us from the animals was our ability to accessorize. She taught me to apply makeup; we did not technically use a trowel. We also learned what utensils to use when dining, how to engage in polite conversation, how to facilitate graceful introductions. I learned how to walk and how to sit with my knees together.

I didn't mind. It was something to do.

One day in the spring of 2000, Miss Vivian took us, one by one, into the dance studio to see a man who was visiting the school. They'd set up a table in front of the barre. There, flanked by mirrors, sat The Scout.

He leaped to his feet when I walked in. "Oh my God, you're gonna be a supermodel!"

"Nice to meet you, too," I replied.

He laughed and explained that he was a modeling scout visiting from New York City. I told him that I didn't know much about modeling. And I didn't. I wasn't one of those girls who read fashion magazines like runes, or tracked models' careers on blogs and websites. I'd never watched *House of Style* on MTV.

The Scout pulled out a magazine and showed me pictures of Gisele. She was barefoot. A one-shouldered white Donna Karan dress clung to her curves. Her windswept hair framed her face like a lion's mane. She looked strong, challenging. Her eyes were piercing. Everything about her was expressive—even her hand, resting on her bare thigh below the hiked-up dress, looked elegant. She looked like a combination of wild animal and ballerina. I didn't know women who looked like that.

"That could be you," he said.

"Are you joking?"

"I don't joke."

The Scout was one of the best in the business. He wasn't one of those slick, dimpled operators who preys on vulnerable hick girls in Lifetime miniseries. His job really was to find the next Gisele. On that mission, he traveled four hundred thousand miles a year, 288 days a year, powering through tiny towns you've never heard of. His superpower was instantly knowing whether a girl was model material. He was like one of those forensic scientists who takes a skull found at a murder scene and builds it up slowly with clay into a recognizable face, a three-dimensional representation of what the victim must have looked like—except The Scout could look at a twelve-year-old's face and see a twenty-two-year-old beauty. He could spot potential grace in a string-bean body. He could see bone structure under layers of baby fat and natural beauty beneath streaks of cheap, chalky blush or a gel-frozen pouf of bad hair.

He took Polaroids of me and studied them. "There's just one thing," he said diffidently. "You'd have to lose a bit of weight." He told me I'd need a thirty-four-inch hip. If I could get mine down to that, I'd be a superstar.

He handed me his card. "I'll come back in a few months," he said, looking into my eyes. "I'm willing to gamble the price of a plane ticket on you."

Later that afternoon, in the privacy of my room, I measured my hips. Forty-three inches. Only nine inches too big. Nine didn't sound like a particularly big number. I wasn't inordinately fond of my body as it was. I was too tall for back handsprings, and my curves were attracting unwanted attention. Seniors stared at me and invited me to go cruising on Saturday night, to sit in the passenger seat as they trawled College Street in their Camaros and Firebirds.

I hadn't devoted myself to anything since cheerleading. And I hadn't been thrilled by anything since martial arts back in Miami. Maybe modeling was something I could do and do well. Besides, opportunities for poor girls from the South don't come around so often. I knew I had to grab this one.

That night Mom and I went to Applebee's for dinner. I told her, "I want to do this." I explained that until my hips were thirty-four inches, weight loss would become my job. "Mom," I said. "You might get scared when you see me get skinny. But you know I'm strong. And who I am won't change. So don't worry about me."

She took my hand and said, "I love you."

I think Mom thought I'd outgrow this obsession the way I had so many others.

The next day, after school, Mom drove me to the bookstore. I got every diet book on the shelf, plus an Elle Macpherson exercise tape: *Your Personal Best Workout.* Later, I learned that other models called Elle "The Body." On the cover of the tape, she was all broad shoulders, slim hips, endless legs. I popped the tape in the VCR and followed the routine. Compared to cheerleading, it wasn't hard. Then I rewound it and did it again. I did the tape five times in a row that night. The next morning, I asked Mom for a gym membership. I knew it was expensive, but I needed it. I was now five-eight and weighed 165 pounds. That was fine for a regular girl. But not for a supermodel.

I began reading fashion magazines to learn the names and faces of models and to copy their poses. Mom would catch me vamping in front of the mirror, surrounded by glossy pages. "It's like you're in modeling college," she told me.

I took down the pictures of outer space—those black holes and stars and quasars—that had plastered my bedroom walls since elementary school. I blanketed my room with cutouts of models from fashion magazines. I'd wake to see Maggie Rizer staring at me in the middle of the night. I did not find this disturbing.

In the past, I'd never paid attention to what I ate. If I wanted a cupcake, I'd have two. I'd never voluntarily consumed whole wheat bread. I'd no sooner have eaten tofu than a bathmat. But I read those diet books and began trying to eat healthily. Once I tuned in and started eating mindfully, it wasn't hard.

I started looking forward to fall, when I'd start Sumner Hill Junior High, a one-year program. (In Clinton, kids went to junior high for seventh and eighth grades, then to Sumner Hill for a year, then to Clinton High for tenth through twelfth grades.) Since it was a different school, there was a different cheerleading coach. I wasn't sure whether I wanted to audition. Should I just concentrate on weight loss? Maybe I should look for a martial arts class and get back in touch with a sport I'd truly loved. Or gee, since Tina would be going to a different school, maybe the thing to do was focus on making new friends. I waffled.

As summer approached, one of the other CJH cheerleaders said, "Hey, Crystal, you're gonna cheer at Sumner Hill, right?"

I shrugged. "I guess." I pushed the decision out of my head. I'd figure it out later.

When tryouts rolled around, I made a spur-of-the-moment decision to go for it. But I wasn't focused, and I didn't memorize the routine. Was it because I was ambivalent or because I'd gone off my ADHD medicine? I don't know. I just screwed up. I still turn red when I think about standing there, wishing I could teleport to another planet while the other girls leaped and danced around me. I stood stock-still, completely forgetting the moves I hadn't paid attention to in the first place, while some coach I didn't know tapped her pen on her clipboard. I was humiliated. I wept in the girls' bathroom. I insisted to the other girls that I didn't care about not making the squad, while in fact I cared all too much. I wasn't sure I wanted to cheer anymore, but I also wasn't sure I didn't.

That summer, with no cheerleading practice to occupy my time, my only project was weight loss. It was one mission I was determined not to fail. I was in full-blown Macpherson Mania. I did Elle's tape every night and an hour at the gym three or four times a week. I became vigilant about dieting, limiting my splurges to fat-free Pringles, Diet Coke, and dozens of jewel-toned cups of sugar-free Jell-O. I loved sugar-free Jell-O. All chemicals, no heft! Six little containers, only sixty calories! So I'd eat six. Then I'd loll around, glassy-eyed, logy on gelatin and maltodextrin.

I lost twenty-eight pounds in three months.

On my first morning of ninth grade, Mom drove up to the entrance of Sumner Hill. It was a long, low, depressing cement building, like a stretched-taffy version of a motel, with a near-infinite row of windows that often had their blinds pulled down. There was a huge grassy area where all the kids hung out, watching everyone else get dropped off. It was a gauntlet of cliques and hairy eyeballs. The popular blondes, the black kids, the geeks, the Goths—they all had their designated territory on the green. Even on the first day of school, all the kids knew their assigned spaces.

I slammed the car door behind me, whipped my hair around, and sashayed my skinny ass into school. As I saw the heads swiveling and the eyes upon me, I knew everything had changed. I could see it in those faces. In the great board game of high school rank, I'd just jumped ahead a few cafeteria tables.

On that warm August morning, I'd chosen my outfit carefully: dark brown suede Nine West boots with a three-inch heel, flared gold pants, a tight brown scoop-necked long-sleeve T-shirt, and a bunch of dangling gold-plated necklaces from the Metrocenter mall. Heads swiveled. Jaws dropped. Guys in camouflage pants with Confederate flag stickers on their new notebooks gaped. The cheerleaders, in their flares and Tims, stared. Choose your sound track: "All Star," "No Scrubs," "Baby One More Time," "Smooth." I was the girl in the close-up.

As I walked into school and saw everyone looking at me, I knew I had power.

Today thinness trumps almost every other source of power in high school. A few years ago I read a book called *The Body Project,* by a historian named Joan Jacobs Brumberg. It's a collection of girls' diaries throughout American history. Once upon a time, those diaries were full of ambition to be better, kinder people. But now teenage girls' diary entries are all about being thin. They equate thinness with strength and goodness. Weight loss is seen as a direct correlation with virtue.

When I got thin, the nature of my conversations changed, and it was clear that my role in the hierarchy had changed as well. Everyone wanted to talk to me. And they wanted to talk about getting, being, *staying* thin.

In the cafeteria, the epicenter of teenage angst and pecking-order validation, I was suddenly a carnival prize. At lunch on that first day, kids at half the tables beckoned me over. I'd worried needlessly about whom I'd sit with now that Tina was gone. In the past two years, I'd often eaten alone, my nose buried in a book. Clearly, that was not going to happen this year.

At fifth period, as I slammed my locker door shut, the illustrious Madysson Morgan materialized at my side. "So, Crystal, what are you doing this weekend?" she asked. I didn't think I'd ever heard her say my name aloud before. Now she was inviting me for a sleepover.

I'd arrived.

Within days, a popular boy named Zac Higgins asked to be my boyfriend, and I said okay. The A-list girls made it clear that he was a sought-after trophy. Alas, he was also a douche. He knew I wanted to stay a virgin, and he thought that was hilarious. He kept teasing me about it. I put up with it because he was popular.

One afternoon we were doing homework in his room, and he

kept saying, "I'm gonna whip it out!" I rolled my eyes—until he actually whipped it out. Then I marched downstairs to his mother and said, "Your son is being . . . inappropriate!" As she went upstairs to yell at him, I called Mom to pick me up.

I decided to end it with Zac, even if he was one of the cool guys. This kind of cool I didn't need. But one of the popular girls, Jessie, said I should wait until after Christmas, a week or so away. "He got you an awesome present!" she confided. So I waited. A couple of days later, Jessie whispered, "It's a *seriously* awesome present. He's totally sorry he was a dick. You should probably get him something nice, too."

I wasn't sure I wanted to get back together. But I wasn't sure I didn't. I bought Zac a $125 hunting knife, erasing my savings. If he begged like a dog for forgiveness, a great gift would make me look openhearted and generous. And if I decided to stay broken up, a great gift would make me look like a mature, forgiving person. Such was my demented thought process.

On Christmas Eve, Zac rang my bell. I gave him my gift, and he smiled. Then he handed me a plastic bubble with a crappy tin ring in it from one of those dispensers at the front of the supermarket. "You are so dumped," he said.

The next morning, as I climbed the cement steps to school, one of the girls from the popular table grabbed me. "Omigod, I can't believe what Jessie did to you," she said.

"Jessie?" I asked. "You mean Zac."

Her eyes widened with the joy of realizing that I had no clue. She was going to have the privilege of telling me. "No, Jessie has had her eye on him forever!" she said. "The afternoon you wouldn't touch his thing" (*wait, she knew about that? did everyone?*) "he went right to her house. They've been together for a week! They planned this whole thing together, making you think you were getting a cool present, then giving you that gumball ring!" It had to be Jessie's fault. In junior high cosmology, as in the Book of Genesis, girls are the temptresses. It took years for me to understand that this was a pretty reductive way of looking at gender relations.

Right then I was imagining Jessie planning this on the phone with Zac, cackling. Or worse, plotting it while lying in his bed. I could visualize their makeout sessions, both of them mocking me between bouts of tonsil hockey.

Forget it. She could have him. I was done with boys.

I fervently believed this to be true until I got back together with Joey a couple of months later. He'd written me a romantic, if execrable, poem that started:

I am alone
As alone as a stone.

I welcomed him back. A boy who took relationship directives from his Heavenly Father was not likely to pressure me into sex. He was easy to be with. And if you were popular, you needed a boyfriend. Having Joey in that role was one less thing to worry about.

Frankly, I had bigger concerns on my (figurative) plate. My weight loss had stalled. I'd hit a plateau at 138 pounds. I calculated that I needed to get to 110 to win my ticket to New York: 110 pounds would deliver the coveted thirty-four-inch hip. But the scale had frozen, refusing to tick down. I knew The Scout would be disappointed.

I wasn't about to be defeated by a bathroom appliance. I cranked up my diet and exercise intensity like a lab rat pressing a lever for a pellet. Instead of going to the gym every other day, I went every day. I got an old-fashioned calorie counter that I carried everywhere. Once again the pounds started to come off. When I dipped below 130 pounds, I lost my period. I wouldn't get it back for three years.

By February, I'd stopped reveling in my A-list status. At lunch, I tuned out the Yorkie-like yapping around me (*"That guy is slicker than snot on a doorknob! So I told him . . ."*) and sat flipping through my calorie counter, obsessing about lettuce. Which had more calories—iceberg or green leaf? In third grade, I'd read *Hamlet* for fun. In ninth grade, I read the backs of fat-free salad dressing bottles.

My fuse got shorter as my weight dropped. In March, I was suspended for telling off a teacher. I'd asked a question in math, and Mrs. Block had replied, "You were talking and not paying attention, so I won't be answering you."

I couldn't believe the injustice. I protested, "I wasn't talking!"

"You were, or you wouldn't be asking that question."

"You're a teacher, and you're not going to teach me?" I sputtered.

"That's enough, Crystal," she said, turning her back.

Before I knew it, it was out of my mouth: "You're a bitch!"

I was on my way to the principal's office before Mrs. Block could even say, "Go to the principal's office." I told Mr. Jarrett exactly what happened: I'd had a legitimate question, she'd refused to answer, and she'd falsely accused me of wrongdoing.

He sighed. "You're suspended for two days."

I was furious. "What I said was wrong, but we should both be punished!" I told the principal. "Yes, I mouthed off, but she failed to do her job!"

Mr. Jarrett tried to pat my arm reassuringly, but I yanked it away. I did my suspension, steaming, and tuned out of that teacher's class for the rest of the year. I think I still pulled a C, but I learned nothing.

As ninth grade ground onward, my eating grew more disordered. I found it harder to eat in front of other people. I look weird when I chew food, I thought. Food is going into my mouth! People must think I look like a freak! In the cafeteria, I forced myself to stab a few pieces of lettuce dressed with lemon. I didn't need the calorie counter anymore, because at school I only ate lettuce, drank Diet Coke, and chewed gum. My throat was starting to hurt all the time.

My friends were plastic friends, I thought. Barbies. I finally had that sleepover at Madysson Middleton's; I discovered we had nothing to talk about. Because of the way she carried herself, I'd imagined she lived in a spectacular house like the fancy ones in magazines, but she didn't. It was a normal house. It was not a mansion with long blond hair.

I'd sit in the corner booth at Applebee's in the center of a big group of toothy blondes, wondering why I was there. We smiled the empty smiles of beauty queens. I got quieter and quieter. I'd squeeze mustard onto my salad. I'd chew the ice in my drink, which kept the throbbing in my throat to a dull ache. I liked how it felt when my mouth was frozen. I'd also chug ridiculous amounts of water. Holding a cup the size of a vase made me feel secure. I'd dump in packet after packet of aspartame and pretend I was drinking a milk shake.

I had one real friend then—Clover Rivers. Her parents were artists, and she wanted to grow up to run a gallery. She was blond and pretty and flirty, but she had her eyes on the prize, just as I did. She wanted out of Clinton, too. (No one else seemed to.) Clover didn't judge me, because she was just as hungry as I was.

By the end of ninth grade, I could eat only with Mom. I'd make a batch of steamed veggies, and she'd make a normal dinner and we'd eat together. She'd cook tricolor pasta and chicken with barbecue sauce—my favorites. I could only look at them longingly. In the winter of 2001, I'd have a few bites, but by the spring, I was no longer eating pasta or sauce of any kind. My chicken had to be naked as a jaybird. I ritualistically cut it into tiny pieces, putting down my knife, spearing a piece on my fork . . . I could make a tiny amount of food last forty-five minutes. From time to time, Mom tried to talk to me about my behavior. I'd say, "I'm fine." She would sigh.

Late at night, when I was in bed, I'd remember the special trips Mom and I used to take to Cracker Barrel in Jackson. We'd each order a giant fried-catfish platter and biscuits. Sometimes we had apple dumplings for dessert. I loved Cracker Barrel. There was something to see everywhere you looked: vintage farming tools and Burpee seed signs on the walls, rusty old bicycles hanging from the rafters, pottery jugs, deer heads, squeeze boxes, and wicker snow-shoes. There was no point in going there now. I wouldn't even allow myself to think that one day there might be a time when I'd eat fried catfish again.

My life revolved around being hungry and obsessing about my body's flaws. Unfortunately, I had a lot of company. In 1995, 34 percent of high school–age girls in the United States thought they were overweight; today 90 percent do. Ten million Americans have eating disorders, though anorexia wasn't even officially classified as a psychiatric disorder until 1980. I suspect that not eating is something girls have always done; it just didn't have a diagnosis until recently. You don't have to be a budding model to feel that you don't have the right to take up space.

Every day after school, I went to the gym. I needed to use the same treadmill every time. If someone else was on it when I arrived, I'd feel a stab of panic and anger. I'd wait until the person was done, then I'd swoop in proprietarily. The treadmill was in front of a picture window, facing a field and wide-open sky, but I didn't see those things. I just walked, staring into space. I also swam, used the inner- and outer-thigh machines, and marched on the elliptical. I was terrified of the stair-climber and steered a wide berth around it. I knew it would make me bulk up and get muscular, which would be like death. Muscle weighed more than fat. Muscle was bad. I needed my treadmill.

I treadmilled and calorie-counted my way down to 120 pounds and thought, I can do more. As I got skinnier, even the cheerleaders, normally not the most supportive cohort in school, expressed concern. In pictures from ninth and tenth grade, I was always hunched, because I hated being so much taller than anyone else. I felt like a giant. I hated everything about my body. I stopped wearing tank tops because my arms weren't a straight line; I was determined not to go sleeveless again until I was under a hundred pounds. (Had I once thought 110 pounds was the goal? That was crazy! One hundred and ten pounds was huge!)

The only people besides Mom with whom I felt secure were Clover and Joey. But Joey was getting worried about my mania. One day, meaning well, he put his hand on my hip and said, "Hey, it looks like you've gained a little weight. You look good."

He'd meant it as a compliment. But I could feel the place where his hand had been, burning on my hip, through my clothes, for hours. I broke up with him the next day.

More than anything, I bemoaned the fact that I didn't have a gap between my upper thighs like the models on my walls. That gap was the golden triangle—that space, that nothingness. Out of nothing, something. I stared clinically, asexually, at Kate Moss's crotch. I needed her gap. I wanted it the way other people want wealth, fame, love. My life was winnowed to that one little triangle. My own thighs felt huge, unwieldy, like tree trunks. I went to bed and woke up gazing at slender reeds.

I prayed for guidance. My old friend Tina, who came from a religious family, took me to a traveling church in the boondocks. Itinerant preachers came and whipped the faithful into a frenzy. During one sermon, the preacher thundered, "If you pray to God and believe in Him, gold dust will rain down upon you!" People were waving their hands, calling, "Yes! Yes!" The next day, Tina invited me over and said, "Let's pray for the gold dust!" We giggled.

We were 99 percent kidding around, but a tiny part of me thought that if I prayed for a gap between my thighs, my gold currency, it might appear. Tina brought me into her bathroom and turned off the light. We closed our eyes and prayed fiercely; then she turned on the light and there was gold dust everywhere! We stared at each other wide-eyed . . . until she cracked up. She'd filled her hand with gold eye shadow and thrown it in the air while my eyes were shut. She wasn't trying to be cruel; she was joking around. After a few seconds, I managed a hollow laugh. I swallowed my disappointment that there was no miracle. I was still fat.

Once I went on vacation to Alabama with my new friend Nevaeh, a popular girl, and her family. We went to bebe, a clothing store we didn't have in Clinton. I was too self-conscious to try on clothes. I was much too huge. (I never felt fat when I was 165 pounds. It was only when I got below 138 pounds that my body image went fun-house-mirror crazy.) After the trip, I slept over at Nevaeh's. In her bedroom, with the lights out, I let down my guard. We shared a whole bag of Oreos. Afterward, I felt like Lady Macbeth with blood on her hands. What had I done? I went to the bathroom and puked. When I came out, I could see in Nevaeh's face that she knew and that she was horrified. She asked me if I had an eating disorder. I said, "Of course I do! I have to, if I'm going to be a model!"

After that, Nevaeh was always too busy to hang out. I got the hint.

I became more secretive than ever. (Who was I fooling?) By the time I got to tenth grade, in 2001, I was a little sealed-off ball of mistrust. I lived for the dream of escaping to New York. In my head, I was already there. In Clinton, I was in suspended animation, waiting for The Scout to rescue me, waiting to be thin enough to deserve that rescue. I couldn't have been less interested in the culture of Clinton High; as in most southern high schools, everything centered on sports. We had an amazing stadium and baseball field, better than those of many minor-league teams. If you're a Mississippi boy and you want any place of significance in the high school hierarchy, you play football. Failing that, you play baseball. If you're a girl, you're a cheerleader.

There's only one high-status option for nonathletes: show choir. Clinton has the number one high school show choir in the United States. It's even spawned its own hairstyle, the Clinton Pouf. Just pull up a little hair from the sides to the crown of your head, then tease and curling-iron the front into a fluffy meringue, then set the back on hot rollers to create tons of ringlets. It's certainly distinctive.

In the years since high school, I've learned that show choir isn't a feature in all communities; that news astonished me, since it was a centerpiece of mine. Imagine chorus crossed with drill team crossed with a whole lot of hair spray. Imagine a lot of über-perky, Up with People–style dance moves, such as spirit fingers and "chugga chugga choo choo" arm circles. Imagine rhythmically flung hair. Imagine choreography by Corky St. Clair in *Waiting for Guffman*. The key to the movements is "facials"—emotive expressions of surprise, sadness, and openmouthed joy designed to help convey the essence of a song. If none of this sounds familiar to you, rest assured that hours of show choir videos await your delectation on YouTube. Clinton's most famous show choir alumnus, incidentally, is Lance Bass of 'N Sync.

When I was in tenth grade, show choir had forty-three performers, thirteen pit members, and fifteen tech crew members. The girls of show choir rivaled the cheerleaders in prettiness and popularity. If you had the voice of an angel but were hideous, no way could you get in. But rumor had it that if you were truly gorgeous and had a voice like a hacksaw, you could be in show choir if you promised to lip-synch. They usually took one black girl, but it was pretty much a blond thing. Auditions were held at the beginning of tenth grade, and those who made the cut had to make a three-year commitment to the choir.

As was my wont, I waffled until the last minute, then decided to audition. I sang "Colors of the Wind." (*You want Pocahontas? I'll give you Pocahontas!*) I told the director, truthfully, that I was planning to quit school if I got a modeling contract, so I was rejected. But I really didn't mind. I was a whisper from 110 pounds. I was halfway out the door.

Every day I fell asleep in Spanish. It wasn't so much that I hated Spanish as that my body crashed at around one-thirty P.M. I was always up late exercising—I couldn't go to sleep until I did Elle first, which meant I was too sweaty and wired to sleep, which meant that I was frequently up until three A.M.

Once I had a panic attack in algebra class. We were taking a test, and I'd zoned out. When the bell rang, I wasn't finished. I asked the teacher if I could have a few more minutes; I knew she had a free period next. But she wouldn't let me stay in my seat. She reached out and tugged on the paper as I desperately held on and continued scribbling. She pulled it away.

My vision narrowed; my lungs constricted; I fell to the floor under my desk. My breathing was so erratic and loud that everyone turned to look. I wasn't me anymore. I lay on the filthy linoleum under my desk, gasping for air. The teacher crouched and patted my back until I gradually came back into my body and could feel the cool linoleum on my cheek. My vision focused. Kids were standing in the doorway, staring at me wide-eyed.

When would I get out?

By now I was doing two hours of exercise a day: treadmill, swimming, kickboxing, followed by my security blanket, Elle, right before bed. The video was disintegrating from too-frequent play. But my hips were shrinking again. Mom continued to fret about the disappearing me, but I felt triumphant. By definition, to be a model was to have people say you're too thin. Therefore, I was doing my job.

I liked to count the veins in my arms. They were my bread crumbs, a trail to follow home. If they weren't prominent enough, I'd worry that I'd gained weight. I'd press my arm to my side, hoping that it wouldn't touch my boob. I wanted a major arch there, with no extra flesh on my upper arm. I constantly clenched my jaw to make it bulge and look squarer. Whenever I felt anxious, I'd pinch my collarbones for comfort. That soothed me. I wore my hip bones like a trophy. At night, in bed, I'd hold them as if they were the handles of a loving cup. I was proud that not all skinny models had that kind of sharp definition. Now I realize it's because those girls' bodies are meant to be thin.

I wanted to be less, always less. I wanted to be as barely there as possible.

I occasionally looked at the pro-ana (pro-anorexia) websites created by girls to encourage others girls to hug their illness closer. Basically, these sites are cheerleaders for anorexia, urging girls not to listen to the family and friends who want them to eat, telling them they're weak if they succumb to hunger or pressure to eat. They renewed my resolve, just as they were supposed to.

One night in the late spring of 2002, I stood naked in front of my full-length mirror, my feet together. I didn't see that my inner wrists looked like pale blue birds' wings you could crush with a breath. I didn't see my concave chest. All I saw was the gap between my upper thighs. Finally, the gap. I felt the blood rush to my face. I was ecstatic.

I didn't know what size I was. I always wore shapeless sweats and a denim jacket. But that weekend, I went to the mall and tried on jeans in a size four, then a two, then a zero. The zero was too big.

I called The Scout. "Come now," I said.

We arranged to meet in the lobby of the nicest hotel in Clinton. When he saw me, he let out a scream that shook the chandelier. I'd grown another inch, to five-nine, and weighed ninety-five pounds. I'd lost over 42 percent of my body weight.

Like a game show host, The Scout bellowed, "You're going to New York!"

I was too adrenalized—too anesthetized—to feel much of anything except a constant pounding in my chest. Perhaps it was just excitement. Perhaps it was the drumbeat of a body starting to rebel, starting to make its needs known.

3

LIVING THE DREAM

Mom was deeply unthrilled by my decision to quit high school before eleventh grade, but she knew she couldn't stop me. She just hoped I'd go to college eventually. I fully intended to. Even in my fog of calorie deprivation, I still dreamed of one day going to Yale; I knew that if I dropped out of school, I'd better get myself a general equivalency diploma. The GED administrators in Mississippi suggested I wait to take the test, making it clear that most high school–age students didn't pass. Might I want to wait until I was older? No. I wanted that piece of paper in hand before I left Clinton. I took the test and aced it. Then, I felt, I could say goodbye to Clinton without looking back.

I knew I had to move fast. Like gymnasts' and football players', models' working lives are brief. They have a tiny window of opportunity. This was mine.

In a blur, I packed my suitcases. Mom packed, too. She'd told The Agency there was no way she was abandoning her sixteen-year-old daughter in Manhattan, and they'd told her she could stay with me for a little while.

As the airplane dipped below the cloud line, I saw the runways of JFK airport in the distance. I chanted to myself, Everything's starting. It's all starting. I unbuckled my seat belt before we'd stopped whizzing across the tarmac.

As we made our way through the terminal, I was determined to look blasé, but I was practically skipping. In my ears was a steady low buzz; in my stomach was an entire butterfly exhibit. I don't think it was just excitement. My body was starting to react to the months of cruelty I'd subjected it to. I tuned out my stupid, betraying body's flutterings—I was floating above the world of meat and flesh.

Mom and I took a taxi into midtown Manhattan. I wanted to hang my head out the taxi's window like a golden retriever. I was in New York City!

We arrived at the model apartment where we'd be staying. As the doorman handed us the keys, I wondered how many other models I'd be living with, how big the apartment was, where Mom would sleep. The agent I'd talked to on the phone before we left hadn't volunteered any of this info, and I didn't want to look stupid by asking.

We took the elevator upstairs. I turned the key in the door's lock. There was a living room with a parquet floor and a big picture window overlooking Midtown. It was spare, furnished with only a couch and a few chairs, all arrayed around a big-screen TV like satellites orbiting a sun. A bookcase stood awkwardly a few feet from the wall; it held a few abandoned paperbacks and old exercise tapes. Behind the bookcase was a single bed; the bookcase offered minimal privacy and no insulation from the noise of girls staying up late at night and watching TV. Next to the living room was a modest kitchen. Its fridge contained bottled water, a few apples rolling around like tumbleweeds, a smattering of take-out containers, and some sad-looking lettuce.

There were two bedrooms. One contained three single beds, all lined up in a row as if awaiting Goldilocks. The other bedroom belonged to the chaperone. Her door was closed.

Other people would kill to be where I am right now, I thought, surveying the scene. Suddenly, reality bitch-slapped me. I'd spent so much time obsessing about whether I could lose enough weight to get to New York City. Now that I was here, I started obsessing about whether I'd be good enough to stay. I'd need some ineffable combination of the right look, the ability to come alive in front of a camera, and luck. I started to worry: What if I didn't have any of those things?

Most models don't. They're sometimes called "summer girls," teenagers who come to the city in June or July and leave in September, their dreams of multimillion-dollar contracts dashed. They're the spaghetti that gets thrown at the wall and doesn't stick. The agency I was about to sign with was paying my rent (and deducting it from my future earnings) because they were confident about my potential, sure I'd pay back that money. But the summer girls have to pay cash up front, up to four hundred dollars a week. How could The Agency be sure I was better than they were?

Mom could see that I'd gotten very quiet and had my anxious face on. She looked around and said briskly, "Well, this is not bad! Let's unpack!"

In hindsight, I know I was lucky; the apartment offered more privacy than most. In some model apartments, there are multiple rooms with multiple bunk beds stacked to the ceiling, filled with super-skinny long-limbed girls. All those wooden slats make the room look like a giant industrial playpen. Or—I have to say it—like those black-and-white photographs of the liberation of Buchenwald.

I peeked into the non-chaperone room and saw that two of the beds had rumpled sheets; the girls staying there must have been out on go-sees. "Do you want to sleep in here?" I asked Mom. She looked at me wryly. "I can sleep in the living room with noise, or I can sleep in the bedroom with noise!" Good point. (She chose the living room.) In addition to the inevitable clamor of an apartment full of models, Mom and I would have to get used to the deafening honking and squealing brakes of Midtown traffic.

After we unpacked, Mom and I went for a walk to explore our new neighborhood. I gazed up Park Avenue, at the giant glass-and-steel buildings rising on either side of a wide boulevard that stretched as far as I could see, and thought. I'm in the biggest city in the universe. Today New York City feels tiny to me. It's cozier than Clinton, because I'm at home here in a way I never was there. I have a community. I'm always bumping into models downtown and friends in Williamsburg. New York City neighborhoods are like small towns. You have your beloved dry cleaner, your bodega guy, your dog-run dogs, your crazy grumps who sit on lawn chairs in their front yards in Williamsburg next to their plastic flowers, doing surveillance of the hipster newcomers. New York is minute. (Milan, Paris, and London are still huge to me.)

But on this, my first day, I gazed up Park Avenue and had a "freeze this" moment—the kind you know will be an indelible memory even before the moment itself has passed.

Mom and I went to a salad bar in the theater district for dinner. Manhattan salad bars were like nothing I'd ever seen in Clinton. This one, like most, was an astonishing, riotously colored palette of different kinds of greens, beans, grilled veggies, roasted veggies, pine nuts, potato salads, cheeses, olives, chickpeas, fried eggplant, pastas.

I had the lettuce.

That evening, Mom and I met the chaperone and the other two girls staying at the apartment. The chaperone was perfectly nice—a young woman with a chic cropped haircut and thick-framed black glasses. She had some kind of low-level job at The Agency. (Lots of chaperones are bookers or scouts for the agency that sponsors the apartment; they do the job for free rent in the most expensive city in America.)

Both of the models were around my age. One girl I don't remember at all. The other girl was Hope.

I took one look at Hope and knew she was anorexic too. We can always find each other, we girls with secrets. She was thin the way I was thin—she looked ill, as if her head were too big for her body. Some models have an organic, gazelle-like slimness to them; you can tell they're the size they're genetically supposed to be. But Hope was emaciated. Her limbs looked like a botanical drawing of bluegrass.

As all of us new housemates made polite chitchat, I could tell that Hope was sharp and funny. Then the chaperone went to the kitchen and got herself an apple. As the chaperone ate it, I watched Hope. She had fallen silent. She couldn't take her eyes off that apple. The way it tempted her was positively biblical. Her mouth hung slack.

That night, as we got ready for bed, I whispered to my new friend, "Girl, you have a problem. And I like that."

We quickly became close. Hope was the performer; I was the audience. She did impressions of Renée Zellweger's squint and Reese Witherspoon's chin that made me laugh so hard I could barely breathe. She dished about other models and gabbed late at night about what our lives would be like when we were walking in Gisele's and Kate Moss's Louboutins. We'd share an apartment, date rock stars, travel the world, trash hotels. Remember when Linda Evangelista told *Vogue* she didn't wake up for less than ten thousand dollars a day? That was nothing. We'd make twenty-five thousand a day. I loved hearing Hope's stories.

But sometimes Hope stopped performing. She went utterly silent. Her eyes were red-rimmed. That's when I knew she was kicking herself about her failings, her weakness. I knew not to address her feelings directly; I hated it whenever anyone tried to talk to me about my disorder. Truthfully, in some ways, I preferred her when she was quiet. She was less exhausting. When she was in her own shame spiral, I just sat with her. We were anorexia bunnies, huddled together and twitching and blinking in the corners of rooms. Other girls thought we were weird. On shoots, while other models were all noise and giggles and open mouths and wild hair, we were stoic and watchful.

Bright and early in the morning of my first full day in New York City, Mom and I went to meet my booker at The Agency for the first time.

I'd never hailed a taxi. I felt hyperaware, walking to the corner and putting up my hand. Characters in movies did that. Who did I think I was, Audrey Hepburn? Would a cabbie recognize what I was doing? Was this the correct semaphore? Was I leaning out too far? Should I stand on the curb or in the gutter? Should I extend the heel and point the toe of the supporting leg? I couldn't do the simplest thing without second-guessing myself a million ways from Sunday.

The cab pulled up at The Agency, and Mom and I walked under the swooping metal overhang past the small sign by the door with its spare, minimalist lettering. The security guy waved us up. As the elevator swooshed silently aloft, I fidgeted like a toddler who had to pee. My whole life had led up to this moment. The Scout had told me he'd praised me to the skies, but what if The Agency didn't like me in person? When the elevator doors swished open, The Scout was waiting. And he screamed like a banshee.

"You are so thin!" he squealed, throwing his arms around me. "You look incredible! You're perfect!"

Standing next to him was a short, curvy, smiling woman with

freckles and a shiny bob. She was like a little pocket lawyer, all corporate and cute. She wore a form-fitting white blouse, sky-high heels, and wide-legged tweed trousers—she'd clearly read those articles in fashion magazines about how to dress to look taller, but she was so adorably compact, she could have been standing on Yao Ming's head, and she still would have seemed wee. This was The Agent. She gushed about how beautiful I was, how happy she was to work with me, how successful I'd be, while she escorted me to her office. As she bubbled at me in her midwestern accent, with Mom and the Scout trotting along behind us, I could see she was appraising me like a rump roast in the butcher's case. Before I knew it, she'd whipped out a tape measure and wrapped it around my bust, then my waist, then my hips. She chattered all the while. How was my flight? What did I think of the apartment?

I felt like my mouth was clogged with peanut butter. I answered in monosyllables. Fine. Great. Thanks.

"Hmm," she said, studying the tape measure. "Thirty-three. How much do you weigh?"

"Ninety-five," I told her truthfully.

"That's great. Just don't lose any *more* weight. We don't want you to get too skinny to fit the clothes!" She reflected for a moment. "A thirty-three-inch hip is a little bit small."

My heart skipped a beat. What if they decided not to sign me? Then The Agent smiled at me. "We'll just put thirty-four on your comp card."

Comp card is short for composite card, a five-by-eight photographic résumé. There's a single image of the model on one side and a bunch of different shots on the other, along with the model's name, measurements, and agency contact info.

The Agent, Mom, and I sat in a conference room while a lawyer put papers in front of us. Mom signed. I signed. I had no idea what my signature meant. I was a minor. But who cared? I would have put my John Hancock on anything anyone put in front of me if it meant I could model. Hey, Crystal, will you sign away your immortal soul? You bet! Will you give us your firstborn in exchange for this pottage of lentils? Where do I sign?

They signed me for $250,000 over the first three years. I could barely wrap my brain around that number. That was probably more than the cost of our entire apartment complex in Clinton. Plus Lana's house. Plus all our neighbors' houses.

With hugs and kisses all around (thank heavens The Agency people were kind and did the familiar American one-cheek kiss, since I would have been flustered by the industry standard, the two-cheek mwah-mwah Euro-kiss), they sent Mom and me back out The Agency's doors and into the world.

We strolled for a while, taking it all in. The soulful singer-songwriter Antony Hegarty of Antony and the Johnsons said of New York City, "It's like a bird sanctuary for oddballs." And it's true. Just looking at the flora and fauna—the outfits on passersby, the graffiti, the windows of stores and apartments—was great entertainment. In Clinton, I'd never seen an out gay person; here, men sashayed down the street in neon leggings and platform heels. Old people had blue hair—and not the pale blue rinse of a southern salon set, covered with a chiffon scarf, but bright blue and bright pink Manic Panic hair. They rode scooters! Buff men walked around shirtless with parrots on their shoulders! It was bliss. I belonged.

I turned to Mom. "I'm ready," I said.

"I know," she replied. She'd had her fill of me posing in front of mirrors, copying the positions of the models in *Vogue, Elle,* and *Harper's Bazaar*. She'd seen me striding around the apartment complex in Clinton at night, loping along like the girls in the fashion shows I watched snippets of on television. It was time to show everyone what I could do.

The Agency immediately started sending me to photographers and on castings (also known as go-sees) to build my portfolio. I settled into the life of supplication: Do I look the way you want? Will you put me in your magazine?

Mom helped me study the subway map and quizzed me on the names of streets and avenues. I memorized the layout of the city. When I had trouble finding a subway stop or an address, I asked people on the street. I quickly learned that the stereotype of New Yorkers as rude, nasty brutes was an urban legend. I'd arrived a year after 9/11. I don't know what the city was like before that terrible day. But afterward, it seemed to this newcomer, New Yorkers were eager to be kind. They looked for ways to help one another. Giving directions was something they could do, a way to reach out.

I joined the ranks of the thousands of leggy young girls who trot around the city all day, lugging a portfolio hither and yon. A beginning model may walk 120 blocks in a single day. My feet were quickly covered in raw red spots and Band-Aids. Battered feet were a badge of honor among models. But even with all that walking, I'd panic about not getting to the gym. All day I ran calculations in my head, adding and multiplying obsessively: How many calories had I burned so far? How many blocks? How many miles? How fast? My brain clicked away like an abacus. If I'd walked a lot, with adequate speed and power, I had to do only an hour and a half at one of my gyms and an hour at the other. By the time I left the second gym, the sky was usually dark—or at least as dark as it gets in New York City, with its millions of twinkling windows and streetlamps.

I joined two gyms the day after I arrived in New York City. I needed two so I could toggle between them all weekend without anyone suspecting I had an exercise addiction. Every Sunday I'd spend four hours at one gym and then four at the other, pounding away on the treadmills and ellipticals, swimming, maniacally scissoring my legs on the thigh machines.

The next day I'd run from casting to casting, handing over my book to a photographer, editor, or catalog producer, who usually glanced at it, handed it back, and said nothing more than "Thanks." If he or she said, "I like your book," that was a good sign. If someone tried to engage me in conversation, that was a great sign. I was so awkward in my own skin in those days, I was about as communicative as a clam. Cattle calls terrified me. Milling around with dozens of other models, all of us giving each other the fisheye as we waited for a harried assistant to call our names off a list . . . I invariably had to take deep breaths to forestall panic attacks.

I usually had eight to ten castings a day and up to fifteen during fashion-show season (every fall and spring). I had to race everywhere. There was only one problem: I couldn't skip lunch. I needed to sit down and savor my sugar-free carrot-orange Snapple and lettuce. I liked to go to Café Europa, a mini-chain with several locations in Midtown. They had steamed vegetables that seemed oil-free. I suspected, in my darkly compulsive and paranoid way, that some salad bars put oil on their steamed vegetables. But I could run my finger over Café Europa's vegetables without feeling any grease, so I needed to eat there. I required at least a half hour for lunch, because I had to cut my vegetables and lettuce into tiny, tiny pieces, and I had to eat the pieces very, very slowly. I took my needs seriously. They were all I had.

One afternoon as I headed to Café Europa, The Agent called and said, "Hey, you have an extra casting in forty minutes. Take the subway to Union Square right now."

My stomach lurched. "I need to have lunch," I told her. "I'll be late to the casting."

"Don't be late," she said. "Have lunch afterward."

She didn't understand. The lettuce, steamed vegetables, and Diet Snapple were the only things that reliably made me happy. They didn't judge me. I looked forward to them all day. "I can't! I can't!" I babbled to The Agent. My voice was rising in desperation. People on the street were staring at me. The ever present pain in my throat was getting worse.

"Miss Renn, do what the other girls do," she said with elaborate patience, as if talking to a very stupid preschooler. (The Agent always called me Miss Renn in an arch, sardonic way.) Despite her sweet tone, I could tell she was gritting her teeth. "Have a bar."

Other models lived on nutrition bars from health food stores. How on earth could The Agent ask me to do that? I couldn't peel some extruded brown thing out of a wrapper and just *go*. I couldn't eat and walk at the same time! This was crazy talk! I needed to sit! I needed a little white plastic knife! I needed to cut tiny pieces! Clearly, The Agent was insane.

I thundered, "*I DON'T EAT FUCKING BARS.*" My voice had deepened at least an octave. I sounded like Zuul, the demon in Sigourney Weaver's refrigerator in *Ghostbusters*.

On the other end of the line, shocked silence.

"I'll only be a few minutes late," I said in my normal (albeit slightly quavering) voice. I heard The Agent sigh and take a breath. Then I hung up on her. I ran to Europa, ordered my usual, and sat down, determined to enjoy my fucking lettuce. But I didn't. My heart was pounding so loudly, I was sure the people at the surrounding tables could hear it.

I was only five minutes late to the casting. But I didn't get the job. Most models don't get most jobs. Maybe the client didn't even notice I was late. The Agent never mentioned the incident.

Unlike some girls with anorexia, I was aware that my relationship with food was dysfunctional. As the parade of new models marched in and out of the apartment in the usual way (one girl would leave to go back to school or build her book in Europe; another girl would replace her), I stayed, filling the fridge with my lettuce and raw vegetables.

Sometimes someone would ask me out to dinner. "Hey, Crystal, we're all going to the Indian place on the corner—wanna come?"

"Oh, that's sweet, but I can't," I always said. My excuses varied: I want to finish this magazine. I have an early casting tomorrow. I already ate. I'm having dinner later with my mom. I had a late lunch.

The girls almost always understood. Everyone knew someone with a similar problem.

Once, though, a new model eyed my giant breakfast bowl of steamed cabbage and carrots and yelped, "God, you eat that twice a day! Ew!"

My white flash of anger flared up so quickly, I didn't see it coming. It wasn't fair that she could have toast for breakfast. I wanted to punch her in the face. "It's none of your business," I answered through gritted teeth. In my head, I added, *Drop dead.*

It was hard for me to watch the youngest girls eat. There weren't many fourteen-year-olds at the apartment, but there were a few. When you're fourteen, your metabolism hasn't caught up with you yet. I once watched a sylphlike thing nestle on the couch, her long legs folded under her like a praying mantis's, as she ate peanut butter from the jar. She'd dip one crooked finger in, bring it out heaping with brown glop, and shovel it into her mouth. She ate half the jar. I was hypnotized. It was gross, and enticing, and forbidden, and everything I wanted.

Hope watched as hungrily as I.

I was glad we had each other.

I woke up regularly in the middle of the night, my mouth watering, craving peanut butter. I would have killed for it. I'd run to the kitchen, fill a spoon from one of my roommates' jars of Skippy, and cram it into my mouth. I'd smoosh it around with my tongue, feeling its oily, greasy deliciousness coat my palate while the smell filled my nostrils . . . and then visions of being on a runway would flash in my head, and I'd run to the sink and spit desperately. I'd rinse my mouth over and over until I was spitting pink from bleeding gums. I'd return to bed with a growling stomach. My whole body *felt* peanut butter. I wanted to bathe in cheesecake. I cried because I wanted ice cream so badly. My tongue, my brain, my every cell yearned for calories. I refused to take even a multivitamin because I didn't want the extra calories in that little tablet.

I never partied with the other girls. I couldn't drink, because alcohol had calories, and I couldn't do drugs, because I was too addicted to control. I couldn't go to restaurants, because even if they gave me my lettuce with balsamic, how would I know they hadn't secretly put on a tiny bit of oil? No, I needed to dress the salad myself. Wasn't that obvious?

Sometimes The Agency wanted us to go to industry parties to show us off to clients. I did what was expected of me. I put on makeup, climbed into my one pair of high heels, and tried to smile. Invariably, I stood in the corner, clutching a glass of water, wishing to be somewhere, anywhere, else.

On nights and weekends, the other girls would sit around looking at fashion magazines, calling home, window-shopping, watching DVDs. They'd shoot the shit about their own relative merits and demerits—should this one get her ears pinned? Should that one get the microscopic bump on her nose shaved off? They'd talk about their bow-legged runway walk, their disappointingly flat butt, their fabulous shiny hair. I listened silently, too self-conscious about my own failings to participate. I knew the girls weren't boasting. Bodies are our business. Models talking about bodies are no different from mechanics talking about parts of a car. For me, the dilemma was about my dark, thick eyebrows. Agents, editors, photographers, and catalog producers talked about my eyebrows with all the seriousness and intensity of Middle East peace negotiators. Should the brows be pruned? How should they be shaped?

Now clients embrace my prominent brows as an integral part of my look. If a makeup artist comes at me with a Tweezerman, I'm confident enough to say, "We don't pluck. If you have a problem with that, call my agent." But back then the endless brow dialectics were a huge source of sweat and anxiety.

Believe me, I know how all this sounds.

Like the decision to pluck or not to pluck, my eating disorder was all about business. Anorexia was how I got a modeling contract. The whole reason I never got into puking (that one Oreo binge in Clinton notwithstanding) was that I didn't want the red eyes and disintegrating teeth that went along with bulimia. Not only was vomiting gross, it wasn't a good long-term marketing plan for Product Crystal.

During my first two months in New York City, I got one big job. It was for *Seventeen,* which was a pretty big coup. The photographer was Didier Malige, who was French and funny and charming. The shoot was at his country house, which was gorgeous. As soon as I arrived, a cat wound itself around my ankles. I reached down to pet it and saw another cat across the room. Then I saw another. Then another. Kitties were everywhere! I looked around and saw that the walls and surfaces were covered with cat photos and cat drawings.

Didier shared his house (and life) with Grace Coddington, the creative director of *Vogue.* At the time, I was ignorant of that fact. I knew Coddington's work—she's a legend. But I had no idea she and Didier were a couple. A few weeks after the shoot, I remembered I'd read somewhere that Grace Coddington loved cats. (An inordinate number of *Vogue*'s fashion features seemed to involve Karen Elson and a Persian cat.) I excitedly told Hope, "You know, Didier

Malige should go out with Grace Coddington! They both love cats!" Hope rolled her eyes and said, "They've been a couple for years, you moron." Which shows that I may be clueless, but I'd make a great matchmaker.

One thing I was not, in 2002, was a good model. Didier is a terrific photographer, but now I look at the pictures of myself from that shoot and cringe. In the opening shot of the story (which was called "Born to Ride"), I'm sitting on a vintage motorcycle. The tag line on the page is "Black denim looks its raciest on top of a Harley." Except I don't look racy at all. I look utterly self-conscious. I have a tiny smile, but otherwise my face looks anxious and blank. I'm sitting on the bike, slightly slumped, completely disengaged. My body language says, "I have been told to sit on this motorcycle. I do not know why. I am wearing black jeans. My arms are like noodles." I might as well have been sitting on a Barcalounger. It was not a shining moment in the annals of modeling.

In late 2002, I did a shoot—I think it was for *Flair* magazine—with Liya Kebede, one of the world's top models. In 2007 *Forbes* magazine wrote that Liya was the model with the eleventh highest earnings in the world. (She earned $2.5 million that year.) She's landed the covers of French, Italian, Japanese, Korean, and Spanish *Vogue* and has appeared three times on the cover of American *Vogue,* which is not always considered the most welcoming outlet for non-white models. Back in my bedroom in Mississippi, I used to look at pictures of her and think, How can I *ever* be that? Then I got to a shoot, and there she was. Lo and behold, I was thinner than she was.

I was manic for the rest of that day. My head was filled with a triumphant little song: I'm thinner than Liya Kebede! I'm thinner than Liya Kebede! In retrospect, I'm horrified by my reaction. Here I was, working with a woman who came from Ethiopia, became the toast of the modeling world, and worked for the World Health Organization to raise awareness of maternal and child health in the developing world. I could have asked her about her activism, but all I could think about was her hip size.

Most of the work I got in 2002 was for edgy magazines. Given my strong features and dark, intense gaze, my look wasn't mainstream or accessible, even though my body type was what every magazine wanted. I was always "editorial"—fashion-biz code for "not conventionally pretty." (A more approachable look—what Tyra Banks on *America's Next Top Model* would call "pretty-pretty"— is described as "catalog" or "commercial.") Editorial is where the prestige is. It also usually pays less than catalog work. (Why? Because editorial work isn't explicitly about selling, the way catalog and advertising work are. Editorial pays less because it purports to be about art, not about the obvious pushing of clothes and cosmetics. Sometimes it actually *is* about art.)

At another shoot for a tiny avant-garde magazine, I played a topless, evil Red Riding Hood in jet-black makeup. I wore red balloon pants with a huge hood attached to them, billowing swaths of fabric protruded from the butt of the pants and terminated in a pointy cap. The outfit is hard to describe and was even harder to take seriously. A friend of mine was in the same shoot. She was a horse. (Don't ask.) Unfortunately, that shoot never saw the light of day. The photographer, who was perhaps a little *too* creative, didn't think to ask my age. This was an amateurish mistake on his part. I was a minor and looked it. No magazine, no matter how edgy, was going to display my dewy little boobs. Pornography charges can put a real damper on business.

Then there was the shoot on the grungy Brooklyn rooftop with the sniffling, twitching drug-addled photographer. He had his assistant dangle a plush Uglydoll from a fishing pole above my head while he screamed, "You are an octopus! You want to touch the doll, but you don't want to touch it! You are afraid of it, but you are attracted to it!" I was twitching and recoiling and making yearning faces and reaching out and pulling back and looking frightened and then trying to look aroused (a feeling I was still pretty clueless about). I was terribly self-conscious and afraid the herky-jerky photographer was going to fall off the roof. If *Punk'd* had been on the air at the time, I would have thought I was being punked.

Then there was the photographer who kept screaming, "I need to SEE WHO YOU ARE! Show me EMOTION!" He wouldn't tell me which emotion he wanted. He just kept repeating, "EMOTION!" Finally, I started screaming about wanting a fat-free blueberry muffin. I started out just yelling about the muffin, but then I started to luxuriate in it, pounding out a prose poem about the muffin like a beat poet at a coffeehouse in *Funny Face*. I wound up weeping for my fat-free blueberry muffin.

Afterward the photographer clasped my hand, looked deeply into my eyes, and said, "Beautiful, beautiful blueberry story, man."

A few hours later, I realized how funny the entire scenario had been. But at the time, it felt deadly serious. I needed to get this right. The only genuine emotions I could tap in to were yearning and fury. My yearning was right there on the surface; I wanted to eat. My fury was buried deeper. I was enraged at my body, at my lack of success, at the daily humiliations of my job.

The only real validation I felt was when stylists told me how skinny I was. They pinned back the clothing that dripped off me, and I reveled in the sensation of loose fabric being pulled taut across my ribs. I loved when photographers told me to push my hips forward or push out my stomach so I didn't look as emaciated.

I was determined to remain the smallest girl in the apartment, no matter how many girls came though. Whenever I wasn't working or precisely carving up my pile of veggies, I'd disappear to the gym. It was exercise or die. Then I'd go sit on the floor of Barnes & Noble, looking at every single fashion magazine. Feeling my heart pound from exertion and want, I'd imagine myself in each shoot. When it was time to leave, I had trouble straightening my legs to stand up. They shook for a moment, like Buster Keaton's legs in an old silent movie before he gets his footing or falls down in a heap.

I wasn't the only teenager having a hard time. One crisp fall day at the apartment, a girl whose name I've forgotten snubbed another girl whose name I've forgotten. It was nothing. It was infantile. Girl A thought Girl B had taken her magazine. Girl A began theatrically pretending to stare through Girl B, saying stuff like "Maybe I'll go take *that* bed, since there's *no one* in it." It was the kind of thing dumb seventeen-year-olds do to pass the time and feel powerful. Hope and I just rolled our eyes at the pettiness.

As Girl A swanned out, I said to Girl B, "Just ignore her. Moody, crazy models!"

Girl B walked slowly out of the bedroom and went to the living room window. It was open about three inches, and she started to yank it to the top. She put her leg over the sill. We were thirty flights up. Hope and I pulled her down as she sobbed, "They all hate me."

I don't think she was being theatrical. I think she really wanted to kill herself. The stress of the business was too much for her. I cradled her as she cried, then we sat on the couch wordlessly. I held her hand tightly, afraid she might bolt for the window again.

Hope and I told the chaperone. The next day the girl was gone. The Agency had sent her home. They didn't think she was healthy enough to stay. Hope and I felt guilty but also a little relieved that we wouldn't have to cope with her lunacy. We had enough of our own.

Shortly afterward, Hope left, too. She wasn't making enough money, and The Agency stopped advancing her rent. We kept in touch for a while, but her career wasn't going the way she'd wanted, and things became increasingly awkward between us. She quit modeling a few months after leaving the apartment.

It was a tough time for a new girl to break in. The fashion business, like most American industries, was hurting after 9/11. Top magazines weren't taking many chances on new models. People wanted what was comforting and familiar, what they knew, because the world seemed so upside down. Everyone wanted to hire established girls who were already proven to sell. I went to a lot of castings, and I got some work—the *Seventeen* gig, jobs in some avant-garde magazines, and a two-page German *Vogue* spread (a big deal for a sixteen-year-old). But nothing really popped me through the waves of new models who crash into New York City regularly, pounding the city like the surf at Montauk.

People say toll collectors have the most stressful job in the world, but if you ask me, that honor has to go to the casting directors at American *Vogue*. There have been three of them in the past five years. And I didn't win any of them over. They liked me enough to keep seeing me, but the calls never resulted in a job.

I couldn't simply blame the economy. The problem was me, too. One magazine told The Agency I had a "weird personality." And I did. I had an eating disorder! Some days I radiated anxiety; other days, when I was especially hungry, I reflected nothing.

On jobs, I had the tools to excel, but I couldn't use them. I was uncomfortable in my skin. I had a vacant, faraway quality. I'd try to create a narrative for myself—who was the girl wearing these clothes? what would she think and feel? how could I convey that to the camera?—but then a stray movement or a harsh laugh from someone on the set would break me. I'd sense the frustration from the photographer, which made me close up more. Models have to be open to be successful.

In mid-October 2002, The Agency sent me to Europe. It's common practice for agencies to send new girls there to build up their books, to work for small magazines, maybe to get discovered by the international edition of a major fashion rag.

Mom and I went to London first. For a month, we stayed in a midpriced hotel, and Mom went sightseeing while I went out on castings. I was starting to freak out. I knew I wasn't becoming the rock star The Scout and The Agent said I could be, which made me even more controlling about my weight. At least that was something I had power over. I found a gym near my hotel and exercised nearly every minute I wasn't going on calls. London felt miserable to me anyway—it was cold and rainy the entire time I was there, the kind of cold I'd never felt in Mississippi or Miami. The chill crept into my bones, dug in, and wouldn't let go. The only place I felt warm was at the gym, when I was sweating.

I swam every day. I hit the pool at six A.M., before my dreary round of go-sees began, when I was the only person in the water. Lap after lap, I sobbed in my lane. I bawled as I powered across the tiny ice-cold pool, back and forth, back and forth, sometimes gagging on the chlorinated water as I gasped and shrieked soundlessly underwater. The few times someone else was there, I was furious. I needed to scream into the water, and I couldn't do it in front of company, just as I couldn't eat with someone watching me.

I hated my life. I didn't want to be working out in a freezing pool in a foreign country in the early dawn. I didn't show well in London, and I knew it. I silently handed over my book, and the clients silently looked back.

One day I was really sick. The constant damp and drafts were taking their toll, and my immune system was toast. My nose ran all the time; I was covered in bruises, since I lacked any kind of insulating fat and was woefully vitamin-deficient. I had a fever, and my entire body ached. So I called my London agent and booked out, even though I had eight or so castings that day. I was barely able to stay upright. But I went to the gym. And there was my agent on the chest-press machine.

"What are you doing here?" he demanded. He thought I was shirking. I mumbled that I truly was sick, but I needed to get in a quick workout to sweat out the toxins. I got on the treadmill and began to walk in place, going nowhere, as usual.

And then Christina Aguilera's "Dirrty" came on the TV in front of the treadmill. I was dumbstruck. I was drawn to her lank, twisted hair, her piercings and tattoos, her curvy little body. Most of all, I was drawn to the power she projected in that video. She seemed so in control—of all the tough men in the *Mad Max*–like, ultimate-fighting cage-match setting; of her own sexuality; of her sinuous movements. I was always drawn to tattoos, but I knew I couldn't get one. My body wasn't mine; it needed to remain a blank canvas for clients. Christina, on the other hand, seemed to own herself fully. I wanted that kind of self-possession but had no idea how to get there.

The London agent called The Agent in New York to complain about my going to the gym when I was supposedly sick. I reiterated to everyone in London and everyone in New York that I wasn't faking. I was ill. But I would get better. And I would do better.

In mid-November, The Agency sent me to Paris for a month, hoping I'd get some work there. My book still needed more pictures. Paris meant new possibilities, new potential clients. Mom and I took the Chunnel from the United Kingdom to France. The train went faster than any train I'd ever been on, through the longest undersea tunnel in the world. My old, healthy self would have been full of questions about how they'd built this wonder of the modern world. My new, starving self was dimly aware that once upon a time, I would have been full of questions.

There wasn't a gym or a pool in walking distance of my apartment-hotel (an *apart'hotel,* the company called it). So I walked back and forth in the hallway for hours after my castings, until two or three A.M. At night, Mom would beg me to come inside as I speed-walked back and forth, back and forth, down the hall outside my room. I needed to walk for an hour. It took me fifteen seconds to walk the length of that small hallway. That was four half-laps per minute, 240 per hour. Back and forth, back and forth. I made my strides as long as I could and swung my arms as widely as I could to maximize the calorie expenditure. I was a wooden soldier. I ventured outside for exercise only once. As I loped past the Bastille, I got chased down by a group of guys, hooting and catcalling. I'd been whistled and muttered at in New York City, but I'd never been chased. Were they going to do something to me? Were they only teasing? I didn't know. I didn't speak French. They seemed threatening. I ran back to the hotel. After that, I stuck to the hallway.

In my hallway-gym, I alternated two hours of back-and-forth tin-soldier walking with jumping jacks. I'd also practice runway, striding icily down the hall. I can only imagine what the Parisians thought as they walked by in their jaunty little scarves, holding their jaunty little dogs. And I did the Elle Macpherson tape in my room. I knew it by heart; I didn't need the visuals.

I didn't do all that well in Paris, either. More small jobs. More arty magazines with tiny circulations. I needed something major.

By now it was almost Christmastime. The fashion industry pretty much shuts down between Christmas and New Year's. So Mom and I went to Seattle to spend the holidays with one of my uncles and his family. Everyone else ate ham and turkey and sweet-potato casserole with marshmallows. I had the lettuce.

Just after New Year's, Mom and I returned to the model apartment in New York City. The Agent asked Mom to come in for a meeting. I worried that I was going to be sent home.

I wasn't.

Mom was.

"Crysti, The Agency thinks you'll do better if you're on your own," she told me afterward. "The Agent said if I really want you to succeed, I have to go."

The Agency felt that Mom was holding me back. Clients knew she was living with me, and that made them see me as even younger than I was. (Being a new model is a balancing act. Editors love the notion of freshness and novelty, but no one wants to shoot a babyish girl in haute couture. You have to present yourself like an adult at castings and on jobs, and you have to look youthful but not so child-ish that you appear to be playing dress-up in the ten-thousand-dollar dresses.) I was coming across as a girl, not as a woman. I needed to convey more maturity. If Mom left, I'd be forced to mature. And then my career would take off.

The Agent reassured Mom that The Agency would look out for me just as Mom had. Mom would be only a phone call away. But she needed to cut the apron strings. The Agent was insistent.

How could I give up my dream? I helped Mom pack.

"I don't feel good about leaving you here," she said. "I know you're capable. But you're sixteen years old! I don't want to go!" She knew I wouldn't get whacked out on drugs or contract sexually transmitted diseases. She trusted me. But I was her baby.

I walked her down to the curb and put her in a taxi. She didn't cry. But years later, she told me that the moment the cab pulled away from the curb was one of the hardest of her life.

At first I called her every day. Then I called twice a week, then once a week, then once every two weeks. I missed her, but I had my eyes on the prize. I focused on work.

Mom moved back to Miami to live with one of my aunts; Lana wouldn't let her see her grandkids in Mississippi.

I kept going on castings, but whatever momentum I might have had after the *Seventeen* shoot three months earlier was gone. I knew my spark was missing. I had a personality in me somewhere, but it was locked away in a tower, inaccessible to me. You can be as beautiful as anything, but if you can't show people a little of your soul, you'll never make it. It wasn't until I became the weight I was meant to be that I figured that out.

Now all I thought about was food. I'd call Mom late at night, sobbing about pecan pie or Cap'n Crunch or a big, juicy Mississippi peach. "Oh, honey," she'd say. "I'm sorry. I'm so sorry." For long minutes, there would be no sound except her gentle cooing and my sobs. Finally, she'd suggest, "Maybe just have what you're craving?" I'd just shake my head, though she couldn't hear that over the telephone wires: *NO NO NO NO NO.* She understood my silence.

All the *NO* was taking its toll. It was getting harder for me to get through my eight-hour weekend workouts. One day in February, another girl recommended I try diet pills, so I picked some up at the drugstore and popped one.

Within an hour, I was buzzing like a bee on a dozen venti quattro macchiatos. I went to both gyms, did Elle's video, and cleaned the bathroom in the model apartment. The fact that I was simultaneously shaking, seeing stars, and on the verge of vomiting didn't much bother me.

That night, I barely slept. There was a roaring sound in my ears. My jaw was clenched so hard I was worried I might dislocate something. I resolved to take the diet pills no more than once a week, just to make it through one eight-hour workout. I never told Mom about the pills. I didn't want her to worry.

I booked out and went to visit her in Miami a couple of times. She always had a pool party in my honor, and the aunts and uncles and cousins in the area would come. Everyone else would be laughing, eating burgers, drinking out of brightly colored plastic cups, but I'd spend the entire party in the pool. I made myself stay in the exact middle of the pool, as close to perfect center as I could get, just treading water. That way I could listen to the family's conversations and chime in when asked a question, but I could exercise at the same time. My rule for myself was that I was never allowed to touch the side of the pool after I'd gotten into the water. If I accidentally touched the wall, or got tired and put my hand on the lip of the pool, I'd punish myself by making myself do hundreds of backflips. I had to touch the bottom of the pool with my hands, propel myself upward, kick my feet against the wall, and flip over backward again. After the guests left, I'd do it for up to two hours. In the warm Miami night, I'd frog-kick the length of the pool and back, over and over. I was obsessed with making sure my legs were extending fully as I kicked, creating as long and lean a line as possible. As I swam, I imagined myself lengthening and getting skinnier. I was experiencing a lot of muscle aches in my inner thighs. I was happy about that. If exercise didn't hurt, how could it be working?

I still have to be careful not to go down that rabbit hole again. Seven years later, I do yoga. It makes me feel in touch with my body, not angry at it. But occasionally, I get a sharp, stabbing pain in my inner thigh when I stretch, perhaps from some tendon or muscle I messed up in the crazy-workout years. My visceral, unmediated, knee-jerk reaction to that pain is: Oh, good. Even today, my first reaction to pain is that it is punishment, and punishment is deserved. No girl should feel that way.

Back in 2002, I didn't know any better. I didn't know how *not* to feel pain.

By this time, modeling no longer seemed so glamorous. I knew that behind every picture was a team of hardworking people. At fourteen, I'd thought the women in *Vogue* looked as beautiful walking down the street as they did in pictures. But now I knew the artifice. I knew there was a fan to the left to make the girl's hair billow out dramatically. I knew some poor assistant was off to the right throwing up the dress to give it volume and then running out of the picture. I knew the serene-looking model might have just yelled at her boyfriend on the phone or thrown up in the toilet on location. At this moment in my life, the artifice felt oppressive and miserable. Years later, when I was happy in my own skin, I could see the art and the beauty in the pretense.

I'd educated myself about who all the top photographers were, but now I despaired that I'd never work with them. I wanted to help make intriguing pictures, though I couldn't figure out what I was doing wrong, what was keeping me from getting the opportunity. I was treading water (and swimming one lap after another, and scissoring in one place on the elliptical, and running in one place on the treadmill—the metaphors write themselves), loathing the very life I'd stopped eating in order to get.

I thought about the pictures I'd seen and loved in fashion magazines. The ravenous lipstick-smeared mouths; the fantastic broken-doll poses; the portrayals of sexual hunger and kink; the gender-bent outfits; the burned-out, sharp-edged, brutal Walker Evans–like photographic landscapes; the crisp, precise look of minimalism and the over-the-top images of fabulous candy-colored fantasies.

The best fashion photos make you look twice. They have an ethereal, ghostly beauty or an acid-trip pop. They recall seedy truck stops or the powdered silk-draped court of Marie Antoinette. They make you think of the way your grandma looked, all dressed up, when you were a very little kid, or they make you wince and think about dead dolls. Great fashion photography brings up associations you might be uncomfortable with or unsure about. It can juxtapose stuff that makes you happy with stuff that freaks you out.

I still wanted in.

Would I be okay if I never got to make pictures like that? Intellectually, I knew that a girl who doesn't make it big in editorial can still have a great experience modeling. She can do catalog, see the world, get braver at talking to strangers, make a little money, get confident in her ability to navigate a metropolis by herself, learn to rely on herself for entertainment. If that girl is strong, she can deal with the steady flood of rejection, the numbing repetition of trotting along a city street or pushing into a crowded subway car to show indifferent people pictures of herself. If that girl can keep perspective, she'll realize that looks and beauty aren't everything, that even when you're making beautiful pictures, girls are still just the raw material that feeds a great commercial machine. A sane girl will appreciate what the machine can give her: money, experience, cute clothes.

But I was not that girl. I wanted more. I was still hungry.

4

THE FROG IN THE POT

Robin Givhan, the Pulitzer Prize–winning fashion writer for *The Washington Post,* recently said of the current vogue for skinny models, "It's like the frog in the water: If you slowly turn up the heat, it doesn't know it's being boiled to death. After a while, a size 0 starts to seem normal, not cadaverous."

I was that frog. And I didn't want to get out of my little lunatic soup pot.

I loved my pathology. I loved the veins running up my arms. If one didn't protrude as much as I wanted it to, I panicked. If my upper arm could touch my breast when my arm was by my side, I panicked. If I couldn't grab my hip bone like the handle of a coffee mug, I panicked. If I bumped into someone on the street, I wanted him to scream in pain from the lethal-razor sharpness that was me.

In 2002, this was my typical day's diet:

BREAKFAST: A giant pile of steamed vegetables with bottled fat-free dressing and a stick of sugar-free gum

LUNCH: A head of lettuce or steamed vegetables, a can of Ultra Pure protein shake (vanilla cream flavor, 160 calories), a sugar-free Snapple, an apple, and a stick of sugar-free gum

DINNER: Steamed vegetables with bottled fat-free dressing and a stick of sugar-free gum

SNACKS THROUGHOUT THE DAY: Six sticks of sugar-free gum, two Diet Cokes

I perpetually needed something to do with my hands and mouth. I nursed my Diet Coke and clutched my can of chemical shake even after it was empty. I bit my nails obsessively, relentlessly. It was like a craft project. My fingertips looked like a war zone, with infected red ripped-open cuticles and nails that were barely a quarter-inch long—these itty-bitty islands surrounded by puffy, infected bits of tissue.

Sometimes I became terrified that sugar-free gum actually had calories. Then I'd run and check the pack. I could feel the blood rushing to my head. I'd read the ingredients a few times and heave a sigh of relief. It took a few minutes for the thudding in my chest to go away. This happened at least once a week.

On my calls and shoots in those days, my eyes locked like a laser with those of the other girls who had eating disorders. We could always spot each other. How? It's not as if we said, "Oh, I'm gonna go throw up now—save my seat!" But you can tell when someone's not naturally ultra-thin. And when you're full of self-loathing yourself, you can usually pick up the neurosis in other people. Genetically thin girls don't have veins running up their arms. So I looked for girls with networks of blue veins—as in those *X-Men* scenes when Rogue touches people and they get etched with blue lines and the life force gets sucked out of them. I looked for dark circles under the eyes, like my own. I looked for girls who excused themselves to talk on the phone when everyone else was eating lunch during a shoot. I could tell by the way someone looked at herself in the mirror—was it a normal, appraising look or an "I hate myself and everyone around me" look? I was compulsive, I was obsessive, I was anxious, and I was attuned to those qualities in others. Those hungry girls were my sisters. But after a shoot, we usually went our separate ways. There was no power in our numbers.

From 2001 to 2003, I walked around in a fog. Sometimes I bolted upright in the middle of the night: "What if there are calories in Diet Coke?" I'd lie in the dark and panic. What if the manufacturer was lying? How many cans had I drunk that day? Was it one or two? Had I had a cup of tea? What if that had calories, too? How hard had I squeezed the tea bag?

I was in a constant state of panic. I had no energy, felt no joy. I was freezing all the time. I was constantly constipated; my stomach pain was so ever-present that I took its constant thrumming for granted. I had trouble sleeping. I experienced regular heart palpitations. My joints, especially those in my knees and jaw, ached terribly. My hair was breaking off and falling out. My skin developed a gray tinge. I had a perpetual headache. I often heard ringing in my ears. I sometimes had trouble breathing. My skin was Sahara-dry. My throat and joints ached badly enough that I often wanted to cry. If I stood up too quickly, I'd get so dizzy that I had to put a hand on the wall to make the room stop spinning. I was always exhausted. I needed loads of caffeine to make it through my eight-hour workouts. My legs were so covered in bruises that I looked like I had an abusive boyfriend. My pathology was my lover. I don't know what death feels like, but this had to be the beginning. I wanted to claw off my own face.

I barely talked. When I did speak, I'd sometimes lose my train of thought midsentence. How could I be the same person who'd aced her GED?

The stereotype of models is that we're brain-dead, but some of us are just starving.

Once in mid-2002, I keeled over on Madison Avenue on the way to a casting. I felt my heart leap and thud; my vision turned sparkly, then narrowed and went gray, as if I were looking through a paper-towel tube. I hit the filthy concrete. A woman in navy blue wedges helped me get up from the sidewalk and sit against the side of a building. She waited as I called the chaperone from the model apartment and said, "Please come get me. I can't move."

I sat in the shadow of that apartment building for twenty minutes until the chaperone came. She helped me up and put me in a cab. That was the only time I missed a casting—fortunately, it was a Saturday, and I had only one. The next day, I was back to running. Running to castings. Running on the treadmill. Running from reality. I didn't care if I was unhealthy. I wanted to be a supermodel. It was a careerist sickness.

I look at pictures from that time, and I'm stunned. Not at my thinness—unlike some anorexics who always think they're fat, I knew on some level how thin I was. No, what astounds me in those photos is my blankness. There was no light in my eyes. They had an otherworldly, faraway, George Romero quality. There was no there there. I was supposed to be selling romance and glamour, but the notion of sensuality or sex was laughable. I was a ghost.

Around February 2003, The Agent called me in to a meeting. "Miss Renn, Miss Renn. You wear too much black," she said in a singsong.

Excuse me?

"You look too severe," The Agent went on. "Can't you be more fun? Clients want cute and fresh! Can you wear some flannel? Or hey, buy some red pumps! Have fun with it!"

A few months earlier, I was too young-looking. Now I was too harsh-looking? I didn't want to "have fun with it." I'd loved black since I was a kid. I dressed like a mime. I slicked my hair back or wore it stick-straight (being careful not to comb too much, since it broke off and fell out so easily). I sometimes wore black and white— I had a Ralph Lauren black-and-white-pin-striped turtleneck, a chunky Marc Jacobs sweater with thick black and gray stripes, and a vintage black blouse with polka dots—but mostly, I wore solid black. I was more interested in clothing's shape than its color. I was drawn to architectural pieces, not sweet girlish ones. I collected clothes with shape and structure, I often wore my flowy, haremish Jill Stuart balloon pants with a long tank top and a drapey black tee over that.

"Lighten up!" The Agent trilled. "You should look like a teenager! Like you just rolled out of bed!"

When a product doesn't sell, the marketers redesign the packaging. Clearly, I wasn't selling.

What was selling, still, was thinness. When I started modeling in 2002—and to a slightly lesser degree, today—the look of the moment was nearly skeletal. Starting in the early nineties with the rise of Kate Moss and heroin chic, the fashion industry—and to an extent, the public—fell in love with depressed-looking, emaciated girls. Fashion is a cyclical business, and this wasn't the first time skinniness was big. In the twenties, there was the flapper look, with its narrow silhouette, boyishly bobbed hair, and dropped-waist dresses; in the sixties, there was Twiggy, who looked frail and wide-eyed and childlike. (Today she'd barely register as thin, and flappers look positively portly compared to fashion models now.)

But at the turn of the millennium, models started getting skinnier and skinnier. The real public relations crisis hit in 2006. In a matter of months, model after model died while striving for an impossibly thin ideal. A twenty-two-year-old model from Uruguay named Luisel Ramos perished after living for weeks on only lettuce and Diet Coke. Then twenty-one-year-old Brazilian Ana Carolina Reston died from complications of kidney problems attributed to anorexia and bulimia—at five-eight, she got down to eighty-eight pounds. Then Reston's sister, Eliana Ramos, also a model, died from a heart attack believed to be brought on by malnutrition. Israeli fashion model Hila Elmalich died of heart failure, weighing under sixty pounds—about the size of the average seven-year-old.

There was a huge outcry. Newspapers, newsmagazines, and websites berated the fashion business. The industry responded with a bouquet of face-saving pronouncements. The Council of Fashion Designers of America (CFDA) recommended that runway models be above the age of sixteen and encouraged a limit on working hours. Spain banned models under 123 pounds from taking part in Madrid's fashion week. Israel was the first country to pass weight-minimum laws for working models; those laws required agencies to use only girls with a body-mass index of nineteen or over. This was back in 2004, when the vogue for super-thinness had begun but hadn't yet crested.

Of course, Israel's modeling industry is about as important as Milwaukee's film festival.

Associazione Servizi Moda, the organization representing Italy's top modeling agencies, announced that all models in runway shows would have to produce doctors' letters stating they were in good health. Italy banned the use of models under sixteen and urged designers to use larger models. Letizia Moratti, the mayor of Milan, added that she'd seek a ban similar to Spain's if her city's designers didn't stop using models who "looked sick."

Models began to out themselves as having eating disorders. In

2003, when she was fifteen, model Coco Rocha lost ten pounds in six weeks on a modeling trip to Singapore. "I'll never forget the piece of advice I got from people in the industry when they saw my new body," she told the Associated Press in 2008. "They said, 'You need to lose more weight. The look this year is anorexia. We don't want you to be anorexic, but that's what we want you to look like.' "

In June 2008, *Teen Vogue* ran a story about the seventeen-year-old model Ali Michael, who had been a rising star until she gained five pounds. During the spring 2008 fashion season, she walked in thirty-one shows; the following season, thanks to those five extra pounds, she did only eleven—ten in New York, one in Paris, and none in London or Milan. She told *Teen Vogue* that when she was discovered at age fifteen, she weighed 130 pound but was told to lose weight and dropped to 102 to model. (She's five-nine, like me.) Michael also said that in her struggle to keep weight gain at bay, she experimented with laxatives and purging, and that her diet eventually became oatmeal with water for breakfast, a banana and a few grapes for lunch, and a piece of lettuce for dinner—"maybe with a piece of fish." She said her period stopped and her family doctor put her on hormone replacement therapy. She became worried that she'd lose her ability to have children. On the way back from Paris, after being told she no longer had "a couture body," she ran her hands through her hair, and a clump fell out. She said, "I've always had low self-esteem, and I'm a perfectionist, so I associated being a successful model with losing the most weight possible. When people told me how tiny my waist was or that my stomach was 'so flat,' it made me feel self-assured, almost invincible."

Blatant obsession with skinniness even invaded the Victoria's Secret fashion show, an ostensible celebration of sexuality and curves. True fashionistas look down on Victoria's Secret models because they have breasts and hips; they're considered pinups, not high-fashion girls. They sell sex, not couture. But at a 2008 Victoria's Se-

cret fashion-show taping, *a gossipeuse* for the *New York Post* named
Raakhee Mirchandani overheard an audience member gasp upon
seeing the curvaceous Karolina Kurkova: "She really porked out."
Kurkova (who, needless to say, is not even a tiny bit porky) told Mirchandani her diet secrets: "I wake up and I have a green juice with a
little protein powder and glutamine mixed in. Then two hours later
I have two hard-boiled eggs. Then two or three hours later I'll have
ten nuts, like walnuts or almonds. Then I'll have grilled fish with
vegetables and salads. And then again, a green juice." She added
that leading up to a show, she stops eating carbs and wheat entirely
and does three hours of exercise a day. Mirchandani ended her re-
port on the show by dryly noting, "And then we notice the sumptuous buffet lining the wall, untouched."

In other words, despite the CYA edicts from the international
fashion world, the immediate change was nil. High-fashion models
in countries with prestigious fashion weeks remained as thin as ever.
No one at the Italian shows ever seemed to collect those mythical
doctors' letters. (Hey, wasn't *announcing* it just as good as *doing* it?)
There was talk of banning tobacco and alcohol backstage at American shows, but that didn't happen, either. The CFDA "recommends"
not hiring girls under sixteen for shows and advocates educating the
industry "to identify the early-warning signs in an individual at risk
of developing an eating disorder." But those are toothless sugges-
tions, not rules.

The CFDA official guidelines go on to say, "Models who are
identified as having an eating disorder should be required to seek
professional help, and models who are receiving professional help
for an eating disorder should not continue modeling without that
professional's approval." That's a lot of use of the passive voice. Who
owns the problem here? The subject of the sentence: "models."
(Though even that is followed by that cumbersome "who are inden-

tified" . . . "should be required" . . . "should not continue" . . .) The semantic effect is this: The problem doesn't *belong* to anyone. But if it does, it belongs to the models, who are as passive as the voice in those recommendations. They're the ones whose careers are on the line.

The weight of the entire industry rests on those girls' skinny shoulders. Ask a model backstage at a show about thinness, and she immediately stiffens and blames other girls, nameless ones, who've "chosen not to be healthy." She doesn't blame the business. She needs to work.

Yes, some girls—especially the youngest ones—are naturally that skinny. But some aren't. And those girls may go to terrible lengths to keep the flesh at bay. Some take Adderall as an appetite suppressant. Some take diuretics. I've shared weight-loss strategies with those girls. In 2007, the *New York Times* reported that some models take clenbuterol, a prescription asthma drug that's commonly used off-label to reduce body fat. I haven't met anyone who I know for sure took clenbuterol for weight loss, but it's not as if every girl shares her dark secrets before swallowing a horse pill. After all, I didn't tell anyone about spitting peanut butter into the sink. Secrets are secrets.

I do know that one reason models—and regular girls—smoke like chimneys is to keep their weight down. During fashion week, especially, they subsist on champagne and fumes.

The vast majority of couture and prêt-a-porter designers want to see their clothes worn by skinny models and sold to skinny customers. Even designers who have spoken publicly about battling their own weight—Donna Karan, Karl Lagerfeld, Alber Elbaz, Kate and Laura Mulleavy of Rodarte—don't design for plus sizes. And I can think of one designer, not any of those I just named, who I suspect makes clothes for herself in sizes she doesn't produce for the public;

I don't think she could fit in the largest size of her own line. But God forbid she should make clothes for women who are the same size she is.

The vast majority of fashion editors are thin. Showing how art imitates life, the movie *The Devil Wears Prada* had its horrified, naive Anne Hathaway character ask, "Doesn't anybody eat around here?"

"Not since two is the new four and zero is the new two," answers the magazine's creative director.

"Well, I'm a six," the Hathaway character answers.

"Aha, the new fourteen," the creative director shoots back.

When those pin-thin editors are asked why they don't use normal-sized models, they often blame sample sizes, which constrain them into using girls who fit the preseason samples designers make. Or they blame readers, who they say recoil when faced with healthy-looking girls. Or they blame the culture, some amorphous force that wants girls in magazines to have shoulder blades you could cut yourself on. Or they blame designers for making clothing that looks good only on tiny bodies. Designers, when confronted about why they don't design in larger sizes or use robust-looking models on the runways, tend to stammer about choosing girls who fit the clothes. It's a whole industry of people pointing the finger: The problem is the designers! The problem is editorial! The problem is advertising! The problem is consumers!

Everyone falls back on the old saw about fashion being inconsequential, nothing to think about too hard. "We sell dreams!" that philosophy goes. "Our escapist little world doesn't matter!" As Robin Givhan pointed out in *The Washington Post*, it's disingenuous for designers to dismiss their $47 billion industry by saying. "Oh, it's only fashion." (She made the point that you won't hear an automaker saying, "They're just cars.")

Ultimately, it is the girls—the weakest link in the daisy chain—who bear the brunt of all the denials, demurrals, and buck-passing. As Guy Trebay of *The New York Times* put it, "despite its putative glamour, a modeling gig is more like that of a supermarket checker than one would imagine. Both draw on a work force that tends to be uneducated and young." He points out that models have no union ("and if they did, there would be a lot better ethnic representation on catwalks") and no insurance. In *New York* magazine in 2007, Emily Nussbaum called models "manual laborers with short shelf lives." Indeed, most modeling careers have the duration of a butterfly's heartbeat.

So the girls say there's no anorexia problem in fashion. Or if there is, it's some other model's problem. Not any model in the show they're walking in, and no one at their agency, has a problem, but yes, some nebulous random mythical anorexic girl no one knows, somewhere in the world of fashion, is perhaps failing to eat. If you were in her position, would you bite the hand that didn't feed you? Especially if the money it held out allowed you to feed your family back home in South America or Eastern Europe?

In 2007, at a CFDA panel on eating disorders, Natalia Vodianova, one of the women closest to supermodel status working today (*Forbes* magazine estimated that she earned around $4.8 million in 2008, making her the seventh-highest-earning model in the world), dared to speak out about wispy models and their economic and familial burdens. "They were very young, a lot of them were very lonely, far from home and their loved ones," she said of the models she met on her way up. "Most came from poor backgrounds and were helping their families. They left their childhood behind with dreams of a better life, and for most of them, there was nothing they wouldn't do to live those dreams." Vodianova hails from a poor neighborhood in Gorky, Russia, where her mother ran a fruit stand.

Her sister has cerebral palsy. She understands that the pressure to stay thin can be irresistible if you're the person your entire family depends on.

"One of the interesting things about these models today is that they get used and spit out so quickly," Magali Amadei, a formerly bulimic model, told *New York* magazine in February 2007. "The era of the supermodel is over, so girls working today don't have the earning power. These girls come into the business young, and they are disposable. On top of that, people often talk about your appearance in front of you, as if you can't hear them."

It wasn't always this way. I am not a sociologist, and I don't know how extreme skinniness became chic. Maybe it's a response to the rest of America getting heavier. If you see human heft as déclassé, as a sign of tackiness and (ahem) nonwhiteness (I don't believe it's an accident that the super-skinny look coincided with a super-lack of diversity on runways), then extreme thinness can be a way of distancing yourself from and seeming more high-class than the people you scorn.

Or maybe the mania for thinness is about economic fears—the blankness of these wide-eyed, narrow-framed Eastern European girls becomes a reflection of hunger and uncertainty about the future. Maybe it's a response to terrorist anxiety—if you take up so little space, you're less of a target.

I do know that the last time the economy collapsed coincided with the rise of Kate Moss. Back in the early nineties, she seemed shockingly skinny. Her frailness was the grunge-era equivalent of today's flounder-flat fish-eyed Eastern European girls' interchangeability. Now Kate Moss–level skinny no longer seems novel. So the girls had to get skinnier.

The current skinny-mania is like the platform heel in fashion. One season a designer breaks out with a shape that looks so exciting and novel, everyone wants it. Other designers leap on that basic shape and start taking it further. It becomes a more and more extreme version of itself. The platform gets thicker, the heel gets higher, the pitch gets more pronounced, the accoutrements get more cartoony. Eventually, we're in Balenciaga buckle-and-strap bondage-shoe territory. It's fabulous and scary. Presto, there's nowhere else for that silhouette to go. Everyone's all *bored now* and *Hey, remember the flat?* Or *This summer's all about the gladiator sandal!* Or *Oh, how witty, the revival of the eighties pump! It's bananas! I die!*

I adore fashion, and I'm not mocking fashion. (It's my livelihood as well as my passion.) But the human body should not be held to the same extreme trendiness standard as a shoe. As the flesh-and-blood equivalent of designer shoes, model's bodies will have to reach a point at which they've become so extreme, there's nowhere left to go. And since the technology does not yet exist to reanimate skeletons and have them skitter down a runway "Dem Bones"–style, the pendulum will have to swing back to a healthier silhouette. It's already happening.

Before we look to the future, let's take a quick look back at the past. Jimmy Pihet of the Fédération Française de la Couture told *The Wall Street Journal* in 2007, "You look at the girls, they are not beautiful like models were 20 years ago. The girls are thin, they have strange faces . . . At first, you look at them and you're not sure if they're beautiful or disgusting." Ah, ambivalence is the new black.

I knew that models hadn't always been so skeletal. When I wasn't working, working out, or not eating, I was continuing the Modeling 101 studies I'd begun back in Clinton. To educate myself about the history of modeling, I bought crumbling old back issues of *Vogue* and *Flair* at vintage stores and read how-to books about the business. The most helpful book for me, by far, was Michael Gross's big fat tome, *Model.*

I loved learning about the origins of the crazy world I was part of. I knew that in the dim past, models weren't spectral creatures.

Gross writes that the first true model was Marie Vernet, a Paris salesgirl who married a salesman named Charles Worth and started modeling his designs when he opened Worth, the first designer salon, in 1858. In the pictures I've seen of her, she's wearing a corset, like all women of her day, but her arms are attractively rounded, and she certainly doesn't look skinny.

The first supermodel, according to Gross, was Anita Counihan in the 1920s. (Sorry, Janice Dickinson. But feel free to keep claiming it's you.) Counihan was never photographed in bathing suits because she was considered to have fat legs (my sister!), but she was known as the Face and was the highest-paid model of her time, earning up to a hundred dollars an hour. One memorable month, she appeared on the cover of fifteen magazines, including *Time*. In 1935 she moved to Hollywood to become an actress and changed her last name to Colby. Later, she was the executive assistant to the head of Paramount Pictures, earned a hundred and fifty thousand dollars a year—a staggering sum in the 1940s—then started her own PR agency, wrote a beauty book and was a regular on the *Today* show. She was a trailblazer not only in modeling but in showing how there's life after modeling, if you're smart and you hustle and you make your own opportunities.

Another major model was Lisa Fonssagrives, a Swedish-born ballet dancer in Paris who modeled from the 1930s to the '50s. During her first session with the photographer Horst, she was so scared she was shaking. Finally, it dawned on her to use her dance skills.

"The movements I chose in modeling were arrested dance movements," Gross quotes Fonssagrives as saying. "My training gave me terrific control. It was still dancing, really . . . I would imagine what kind of woman would wear the gown and assume different characters. I would look at the cut of the dress and try different poses to see how it fell best, how the light would enhance it . . . I was terribly serious about being responsible and even studied photography to learn what the problems might be. I would stand before the camera on a set and concentrate my energy until I could sense it radiate into the lens and feel when the photographer had the picture."

That's what I should have been trying to do in 2002 and early 2003. But back then I wasn't enough in touch with my body to tap in to my martial arts training the way Fonssagrives used her ballet background. Today, as a plus model, I'm always aware of where the camera and light source are and how to move to create a compelling shot. "Working your angles" is modelspeak for knowing how to angle your face and body so they jump out of the pictures. When I was straight size (that is, not plus), I had no idea how to work my angles. I wasn't yet attuned to following the light or moving my face and body in ways that created an eye-pleasing geometry. I was too passive.

The first modeling agency, started by an out-of-work actor named John Robert Powers, did represent many women who were considered very thin even for their time. This was the Jazz Age, when breasts and hips were considered unchic. Powers saw an opportunity to connect struggling actors with photographers who wanted good-looking people to shoot for modeling jobs. Powers had the brainstorm to put a bunch of his actor friends' pictures in a book and send it to photographers, advertisers, and department stores all over the city. That was in 1923. By 1929 he had competition: Walter Thornton opened a rival agency and called himself a "Merchant of Venus." (Clever.) Then a third agent, Harry Conover, joined the fray. He saw the chance to offer clients an alternative to the super-thin, super-chic "Powers Girls." So he only hired healthy-looking, all-American girls, and publicly called the Powers Girls "Adenoid Annies, rattling bundles of skin and bones." He wrote, "Frankly, I made up my mind long ago that life was too short for me to kowtow to these Melba-Toast prima donnas whose waspish figures are matched by equally waspish temperaments."

Presumably, he would have loved today's plus-size models. He wasn't alone in his predilection for curvier girls. In 1948 Grace Kelly was rejected as a Miss Rheingold girl—a model for a beer company in a hugely popular ad campaign of the 1940s, '50s, and early '60s— because she was considered too skinny.

Ford, the agency I signed with when I became a plus model, came along in 1946 and quickly became known for its ethical, up-right business practices. Eileen Ford, who'd been a model herself and who graduated from Barnard College, started it with her hus-band, Gerald. One reason I wanted to work with Ford after my unhappy experience as a straight-size model was that I felt I'd be well cared for. The fact that Ford had a well-respected plus division was secondary to me; what was most appealing was that Ford has always had a reputation for considering its models' well-being. Ei-leen was profiled in *Life* magazine in the early '50s, sewing a model's gown before a party while another model soaked her feet in a tub. The headline was FAMILY-STYLE MODEL AGENCY. The Fords, Gross says, tried to help their models improve themselves, encouraging them to study culture, speech, dancing, acting, and languages. They also kept models on a tight leash with partying. I knew I wouldn't be just a piece of (very lean) meat if I signed with Ford.

As recently as twenty years ago, supermodels were both heavier and more distinctive-looking than they are today. Think of Cindy Crawford, with her mole and her glorious hair; Naomi Campbell, with her strong, shapely legs and teasing confidence; Helena Chris-tensen, with her seaglass-colored eyes and dusky skin; Christy Tur-lington, with her serenity and soul; Claudia Schiffer, with her St. Pauli Girl–meets-Bardot overbite and coyness. My favorite was Linda Evangelista, with her catlike eyes, cropped hair, elegant poses, and seemingly infinite expressive range. None of those girls could be mistaken for anyone else on a runway or in a fashion spread. They all had powerful, different looks. They compelled your attention.

Who has that kind of allure today? Can anyone outside the circle of fashion's most devoted acolytes even name the top models now? Is it any wonder that models have been booted from magazine covers in favor of actresses and pop stars? True, we're in a cultural moment that's all about celebrities, but the fact is, few of today's highest-paid models stand out from the pack. Celebrities sell magazines (including the magazines that once had true supermodels gracing nearly every cover) because they sing recognizable songs and act in recognizable movies and TV shows. The public feels they know actresses as people. They want to know about their personal lives. They don't feel that way about models anymore, because models don't spark their interest the way they did back in the '80s.

And back in the '80s, when supermodels were several sizes larger than top models today, the clothes worked on bigger bodies. They were bright, bold, curve-enhancing. Jackets had serious shoulder pads. Hair was sky-high. Earrings were chunky. It was an era when women were gaining power, going to work in their suits and running shoes, and I think the style of the clothing was a reflection of a time when women didn't have to be invisible. I wonder whether today's mania for super-thin, wide-eyed, less powerful-looking girls is tied to fear of female strength. Today's girls take up less space, literally and metaphorically.

Paulina Porizkova told *Vogue* in 2007, "We were pretty unapologetic size 4s and 6s, and there were even a couple of 8s . . . That superskinny thing began with Kate Moss, unfortunately, which was none of her fault, because she's quite naturally thin." A woman who seems very comfortable in her own skin, Paulina says she feels heavy now only when she's around models, even though she's still a size four.

In the past twenty-five years, models have gotten much, much smaller. Twenty-five years ago, the average female model weighed 8 percent less than the average American woman. Today models weigh about 23 percent less than the average woman. And at around five-ten, the typical model is a good five inches taller than models of several decades ago.

Frederique van der Wal, a Victoria's Secret and *Sports Illustrated* swimsuit model from the early '90s and the mother of a young daughter, told *USA Today* in 2006, "This unnatural thinness is a terrible message to send out. The people watching the fashion shows are young, impressionable women."

But does looking at skinny models really cause anorexia in young, impressionable women? The answer is unclear. Sarah Murnen, a professor of psychology at Kenyon College in Gambier, Ohio, reviewed twenty-one studies that looked at the media's effect on more than six thousand girls, ages ten and older. She found that those who were exposed to the most fashion magazines were more likely to suffer from poor body images. But that doesn't answer one vital question: Did the magazines cause their poor body image, or are girls with poor body images more likely to look at fashion magazines? I don't know.

An obsession with skinny models may well be linked to eating disorders, but I don't think looking at skinny models causes eating disorders. If it did, anyone who opened a fashion magazine would have anorexia. We do know that anorexia is linked with depression and obsessive-compulsive behavior, which are caused by abnormalities in brain chemistry. Fluctuating levels of seratonin, a brain chemical that regulates appetite, may contribute to other symptoms of anorexia, such as impulsiveness and mood disorders. The media plays its part, as do family and friends. But leaping to blame the media for everything is reductive.

I've read extensively about the characteristics of people with anorexia. I definitely tend to be a perfectionist. Other qualities—which I don't think I have in spades but I do think are part of who I am— are the desire to always be perceived as being "good" and an overarching fear of being ridiculed. Too many of us feel that we have to be perfect in order to be loved.

It's worth remembering that anorexia predated any kind of media. Think of ultra-religious young women long ago who deliberately refrained from eating to show their devotion and faith. Young women have always found a certain amount of bliss in achieving perfect control.

There are scientists who think anorexia is more about genetics than about dynamics between a girl and her family or peers. I think they may be on to something. Blaming the family for a girl's illness seems wrong to me—and it also seems to boil down to blaming the mother. How familiar this sounds: Not long ago, autism was blamed on cold, undemonstrative "refrigerator mothers." That theory has been thoroughly debunked. The exact causes of autism, as with anorexia, still aren't known, but having a bitch for a mom is surely not one of them.

However, family history is definitely linked to anorexia. About 20 percent of people with anorexia have a relative with an eating disorder. If an identical twin has anorexia, the other twin has over a 50 percent chance of developing it, too. Again, is this nature or nurture? No one knows for sure.

Whatever the cause, anorexia is notoriously difficult to treat. It has a depressingly high fatality rate. Up to 20 percent of people with this disease die of it, according to the nonprofit Eating Disorders Coalition. That makes it the deadliest mental illness, the one with the highest premature mortality rate. (The majority of deaths are caused by complications of starvation.) Once upon a time, the treatment of choice involved separating girls from their families and teaching them, in a residential treatment program, how to eat again. Newer approaches encourage the family to be involved. If a family has meals together, this theory goes, they'll feel that they're all in the battle together, as part of a team. This approach demonizes the illness, nor the child or the parent. Not surprisingly, looking for someone to blame doesn't seem to bring about healing.

Sadly, girls who are determined to stay super-skinny today may have an easier time finding moral support to maintain their sickness than I did when I was a teenager. In addition to pro-ana websites, "thinspo" (a contraction of "thin inspiration") videos have proliferated, because today it's easier than ever to edit and upload videos to the Net. In thinspo videos, images fade in and out of super-skinny, blank-faced girls, all set to an emo sound track. Several feature an anonymous poem: "I want to be so thin, light, airy that, when the light hits me, I don't leave a shadow behind. When I walk across the snow I will not leave so much as one footprint to mar its virgin purity. I can dance between the raindrops in a downpour." That was how wispy I wanted to be, too.

To girls today, thinness equals goodness. The correlation is closer for us than it was for our mothers, grandmothers, and great-grandmothers. The culture of celebrity is also far more intense now than it was decades ago. We're swimming in images of people who are famous merely for being famous, a world in which gossip about actors' and singers' bodies is inescapable. We're simply more awash in media. In *The Body Project,* Joan Jacobs Brumberg points out that as the world got more complicated through the 1920s and '30s, girls got more crazed about self-monitoring and weight. "Inventions increased our level of self-scrutiny," Brumberg says. "Mirrors, movies, scales—the modern bathroom. You have to have a certain environment for that obsessive concern."

A staggering number of people without clinical eating disorders struggle with hating their bodies and feeling anxious about food. According to a 2005 *Self* magazine survey, one in five women have made themselves throw up after eating because they didn't want their bodies to absorb the calories. Having such a fearful relationship with food may not be fatal, but it can kill the joy in living.

Swimming with Mom

Talking nutrition with Grandma

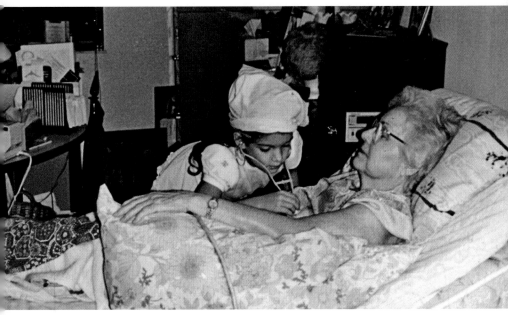

At age six, playing doctor with Grandma

Beginning my career in the arts at age three

Practicing bo staff in the dojo at age nine

Trying to conform in Clinton at age thirteen

Portrait of an 8th-grade cheerleader

Finally skinny enough!

Putting on a happy face in an early Polaroid

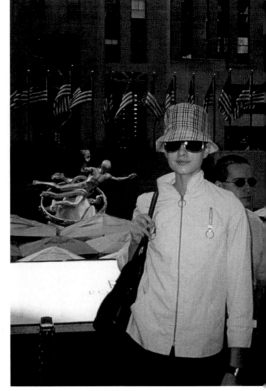

In 2002, becoming a New Yorker

crystal renn

My first comp card with The Agency

crystal renn

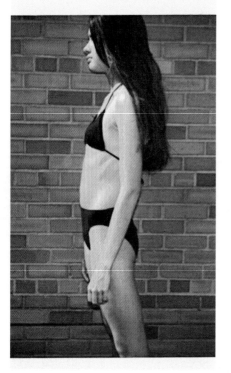

98 pounds, 5' 9"

This is a test photo for The Agency. When The Agent saw it, she winced and said, "You're too heavy here."

A shoot in New York

From a shoot during my miserable stay in London

From the day I had my epiphany. When the head of The Agency saw this Polaroid, he said: "The thighs need to come down."

crystal renn

My last comp card with The Agency

*My first Polaroids at Ford—
note my changed demeanor!*

My first Ford comp card

FORD
12+

CRYSTAL RENN

The shoot that launched my plus-size career: Steven Meisel photographed me for the April 2004 issue of American Vogue.

Walking the finale with Jean Paul

Closing Jean Paul Gaultier's runway show was surreal—by far, the biggest rush of my life. Jean Paul made this dress specifically for me.

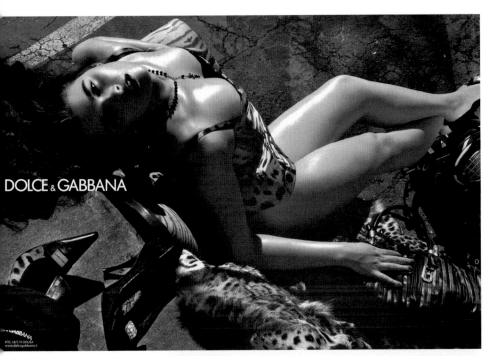

DOLCE & GABBANA

NYC 18177.0 DG.USA
www.dolcegabbana.it

*Starring in a Dolce &
Gabbana ad*

*The famous ad for the
Breast Cancer Research
Foundation. This was the
first time I worked with
the extraordinary Ruven
Afanador (who also shot
my book cover).*

WE'RE MAKING
BREAST CANCER
HISTORY.

At The Breast Cancer Research Foundation,
our targeted funding has led to breakthrough
advances in research, detection, prevention
and treatment.

More than 85 cents of every dollar donated
to BCRF goes to breast cancer research and
awareness programs. And for the sixth straight
year, we received Charity Navigator's highest
rating, outperforming over 5,000 other charities.

At BCRF, we're not just making history.
We're changing the future.

The
Breast
Cancer
Research
Foundation

THE BREAST CANCER RESEARCH FOUNDATION • FOUNDED IN 1993 BY EVELYN H. LAUDER • WWW.BCRFCURE.ORG • 1.866.FIND.A.CURE

COVERS!!!

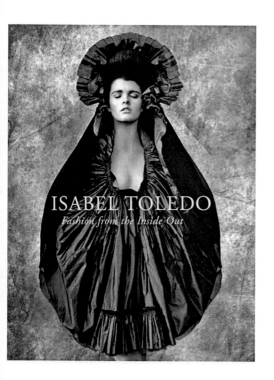

I was honored that designer Isabel Toledo chose me for the cover of her new book, Isabel Toledo: Fashion from the Inside Out. *Ruven shot this cover too.*

MORE COVERS!!!

A happy bride

June 30, 2007: Greg and me on our wedding day

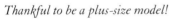

Wedding kiss

Thankful to be a plus-size model!

Enjoying the day with Mom and Greg

A kiss from Ashley

Posing with my beautiful bridesmaids—Ashley and Rachel

Gary walking me down the aisle

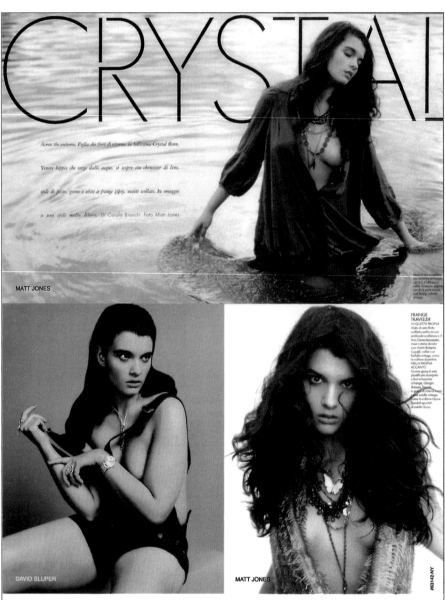

Height 5'9" Bra 38C Waist 30 Hips 42
Dress 12 Shoe 10 Hair Brown Eyes Brown

Grösse 1.75 Oberweite 99 Taille 76 Hüfte 107 Konfection 42
Schuhe 41 Haare Braun Augen Braun

FORD+

My current Ford comp card

The problems begin when girls are younger and younger. According to a 1992 study in the *Journal of the American Dietetic Association,* 46 percent of nine-to-eleven-year-olds are "sometimes" or "very often" on diets. Moms of four- and five-year-olds will tell you that they hear their daughters worrying about being fat and hurling "fat" as an all-purpose insult. There is nothing sadder than the sight of a little girl in front of a mirror, pinching her belly and frowning.

Thankfully, the pendulum seems to be swinging back, at least a bit. The 2009 face of Marc by Marc Jacobs is Daisy Lowe, who definitely has a curvier body than has been in style lately. "I think she looks adorable," Jacobs told *WWD.* The look of the cult show *Mad Men,* set in the early '60s, causes nonstop swooning. Men and women alike can't stop talking about the luscious body of Joan, the show's queen-bee secretary, played by Christina Hendricks. With her impressive bullet-bra-encased chest and ample butt, she's deliriously hot. The looks of Jennifer Hudson, Adele, and Beyoncé are generally admired, not reviled. And the It Girl of 2009 is ample singer Beth Ditto.

Kate Spicer, writing in *The Times* of London, believes the era of super-thin may be over. "Designers such as Antonio Berardi and Roland Mouret have spoken about problems finding girls who adequately fill their womanly clothes," she says. She quotes Berardi as saying, "We have to spend days altering things. We add padding and pieces that work inside the clothes to exaggerate their bodies into a more female form." He goes on to deride "all these young girls with pale skin from Eastern Europe who all look the same, these weird androids with no character," and concludes, "My family is Italian—I am inspired by a womanly aesthetic." For his part, Mouret says, "I see advertising going back to that powerful 1980s mentality, when girls like Linda [Evangelista] were the ideal."

Spicer writes approvingly of Nicole Richie's weight gain and notes that the stick-thin Lindsay Lohan and Paris Hilton have been "disgraced." Designers are hiring the old-school supermodels—Linda, Christie, Naomi—to do more work.

Anita Bitton, a New York–based casting director, told Spicer that for big advertising campaigns, her clients now want strong, complex girls with opinions, not doe-eyed, frightened, interchangeable skinny-minnies. They want "a girl with a voice," she says. "They want a degree of approachability and reality that touches a nerve in the consumer."

Even on runways, 2008 fashion weeks were different from those in recent years. There were girls who were size 2 or 4, not just size 0. The models didn't look quite so scary-thin or quite so young. The styling, overall, was a little less grim. Hair was bouncier; more girls smiled instead of looking as if they were marching to their doom. Furthermore, there was a bit more diversity—the girls didn't look like identical cyborgs. This is undoubtedly a step in the right direction, and I hope it's the beginning of a trend. There should be all kinds of girls on the runway. Difference is gorgeous. Seeing reflections of the great wide world on the runway is good for all of us. I'm not suggesting that we punish the naturally thin girls; I just think they shouldn't be the only game in town.

The fashion industry may not be responsible for eating disorders, but it does play a role in how people view their own bodies. To deny that is disingenuous and dangerous. Young girls idealize modeling—they imagine, wrongly, that it's a world in which a girl is constantly told she's beautiful. They imagine that being a model means being constantly gazed at adoringly and getting to party with rock stars and actors with too much product in their hair.

Fashion can and should encourage all girls to feel beautiful, rather than inadequate, in their own skin. As a culture, we should realize that while a thing of beauty is a joy forever, other things are a joy forever, too, such as education, kindness, humor. We should celebrate those things as much as we do looks.

"I think there's progress," Nian Fish of the CFDA told the Associated Press in 2008. "The girls are still slim. We didn't want them not to be slim. We wanted a projection of health."

I am glad Fish thinks there's progress. But I'm troubled by the phrase "projection of health." I don't want a projection. I want actual health! Maybe Fish just made an unfortunate choice of words, but the effect is to say that we care mostly about image; we don't necessarily want to have anything *grounding* the projection. And many of us in the plus-size and straight-size fashion world *do* want more than that.

The National Eating Disorders Association (NEDA) has recommended that the fashion industry require adult models to have a body mass index of at least 18.5—which is considered the lower limit of healthy normal weight on the BMI chart—and an independent medical certification affirming that they don't have an eating disorder. I have a hard time believing the American fashion industry will go for that. But I think it's worse to pay lip service to a crisis and make rules with no intention of enforcing them just to appear as though something is being done.

Ultimately, fashion is a business, and the market will dictate what's in. If people clamor for curves and continue to get excited about models who don't look like the norm, the industry will expand (hyuk hyuk) to accommodate them. If the industry becomes proactive—if more people in positions of influence stop waiting for a trendsetting photographer to tell them who the Next Hot Atypical Girl is, but as a matter of habit, cast a variety of different-looking girls for more shoots and shows—then the money will follow. Choosing models who don't look like they're at death's door will have all kinds of positive repercussions. To take it a step further, choosing models who prove that beauty comes in all ages, sizes, and colors will energize buyers and trigger new enthusiasm for fashion.

Modeling is hardly the only place to look for diverse images of beauty. There are a few curvy and sympathetic characters on TV (in recent years, we've been able to look to *Grey's Anatomy, Medium, Nip/Tuck, America's Next Top Model, Mad Men, Ugly Betty*, and *American Idol,* to name a few) and in the music business (Jennifer Hudson, Queen Latifah, Beth Ditto, Leslie Hall, Adele, Jill Scott, and Beyoncé come to mind). The Dove ads, with their wide-ranging portrayals of beauty, encourage women of all sizes to feel good about their bodies.

But when I was sick, I wasn't attuned to pop culture or the world around me at all. Perhaps other girls could have been inspired by larger celebrities, but I couldn't see beyond the confines of my own hated, emaciated body.

5

WEIGH IN

'd dieted away nearly half my body weight, gotten out of Mississippi, scored the plum contract, traveled around the world. I was a working model in Manhattan. This was supposed to be the end of my Cinderella story. Swelling violins! Applause! And . . . curtain!

Unfortunately, my life wasn't sticking to the script. I wasn't getting great jobs, and I looked like a zombie in a Sam Raimi movie. (Maybe if I'd eaten a few brains, I'd have felt better.)

Despite how hard I worked to stay thin, despite my hair falling out in handfuls and my skin blossoming in bruises and my heart fluttering like a wounded bird, I began to gain weight.

I don't think I was eating more. (I watched myself like a hawk.) I occasionally had an extra can of Ultra Pure protein shake, but if I did, I increased my workout intensity to accommodate it. For a while, I experimented with eating mango, a fruit I adore, but when I realized I'd gained a few pounds, I freaked out and blamed the mango. I ran around in circles like a cartoon character, screaming, "AAAAAH, MANGO IS MAKING ME FAT!"

I broke up with mango.

Yet throughout the end of 2002 and the first half of 2003, my weight kept creeping up. I prided myself on being the smallest girl in the model apartment, but one day I let myself in and saw a new girl sitting on the couch, painting her nails. She looked up and smiled, and I thought, Oh, no. She weighs less than I do.

My suspicion is that my body was simply changing as I got older. I fought back with tougher workouts, but the numbers on the scale kept creeping up: 105, 111, 123. I was sick with panic, but I didn't know what I could do differently. I tried the cabbage-soup diet and the lemon-juice diet. Since I'd eaten vegetables almost exclusively for over a year, I tried adding a little protein—a couple of slices of fat-free American cheese for breakfast. Only thirty calories a slice! (Thirty calories that tasted like the plastic film they came wrapped in.) Nothing helped. I got the fisheye every time I walked into the agency. All the exclamations about how thin I was and how fabulous I looked faded into echoes.

The agency sent me to a three-hundred-dollar-an-hour celebrity fitness trainer. (His fee was charged back to me.) The Trainer was as buff as a cartoon superhero. He looked like Ben Stiller in his muscled, maniacal *Dodgeball* phase. The Trainer took himself very, very seriously, inscribing "to my youngest disciple" in his workout book before handing it to me. He works with stars when they need to lose weight fast for tours and movie roles, and he is a star himself, selling his own branded workout gear, clothes, videos, books, and supplements.

I worked out with The Trainer only once. It was hard-core. He worked me out until I was close to vomiting. At one point he had me doing jumping jacks. I was on the cabbage-soup diet at the time, and I was as gassy as an Exxon station. You can probably see where this is going. I urgently tried to clench as I jumped, keeping the inevitable within me, but I had to spread my legs to do the "jump out" part of the jumping jack, and I let loose with a blast so loud I think Mom heard it in Miami.

I was mortified. The Trainer was a gentleman and pretended he hadn't heard. But Beethoven could have heard that fart after he'd lost his hearing. He could have heard that fart after he was dead.

I refused to work out with The Trainer again. I was too embarrassed. But I promised The Agency that I'd work out even harder at the gym, which I did. Thank heaven for small favors—they took my word for it. I knew about another girl they made sign in to the gym twice a day to prove she'd gone. Other girls were sent to spas and ordered to lose weight. One girl who was a size 4 or 6 was sent to one of those liquid-diet weight-loss programs at a medical clinic. The clinic wouldn't accept her, saying she was too thin to be a candidate for a supervised fast, but The Agency didn't accept that. A few weeks later, they sent her back. The clinic kicked her out again.

I continued to hope I could exercise off the weight. I was working out for three hours a day during the week and at least eight hours on weekends, still toggling between the two gyms so no one would think I was a crazy-freaky exercise addict. The Agent kept up a quiet, steady drumbeat: Lose the weight. Lose the weight. Lose the weight.

But I kept gaining.

I hit 130 pounds. For a model, it might as well have been 430.

In June 2003 I was booked on a shoot for a company in Chicago. It was a huge-money job for me back then—I stood to earn five thousand dollars. I'd gone to the casting, and they'd loved me and thought my weight was fine, but when I arrived for the job four days later, the photographer flipped out. He screamed at the producer and pointed at me. "I can't use her! She's *huge!*"

The producer stalked over to me. "How fat are you?" he demanded. "And why did the agency send someone who is five-five?"

I am five-nine. This business is rife with girls who lie about their height—I've never been one of them. I'm not statuesque for a model (runway stars tend to be taller than I am), but I'm certainly not short. Did the producer actually think I was five-five? Or was he just trying to be hurtful, hurling a kitchen drawer full of insults at me? Telling a model she's short is like telling a singer she's flat.

While I could shrug off "short," I couldn't deny "fat." For my business, I *was* fat. I was probably a size 4. (That's huge for high fashion, though not so huge for most commercial work.) But the clothes fit! I'd just tried them on a few days earlier. This was a midwestern catalog shoot, which meant that many of the clothes weren't itty-bitty little scraps of fabric. This was not a client that generally required emaciation.

I stammered, "You loved me at the casting, and that was only four days ago!"

The producer snapped back, "Did you gain twenty pounds in four days?" I was speechless. The producer theatrically pulled out his cell phone, flipped it open, and called The Agency. Standing a foot from me, he screamed, "Why did you send me a girl who's so squat and fat?"

I stood there as the he held his phone to his ear, glaring at me. "Fine," he said, then snapped it shut. He whirled on his heel and left me gulping. Without another word to me, he went to work with the other models and stylist.

What was I supposed to do now?

In a matter of minutes, the casting director arrived. (Along with the producer, he was the one who'd chosen me for the shoot.) He walked up to me and, barely looking at me, said brusquely, "You have to leave."

It was the most humiliating moment of my life. But I collected myself. I walked over to the craft services table, feeling everyone's eyes on me. I ate five plates of catered mini-burritos with cheese.

(And I'm lactose-intolerant.) I ate guacamole. I ate everything. I ate until I felt like I was going to throw up. I was beside myself. But my face betrayed nothing. Then I put down my plate, walked over to the casting director, said, "Thanks for the food," and walked out.

I made it as far as the pavement before becoming hysterical. I called The Agent, sobbing. She'd already gotten an earful from the producer and casting director, but she kept her voice calm. "Go to the airport," she told me. "We'll get you on a flight. Come home."

I found out later that the client tried to sue The Agency on the grounds that the agency had misrepresented me. They supposedly told The Agency they were going to bill for the cost of the entire shoot—the studio, the photographer, the catering, the hair and makeup artists—since I'd been hired under false pretenses. I wasn't a model. I was a fat girl.

Sitting alone on the airplane, I thought my career was over.

I got home and called The Agent in a panic. When she answered, her words were soothing, but her tone was oddly without affect or inflection. She didn't want me to come in. She'd call me later.

What followed were a couple of days of radio silence. I spent them at the gym, treadmilling maniacally, unsure what else I could do. At least my digestive discomfort was a distraction—eating heaps of greasy, cheese-dripping food at that shoot after months of starving had made my system scream in protest. My poor body didn't know what had hit it. My brain whirred obsessively.

At the time, my life was all telephoto, no panorama. I couldn't pull back enough to see that I was battling something far bigger than my thighs. I couldn't see that I had something in common with every person who's ever brimmed with self-loathing because of her size, every person who's ever thought her life would be a million times better if she were only smaller. I had no perspective, no shared sense of struggle. It was all about me. But now I can see the bigger (as it were) picture.

In our culture, fat is the devil. It's evil. To be fat is to be seen as a gross, undisciplined, ugly, lazy person. And this perspective starts early. Even children dislike fat children. I've read that kids as young as three characterize fat kids as mean, stupid, ugly, lazy, and unpopular. Heavy kids get teased and mocked. Think about the portrayal of fat in the books we all read growing up: Augustus Gloop in *Charlie and the Chocolate Factory* (a candy-snarfing porker), Piggy in *Lord of the Flies* (a squealing, passive victim), Ermengarde in *A Little Princess* (a slow, pathetic chewer of hair ribbons), Dudley Dursley in *Harry Potter* (a bullying, dim-witted thug), Aunt Sponge in *James and the Giant Peach* (a narcissist with a face "like a great white soggy overboiled cabbage"). If the notion that fat people are weak (at best) or evil (at worst) is a regular meme in classic children's stories, how can we not internalize the message?

In school, where racist and ethnic insults are seldom tolerated, it's generally A-OK to call someone a fat pig. The only other class of insults that generally goes unchallenged in homeroom or gym class is homophobic slurs. Fags and fats, the last remaining refuge of the youthful name-caller.

This kind of cruelty isn't just damaging to kids' mental health; it's damaging to their physical health. Heavy kids who are teased for being heavy are more likely to engage in unhealthy dieting and binge eating than kids who aren't teased.

Today 42 percent of first-to-third-grade girls want to be thinner, while 81 percent of ten-year-olds are afraid of getting fat. These are seven- and ten-year-olds! How tragic that kids so young can't accept their own bodies and see how beautiful they are.

It's not as if the weight-related insults diminish as we get older. Yale professor of public health Kelly Brownell (who coined the term "yo-yo dieting") and his colleagues published a study in the October 2006 issue of the journal *Obesity* in which they found that 72 percent of people enrolled in a weight-loss program had experienced stigmatizing from family members. "Are you sure you want to eat that?" "A moment on the lips; forever on the hips!" And then there's the classic "You have such a pretty face!" Why is it never "You're so pretty"? Why the need to point out, in a classic sin of omission, that there's only one part of you this person thinks could be deemed attractive?

The big question: Why do people hate fat? For more reasons than Jabba the Hutt has chins. Because fatness is associated in our culture with sloth, greed, selfishness, lack of self-control. Because fatness is linked with poverty; rich people are less likely to be fat, and we all want to be rich. Because fatness is associated with the disenfranchised in general; racial and ethnic minorities have a higher rate of obesity than whites. In other words, there's often unconscious racism and classism at work when people speak disparagingly about fat.

The world of modeling is only the real world writ smaller and skinnier. Though our culture has come a long way in terms of accepting diversity, we're not there yet. It's no coincidence that the bodies on runways are pretty darn white as well as very darn thin—the normative ideal is still white and skinny. Plus-size models may be on the smaller side of the bigness spectrum, but there are some people in the fashion industry who think we shouldn't be here at all.

Some people believe that manufacturers shouldn't make cool clothes for plus-size teenage girls, because that will send the message that it's okay to be fat. That's like saying that teaching kids about gravity will make them want to throw themselves off a building. Take my word: Depriving girls of cute outfits will not make them lose weight. Shaming people is neither productive nor kind.

When we talk about fat, there's almost always an element of moral judgment. As I followed the news of the presidential primary campaign in 2007, it occured to me that Governor Mike Huckabee framed the story of his weight loss (he lost over a hundred pounds between 2003 and 2004) in moral terms. He metaphorically waved his old size-50 pants like the American flag, casting his victory over fat as a victory of willpower over weakness. He crafted his own story as a symbol for what he'd do for America; he talked about thinness as a symbol of self-reliance, discipline, and love of country. His book, *Stop Digging Your Grave with a Knife and Fork,* dealt with the notion of food as addiction, weight loss as personal responsibility, and thinness as a religious calling.

People tend to get fervent about fat because they see it as threatening to the social order. They claim obesity is destroying the fabric of our nation, ripping its seams like a butt tearing through the seat of some too-small pants.

Basically, what's going on here is moral panic, a term popularized by sociologist Stanley Cohen. Moral panics start with general concern about how a certain group of people (witches, Commies, crack babies, hippies, Jews, satanic-ritual abusers, fat people, teens attending rainbow parties, immigrants, you name the villain) will have a negative impact on society. Then hostility toward the group in question increases, and a consensus builds that these people are a definite danger. Action is taken that's disproportionate to the danger at hand. (In the case of obesity, how's this: A representative in my own state of Mississippi—go Ole Miss!—proposed legislation forbidding restaurants from serving food to anyone obese.) Then public interest in the problem wanes, and people move on to panicking about something else.

Moral panic tends to have an element of "But think about the children!" For the sake of the children, people get to demean the group at hand. In this case, they get to demonize fat people. Of course kids should be encouraged to eat fresh fruits and vegetables! Of course they should be urged to run and play! No one would dispute that. But making kids feel bad, especially now that we know weight is mostly genetically determined, is plain old mean.

Generations ago, fat didn't have such moral baggage. Fat meant you were rich enough to have food. A fleshy body was fertile, abundant, attractive. Look at all those nude babes in old paintings by Rembrandt, Raphael, and Rubens. The ad I did for the Breast Cancer Research Foundation, after I became a plus-size model, was designed to look like a Renaissance image. Shot by the great Ruven Afanador, it shows me from behind, nude, my hair piled up with one curl falling down my back, draped in a rich red silk wrap; you can see immediately that I'm not your usual skinny model. The BCRF said, "We wanted to create an image of a woman that a large number of women could identify with. And deliver a message that is as much about hope as it is about hard truths. Cancer is ugly. Women are beautiful." I loved doing that ad, for which I volunteered my services. I was thrilled not to be paid. I welcomed the chance to spread the notion that the way I look is classically beautiful, and my body's curves should be a symbol of health.

If you talk to a feminist social theorist (go on, you can pick one up in any bar) about women and weight obsession, she might tell you that our bodies have become our work. Striving for perfection is like having a whole extra job. As the writer Susie Orbach put it, "The body is turning from being the means of production to the production itself." We're supposed to tinker and reduce and perfect—it's integral to the gig of being modern women. When we're focused on our bodies, we don't have the external focus to turn to the outside world. The ironic thing is that if we *did* focus on improving the world—by working for safe streets, public transportation, better health care for everyone, access to low-cost fresh fruits and vegetables, affordable child care, and decent jobs so that more of us would have the time to prepare good food instead of relying on fast food— we'd wind up healthier as a country, and perhaps thinner.

But most of us are in the same place I was during my entire career as a straight-size model: too busy blaming ourselves for our moral failings to have much perspective on the big picture. Our self-hatred keeps us from taking a good hard look at the world outside our bodies. As the writer Naomi Wolf said, "A cultural fixation on female thinness is not an obsession about female beauty, but an obsession about female obedience." When your biggest concern is controlling your body, you're not thinking about all the things in the world—besides yourself—that you might be working to change.

Women aren't the only victims of these "your body must be perfect or you are screwed" messages. Men get them as well. Men's body insecurity is a whole new market; increasing male neurosis builds sales. When marketers sense weakness, they go right for the jugular. There are now a dizzying number of sports drinks, protein powders, underwear designed to show off your manly package and minimize your gut, black-market steroids, and male-enhancement products designed to make men feel better about their bodies by first creating the anxiety that makes them feel worse.

My struggle was the same as that of so many other Americans, just writ small. Whether you're desperate to lose ten pounds or 110 pounds, the feeling of self-loathing is the same; it doesn't matter what your magic number is. I was in a peculiar position compared to most people who want to lose weight, because my career depended on it. I definitely was under scrutiny—by my agency, by clients, and perhaps by the potential buyers of whatever item of clothing I was supposed to be selling. To those critical viewers, I was a failed exemplar of hotness.

But celebrities in America have it worse than I ever did. Celebrity culture is intricately tied to fatphobia. We study famous people's bodies as if they were sacred texts, and we invariably deem them either too fat or too thin. The editors of gossip rags such as *Us, Star,* and *Life & Style,* and websites such as TMZ and The Superficial salivate over unflattering pictures of famous people and comment that they look (a) skeletal, (b) fat, or (c) pregnant.

In the past, we didn't have this level of "celebrities—they're just like us!" intimacy. There was no Internet, there were no blogs. There were gossip magazines, sure, but they were filled with staged photos set up by movie studios that kept a tight rein on both their stars and the press. Now it's the Wild West of paparazzi ambushes and unsubstantiated dark speculation. While the gossip industry mocks bad outfits and skin, that's nothing compared to the way it deals with weight. One cheeseburger, and a size-2 actress is looking at pictures of her midsection in every tabloid, with arrows pointing to the possibly nonexistent "bump" as the editors act like she's expecting octuplets.

I gained weight as I got older, and I'm hardly alone in that. But the media scrutiny of famous people as they age is unrelenting. Heaven help the celebrity who doesn't wear a bra with enough support for gravity-prone bazooms (Susan Sarandon) or who possesses a stomach that bears evidence of childbirth (Victoria Beckham) or displays an aging body on the beach in a bikini deemed too sexy (Donatella Versace). Celebs get mocked for having any suggestion of their age written on their bodies, but they also get mocked if they're considered too reliant on Botox or plastic surgery. Aging, like losing or gaining weight, triggers all kinds of conflicting values and judgments. Hot MILFs, predatory cougars—how can any woman find her way among all these contradictory messages? I was twenty-two when a photographer told me that he was going to make me "look young." I felt like laughing, crying, and bitch-slapping him all at the same time. In what universe is twenty-two old? Besides, when I *am* old, I hope I'll embrace it with grace.

Celebrities' ubiquity means that we feel we own them, and they owe us. We can dish about them the way we would our next-door neighbor because they feel like our next-door neighbor. (This is especially true now that stardom has become so debased; reality-show contestants are considered stars.) If they get to be rich and famous and have lives brimming with goody bags and loans from jewelry designers and red carpets and personal trainers, the least they can do for us is have flawless, unattainable bodies. That's in their job description! And if they fall down on the job, we are all too eager to get angry. How dare they get fat or droopy, with all their money? When they lose weight, we get fake-sanctimonious and tsk-tsk-y, even though the pressure to be thin is what makes them dip too far into skinny territory in the first place.

It's an impossible balancing act. So poor Jennifer Love Hewitt, on a romantic getaway, showed a little cellulite, and the gossip rags acted like she'd eaten a baby seal. When Britney Spears was in full umbrella-waving, head-shaving, tattoo-getting, public-sobbing, non-car-seat-using, in-house-blockading mode, she arguably got more opprobrium for gaining weight than for losing her mind. Kirstie Alley got fat, became a Jenny Craig spokesperson, lost weight, got cheered, gained weight, got fired (hey, Valerie Bertinelli, you look awesome!), announced she was going to launch her own weight-loss program, got eviscerated ("Never take weight-loss advice from someone as wide as a Hummer" said one Internet wag) . . . rinse and repeat. Don't we have anything else to talk about? When Jessica Simpson's jeans size bumps the leader of the free world off the cover of a magazine, our country has a problem. That problem is not weight—it's weight obsession.

Our size-crazed culture has made a reality juggernaut of weight-loss TV: *The Biggest Loser* is the grand pooh-bah of this genre, but it's hardly alone. *Celebrity Fit Club, Fat March, Weighing In, Inside Brookhaven Obesity Clinic, Big Medicine, Shaq's Big Challenge, Honey We're Killing the Kids, Bulging Brides, Bridal Bootcamp, I Can Make You Thin*—just listing all the shows that have put fat bodies up for voyeuristic viewing can leave you as breathless as a *Fat Loser* contestant running a marathon. Alessandra Stanley of *The New York Times* calls these shows "binge viewing for a nation obsessed with weight," "part public health warning, part carnival side show," and "an escalator-age version of the Horatio Alger story."

In the original Horatio Alger stories, poor shoeshine boys, newsboys, and peddlers pull themselves up by their bootstraps and, through hard work, achieve the American Dream of wealth and success. Americans want to believe that if someone merely applies herself, she can accomplish whatever she sets her mind to, and that goes for weight loss, popularity, and beauty.

The Biggest Loser (and, to a lesser degree, its sisters, especially the bridal-workout shows) had the genius idea of combining the Horatio Alger fantasy with the Cinderella fantasy. We all love makeovers and duckling-to-swan, scullery-maid-to-princess stories, and we all want the hard-work-pays-off morality tale. So *The Biggest Loser* is big business. It has 10.5 million viewers and has spawned a big fat empire of books, DVDs, scales, and diet food. The show's executive producer told *Entertainment Weekly,* "I think we could become Weight Watchers for the 21st century."

Indeed, that's a perfect parallel. Diet programs are very likely to have repeat customers, since 90 percent of people who diet gain the weight back within five years. No one has followed the *Biggest Loser* contestants long enough to know what percentage keep their weight off. The show is all about the "big reveal," the triumphant weigh-in as the pounds and inches come off. In the usual version of my own story, the ending would come when I got signed to a contract with The Agency. I lost seventy pounds! No one wants to know that the weight didn't stay off. Reality TV about weight loss is never about the long-term struggle to keep those pounds and inches from piling back on. The *Biggest Loser* producers want to sell the triumphant image of people who've lost hundreds of pounds, pitching branded products associated with weight-loss triumph, even if it means that naive hopeful fat people will end up buying the products again and again, losing and gaining in an endless cycle.

Watching weight-loss reality TV is like pulling off a scab; it's simultaneously fascinating, quease-inducing, painful, and cathartic. We get the immediacy and thrill of one of those "Eye of the Tiger" workout montages with the gross-out factor of a Discovery Health documentary about a giant tumor. As we watch, we identify with the contestants (I want to lose weight, too!) while distancing ourselves from them (At least I don't look like that!). Humiliation is part and parcel of the entertainment. For their weigh-ins, contestants stand on a giant industrial scale, as in a truck stop, wearing unflattering, dehumanizing, identical skintight bike shorts. The show encourages us to put these people in the "them" category, the "other" category, while also inspiring us to drop some pounds, because hey, if *they* can do it, surely we can. It's a dizzyingly mixed message.

There's a concept called false hope syndrome, described by psychologists at the University of Toronto. Dieting is the perfect example of it. People keep trying to do something over and over, despite repeated failures. They explain away each failure and try again with renewed vigor. Overwhelming odds against success don't deter them—hope springs eternal! Diets don't work long-term, but people blame themselves, not the diet. The very act of embarking on yet another diet makes us feel better and more hopeful. This time it will work. This time we'll do it right. We feel empowered. We're finally taking control of our lives. But the ending is always the same.

In 2002, full of false hope, I kept thinking that if only I did something different, I'd have the body I wanted. By 2009 I'd learned that a more lasting path to happiness was to love the body I had.

The nonprofit Council on Size and Weight Discrimination points out that the belief, in the absence of evidence, that fat can be cured through willpower and good ol' American elbow grease helps reinforce stereotypes that hurt all heavy people. Heavier workers are paid less than thin ones. Slightly heavy women make about 6 percent less in wages than standard-weight women; very heavy women make 24 percent less. If fat is something that can be easily fixed—if only fat people weren't such lazy slobs—it's easier to justify discrimination against fat people. After all, they bring it on themselves.

In 2005 Dove commissioned a study called "Beyond Stereotypes: Rebuilding the Foundation of Beauty Beliefs." Its survey of 1,000 girls (aged 15–17) and 2,300 women (aged 18–64) found that two thirds of women around the world avoid activities such as meeting friends, exercising, voicing an opinion, going to school, going to work, dating, or even seeking medical help because they don't like the way they look. What a depressing statistic.

Weight-loss reality shows only entrench this kind of self-negating worldview. The message they send is that life can't begin until you're thin. For most of us, that's not the case. For most Americans, the health risks of being fat are outweighed by the health risks of dieting, as I'll show in the next chapter. The evidence is pretty clear that being slightly overweight is healthier than being underweight. In other words, being my size is statistically healthier than being the size of most models.

The average American woman is exactly my size: a 12. Other than in plus-size modeling and in fleeting appearances on bridal weight-loss shows, we're very underrepresented in the media. I can think of a few singers who are that size; I can think of Sara Ramírez, the hot Dr. Torres on *Grey's Anatomy*. But that's really it. The *Los Angeles Times* guesstimated that Christina Hendricks, the sexy red-headed secretary on *Mad Men,* is a size 8 or 10. America Ferrara of

Ugly Betty, while curvy for a TV star, is smaller than that, even if she looks big when compared to the legions of size-0 celebrities. Anyone who doesn't look like a bobblehead doll on a car dashboard, with a giant head and a narrow little body, is an unusual sight on television.

The media should not have to shoulder all the blame for the challenges we face in accepting our true size, whatever that size may be. The media are only a reflection of the culture. We need to change the culture, and we need to work on accepting ourselves at the deepest level in a way that comes from within, not without.

Let me get this out of the way: Some people like to squeak, "There's thin bias! There's thin bias!" every time someone else mentions that the culture is tough on fat people. Oh, shut up. Saying, "Thin people are discriminated against, too!" is like saying, "Where's the white issue of *Vogue?*" Every issue of *Vogue* is the white issue. Every issue of *Vogue* is the skinny issue. Skinny people do not experience the same level of difficulty in the world as heavy people. The social sanctions of being overweight are far greater than the social sanctions of being skinny.

It took me a lot of reading and soul-searching to burn through my own self-hatred and come out the other side. Back in June 2003, I still thought everything was my fault. I thought I was huge and hideous. I thought my career was over because of my own weakness.

A few days after I got home from the disastrous trip to Chicago, The Agent called, her voice menacingly casual. "We'd love for you to come in and take some Polaroids on Monday," she said. "We just want to See Where We Are. Wear that adorable black Calvin Klein bikini. Have a great weekend!"

I knew what was happening. It was time for the come-to-Jesus speech. They were going to take the Polaroids and rub the truth in my face, like a dog trainer pushing a dog's nose into its excrement.

That weekend, forty-eight hours before the meeting, in a state of abject panic, I essentially moved into the gym, hoping that I could reverse the laws of time, space, and momentum through nonstop exercise. I hit every corner in the gym—from Pilates to thigh machines to swimming to hitting the heavy bag—until my legs quivered as if they were independent of the rest of my body. I worked out for eight hours on Saturday. Exercise is supposed to make us stronger. But I was so weak that I hobbled back to the model apartment like an elderly woman, holding on to brick walls, lampposts, and fire hydrants.

On Sunday I worked out for another nine hours. Afterward, I inched my way along East Fifty-fourth Street to sit in Barnes & Noble, my safe place. I sat for three hours, looking at magazines, thinking, I just want this. Only this. Why can't I have the one thing I want?

On Monday morning, I pulled out the Calvin Klein string bikini and held up the little squares of fabric for examination. No way, I thought, stuffing them back in the drawer. Instead, I found a faded, tacky racer-back lap suit I'd bought in a South Florida strip mall.

I hadn't really looked at myself in years. I'd perfected a trick of letting my eyes glaze over when they flickered across a mirror—the effect was like smearing a thick layer of Vaseline across a camera lens. I saw big brown eyes, strong brows, a smear of dark hair. Otherwise, the creature in the mirror was featureless, borderless. I wriggled into the bathing suit, with its pilled fabric and stretched-out straps, and glanced in the mirror. A black-and-neon blur. I quickly took it off and pulled on my usual ninja uniform: black top, black pants, black stretch headband.

To someone in my state of mind, submitting to a Polaroid is like an execution. Stand against the wall, and they shoot. There's not even a blindfold.

When I got to The Agency and saw that The Agent herself was holding the camera, I knew I was in big trouble. There was one guy at The Agency who usually took the Polaroids for clients. He had a gift. He made the most casual point-and-shoot photo look like something that had been exquisitely styled for a million-dollar advertising spread. The fact that he wasn't going to take my picture meant that no one was interested in trying to make me look good. This was about scrutinizing my body. This was the "black marker" treatment.

I stripped off my clothes. The rhythmic click and whirr of the Polaroid followed. When it was over, I ran into the bathroom to put my oversized sweater and leggings back on.

When I came back into the room, the head of The Agency had joined The Agent. Both of them were scowling at the Polaroid in The Agent's hand. "The thighs *need* to come down," The Agent said. As if this were a news flash. As if I hadn't been frantic about those thighs every waking moment since the day I began communing with Maggie Rizer on my wall in Clinton. "You *need* to go on a diet," the head of The Agency said. "I have a forty-thousand-dollar job for you in two weeks. It could *make* you. But you cannot have it unless you get the thighs down."

The thighs. Not "your thighs." A model's body is parts: thighs, breasts, legs. We are Oven Stuffer Roasters in bikinis.

Something snapped.

I Could. Not. Do. This. Any. More.

The threat of losing the forty-thousand-dollar job meant nothing. I was too hungry. I could not keep running endlessly on the treadmill, the elliptical, the hamster wheel, with my heart pounding, feeling sicker and more hopeless every day. I knew I was never going to weigh ninety-five pounds again.

I was done.

And the minute I truly understood that, I could breathe normally for the first time in years.

The head of The Agency left the room. I told The Agent everything. The eight-hour workouts, the incessant pounding in my head and chest, the muscle and joint pain, the fact that (except for my manic binge in Chicago) I hadn't eaten anything substantial in years. The Agent stared at me. I felt her distant, icy distaste melt. Suddenly, she saw me as a person—a girl—not just a career and a commission.

She locked the door and said, "Here's the deal. As long as you don't gain any more weight, you can still work. You will never be high-fashion, but you can be sexy. You can aspire to *Sports Illustrated* swimsuit or Victoria's Secret, but you're never going to be in *Vogue*. We can start sending you out for catalog. Let me know if that's what you want."

I wanted to eat. But I also wanted to be in *Vogue*. I couldn't help it. I didn't want to be a faceless generic girl selling chenille bathrobes. "Those are my only choices?" I asked.

"Well, I suppose there's plus-size," she said dismissively.

"Tell me about plus-size," I said slowly, an idea beginning to form.

"You can be your natural size," she said. "You can make a lot of money because your career is longer—selling womanly clothes means you don't have to look so youthful. But there's no editorial. Take a day. Think about whether you really want to give up."

As I got up to leave the conference room, the joints in my knees clicked. They were as loud as gunshots. My muscles had clenched tight from the frantic exercise and from the tension of the meeting. My jaw and throat throbbed.

I realized that the promise I'd made to Mom—that I'd still be me no matter how much I shrank—was long broken. I'd been a smart girl, but I couldn't think straight anymore. I'd become too hungry to think.

I was dying.

I didn't want to die.

I walked uptown slowly, gazing at skyscrapers and pocket gardens and water towers and people. My head was floating over my body like a balloon on a ribbon. I wondered whether the determination that had gotten me out of Clinton in the first place could help me redefine what fashion modeling could be. I felt the way you do when you've been up all night and you can barely start to see dawn at the edge of the night sky.

I stopped at Café Europa and bought a salad. With a kind of eagerness I hadn't felt about anything in ages, I put salmon on it. Salmon! Such a goofy thing to crave. Even the name sounds silly. Salmon. But I could hear my body saying, This is what I want. I hadn't heard my body say anything except Help me! in what seemed like forever. But now I was listening. I drizzled a little olive oil on top and tossed in some walnuts.

I don't know how long it had been since I'd tasted salmon. The flesh was sweet and salty, with a texture I had long since forgotten. I wasn't eating out of desperation and panic, as I had at the shoot in Chicago—this time I was eating out of joy. I was experiencing emotions and sensations that had been dormant for years.

And for the first time in years, I stopped eating to say grace.

6

LIFE-SIZE

The next morning I went back to The Agent's office. Her eyes searched my face as she ushered me in. Then she closed the door behind her.

"I want to be plus-size," I said.

The Agent, God bless her, said, "I'll get you a meeting with Ford." We looked at each other for a moment. Then she enfolded me in a giant hug.

Ford Models had the premier plus-size division in the country. The Agent could have been fired for facilitating my departure from The Agency, but she put my emotional and physical health ahead of her fear of her boss. I'll never forget that.

The next day I walked into Ford's airy office on lower Fifth Avenue. Its polished wooden floors were pockmarked with little divots from a thousand stilettos. Gary Dakin, now a VP at Ford, came into the lobby to greet me.

Today he says fondly, "You walked in with this huge mane of hair and this *face*, and we thought, no-brainer!" Gary always says nice things, but not in the fabulous-darling-let's-blow-smoke-up-the-model's-ass way endemic to my business. His style is to make me feel upbeat rather than perpetually anxious—the opposite approach from the folks at The Agency. He knew from the start that helping me feel good about myself would make me a better model. I immediately felt that he cared about my happiness as a human being. In a world where personal and professional relationships are intricately intertwined, not always in a healthy way, I instinctively knew I could trust Gary.

Which was fortunate, since The Agency kicked me out of the model apartment the same day.

Ford promptly moved me into theirs. They'd never had a plus-size model stay there before. (Most plus models are older and choose to live on their own.) I had no money—almost everything I'd earned was still tied up at The Agency—but Gary said I should focus on getting my head together. He was sure I'd be a successful plus-size model, but first I needed to recover.

The Ford model apartment was bigger and fancier than The Agency's. It was downtown, with a wrought-iron spiral staircase leading up to a mezzanine overlooking the living room. It had an expansive outdoor balcony with views of wooden water towers, callery pear trees, and the rapidly gentrifying tenements of the East Village. There was a bedroom on each floor, each containing a bunk bed and a single bed. Downstairs there was an additional tiny room, the size of a walk-in closet, with one bunk bed. I chose that room, because the day I moved was sweltering, and the bottom bunk was flush against the air conditioner. Growing up in Miami means getting used to air conditioners running full-bore, like power generators. Nothing brings me back to my childhood like the sensation of stepping out of a freezing, hermetically sealed home into a physical, visceral blast of wall-solid tropical humidity.

I didn't know what was going on behind the scenes between Ford and The Agency: a scuffle over my contract, over money, over various legalities. Things got heated. Thankfully, Gary and his colleague Carrie kept me insulated from the ugliness.

For months I was too sick to work. But gradually, I got better. I bought books on nutrition. I educated myself about eating healthily and about trusting my body instead of viewing it as an enemy to be vanquished like some fairy-tale dragon. I started buying normal food—organic, real food—for the communal fridge. I shared it with other people. I reveled, once more, in the sensory pleasures of food and in the fun of lingering over delicious meals I'd helped prepare.

I wasn't sure where my career was going. But I wasn't scared. The sun was shining. The bluebirds were singing. (Living Downtown instead of in Midtown, I *literally* heard the birds singing.) Happy Disney mice might as well have been tying my shoelaces. What I had believed for three years to be the only way to model—being a shadow of myself—I now knew wasn't the only way.

I started to think of the models I admired. None of them was pretty-pretty. The ones I thought were the most beautiful were the ones who were a little strange-looking, a little gawky, a little too strong-featured. I was drawn to models who were a bit otherworldly, like stick insects and bug-eyed space aliens. From my reading, I knew that many of the models who wound up doing the most interesting work had once been awkward, weird outsiders—punky art freaks, not prom queens. I admired them for pushing the conventional boundaries of beauty. I started thinking that maybe I, too, could challenge people's standards of perfection.

It would probably make a better story if I told you I went crazy for a few weeks, eating nothing but orange circus peanuts or pork rinds covered in squeeze cheese. But I didn't. I had a few weeks of gorging on peanut butter, my old love, but I never binged and purged or freaked out as my weight crept up. Just as the cliché says, I learned to listen to my body. I used to say no, but now I was saying yes.

One thing that kept me sane was the lack of pressure to earn money. Gary and Carrie said that when I was healthy, and when my body had figured out what size it wanted to be, I'd start working hard. Until then Ford would happily pay my room and board. That made me feel serene.

So did the new friends I was making at Ford. On my very first day at the model apartment, I walked in with my bag of groceries and saw a girl hunched on the couch. She was squatting on her heels as if she were a gargoyle jutting out of a building. I said, "Hi, I'm Crystal," and she grunted. Her head swiveled to follow me as I went into the kitchen to put away my food. I bent to put my grapes, apples, and mangoes in the crisper drawer, then stood up and shut the fridge door. Bam, there she was, next to the fridge, peering at me like an owl. I jumped a foot.

"You stare too much!" I told her.

"I stare?" she asked.

"Like a laser!" I told her.

Her eyes widened even more, then she burst into laughter. I joined in. She apologized for staring. "It's what I do," she said.

Her name was Rachel Alexander. With her penetrating, deep-set dark eyes under straight dark brows, she looked like an existentialist in a French coffeehouse. Once I got to know her, I discovered how observant, quirky, and funny she was. I tend to be shy and oblique; I worry that I'm invading the other person's space if I engage in too much eye contact. But Rachel is completely comfortable with the power of her gaze. I realized I could learn something from her directness.

Rachel had the same obsessive tendencies I had. We'd analyze each other's families, careers, and looks, spending hours chatting late into the night. One day, she called me from her agent's office. Her agent wanted her to get her hair bobbed to play up her eyes and strong features. "Do you think I should?" Rachel asked me. "Absolutely," I told her without hesitation. "You'll look incredible." The very next day, she got her hair chopped into a severe architectural style that worked wonders for her—her career skyrocketed.

As I watched Rachel's career take off, I felt even more hopeful for myself. Rachel looked nothing like those wan, emaciated, bland Soviet-bloc girls dominating the runways. Her beauty was, for lack of a better word, brainy. I'd always known she was a knockout and had always been confident she'd make it. If the fashion world could embrace her atypical look, surely it could embrace what made me different—my real, lush body.

A few weeks after I joined Ford, I met Ashley Graham at a dinner for the agency's "plus girls." She was outrageous, hilarious, and very smart. Whenever I'm feeling tired and dull, it's a huge charge being with her, basking in her charisma and command of a room. Talk about body confidence! She looks like a size-16 Eva Mendes. It's fun to walk down the street with her and become utterly invisible. Guys see her coming and drool as she walks by; by the time we're down the block, they're standing in a saliva puddle. I might as well be in a burka. She's the kind of person who's genuinely hot. I can play the hot girl at parties and on shoots, but for Ashley, that kind of eyeball-singeing eroticism is utterly effortless.

Ashley keeps me from taking myself too seriously. When I'm with her, we delight in cracking each other up. We create loony characters and catchphrases. We like to smoosh our chins down into our chests for the attractive quadruple-chin effect, then stroke our throats and bellow, "PET IT!" like psychotic dowagers. We do a whole routine where we pretend to insult each other in hoity-toity rich-bitch British accents: "What an *interesting* fashion choice, darling! How *deliciously* down market!"

"*Darling!* It's Diooooooooor!"

Then we do a glass-shattering, affected fashionista laugh, mocking the pretentious and label-obsessed people who surround us.

New York City was starting to feel like home. Finally I had real friends, a real community. The only bad thing about having a social life was that I started smoking. It's ironic: I'd resisted the habit for so many years, even when I knew that cigarettes were supposed to help you stay skinny. But now I smoked because it was companionable. Everyone else smoked, so I smoked. It was friendly. It was a ritual to share with others.

I realize this is an exceedingly stupid justification. Within a week of starting, I was trying to quit.

As I smoked and talked and pondered the future, I kept thinking about what The Agent had said about plus models having a longer career than straight-size models, even though they could be only catalog. I didn't want to be catalog. I'd gotten into this business to do editorial; I'd always been drawn to the fantasy, the collaboration among editors, stylists, photographers, and models in a story told with fabric and the body. I wasn't a "money girl"—a model who could rake in the bucks by smiling and selling. I would have been happy to work for free, if only I could be part of the world of high fashion. I wanted to play characters, touch exquisite fabrics and jewels, work with great photographers.

As I gained weight, I stared at myself in the mirror in the model apartment bathroom, this time without my old self-protective glaze. The gap between my thighs was the first thing to go. So much for the triangle I'd worked so hard to earn. That gap was my old status—and by status I mean both "place in the world" and "prestige attached to one's standing in society." In the society of skinny models, the gap is the diamond ring, the Hummer, the mink. But now I was a person waking up, blinking in the bright light of a hangover. I could see how my former values had messed me up.

I stopped pining for Maggie Rizer's thighs. The threat of dying seemed infinitely more real than the dream of succeeding as a straight-size model. I was happy to have books back in my life—I hadn't realized how much I'd missed them. It wasn't until I stopped starving that I had the focus to read anything other than fashion magazines and books about modeling. Suddenly, there was room in my head for something besides a yearning for muffins.

Now that I was befriending my body and treating it more kindly, I was able to assess my face and form, the tools of my trade, dispassionately. I had wide-set eyes, arched and expressive brows, strong cheekbones, full lips with a Cupid's bow. I had curtains of hair, like a girl in a Renoir painting. And I was starting to have a body with soft curves. I was getting breasts—as a size 0, I'd been so flat-chested I was nearly concave. I'd looked like a Pringle. Now I was beginning to have a woman's body, not a boy's.

As I grew shapelier and happier, I craved a little color in my wardrobe. I still loved black, but I was feeling the rainbow. Even though I was nearly broke, I bought myself a vintage multihued, ziggily micro-striped Missoni-style sweater. I got a pale blue vintage T-shirt with a silly caped vampire saying VANT TO NECK? and a pair of broken-in vintage boot-cut jeans. I was excited to show off my new curves. My style isn't flashy, but when I started gaining weight, it got a little bit flashier. I borrowed a tie-dyed miniskirt from another plus girl and wore it with a tank top, a men's vest, knee-high boots, and a mushroom-shaped leather cap with a big poofy crown and a tiny bill. Now the thought of that ridiculous getup makes me laugh. Even then, I wasn't entirely comfortable in such "look at me" garb. I walked out onto the street and immediately felt uncomfortable. After a few months of dressing to attract attention, I went back to my more modest style.

I stopped counting calories the very day I left The Agency. Just stopped cold. I also stopped going to the gym. I knew that exercise was important, but I associated the gym with mania. I needed to go cold turkey for a while. I had to give myself permission to just *be*. I read and strolled (as a form of meditation in movement, perhaps, but not in any sort of goal-directed way) and focused on appreciating the taste and textures of food.

I didn't weigh myself, so I don't know how much I weighed when my period came back in September 2003. But it came back with a vengeance. It was a menstrual maelstrom, an endometrial tsunami, the reproductive equivalent of a twister that could pick up a house and hurl it from Kansas into Oz. It was excruciating; I couldn't get out of bed for days. But I was relieved to know I might still be able to have children after all I'd put my body through. The pain felt like a blessing.

My poor confused corpus took a while to figure out what size it wanted to be. My weight inched up, leveled off, went up some more, went back down. I wasn't worried. I felt as if my body and I were both learning. We were both in recovery!

I was a size 16 for a while before settling in at a 12. By mid-2004, it was clear that that this was the size my body had chosen. It was pretty close to the size I'd been on the day The Scout discovered me in Mississippi.

During my healing process, I did tons of research about dieting, set point (the weight range within which everyone's body is genetically designed to stay) and eating for health. I kept being drawn to articles by Linda Bacon, Ph.D., a professor of nutrition and a physiologist at the University of California at Davis. Her attitudes about being healthy, eating well, and loving your body dovetailed with my own philosophy.

Recently she wrote a book called *Health at Every Size*. In unpretentious, jargon-free language, it distills what my battle with my own body taught me: Drastic calorie reduction simply doesn't work over the long term. More important, Bacon (I know, what a name for a nutritionist!) lays out how to love yourself and have a healthy relationship with food. The book is a delightful mix of hard science and self-help. One thing I especially love is the little contract you're supposed to write to yourself:

The Live Well Pledge

Today, I will try to feed myself when I am hungry.
Today, I will try to be attentive to how foods taste and make me feel.
Today, I will try to choose foods that I like and that make me feel good.
Today, I will try to honor my body's signals of fullness.
Today, I will try to find an enjoyable way to move my body.
Today, I will try to look kindly at my body and to treat it with love and respect.
Signature: _____ Date: _____

It may sound sappy, but that pledge speaks to me. It's the philosophy I stumbled on by myself, on my own, through anorexia and exercise bulimia and suffering and loss and painful trial and error. But that pledge says it more succinctly than I could: Food should be a source of joy, not agony. Exercise should be about enjoyable movement, not penitence. We should respect our bodies' wisdom.

Unfortunately, too few of us do. Fifty million Americans go on diets every year, but only 5 to 10 percent of them lose weight and keep it off for at least five years. When we diet to lose weight, we have to steamroll over the weight our genes want us to be, disregard the hunger pangs that won't go away as we dip below the size that's normal for us, ignore the marketing of junk food and the prevalence of giant slabs of meat and glugs of high-fructose corn syrup and the hugeness of most portion sizes. We may have to struggle to find fresh, affordable food, which isn't accessible in many neighborhoods. We have to find the time to cook and walk more. We blame ourselves for failing to lose weight and we never think, Gee, if almost everyone who loses weight gains it back, maybe the problem is with the concept of dieting, not with individuals.

To a great degree, our genes predetermine our adult weight. Adopted kids grow up to be the same approximate size as their biological parents, not their adoptive parents. That's an indication that our genes want us to be a certain size. It takes a brutal and constant battle with our biology to achieve and maintain a lower weight than that.

Want more evidence that genes, not willpower, are driving the weight-control bus? A researcher named Ethan Sims at the University of Vermont set out to deliberately make thin mice fat. He couldn't do it. Even if he provided them the most delicious mousy goodies in abundance, they didn't gain weight. So he force-fed them. (Sucks to be a laboratory mouse.) They gained weight, but their metabolism also sped up, and they gained much less than they should have according to the amount of food they were eating. As soon as he stopped force-feeding them, they dropped the weight. Sims tried a similar experiment with humans, hiring college students with no food or eating issues and no family history of obesity to gain weight. They just couldn't, no matter how much they ate. Their metabolisms, too, compensated for the extra food.

He tried the experiment again with prisoners, because their physical activity was limited. (Sucks to be a prisoner.) After four to six months of diligent pigouts, some managed to increase their weight by 20 to 25 percent by eating up to *ten thousand calories a day*. They, too, gained less than you would have thought by the amount they were eating.

Finally, Sims got fat people to diet down to the same size as those newly fat prisoners, through total vigilance and in-patient monitoring. But the "genuinely fat" people needed half as many calories as the "fake fat" prisoners to maintain the same weight. What all this means, unsurprisingly, is that fat and thin people are fundamentally different.

Here's what I've learned about what happens when your body dips below its genetically predetermined set point: Your hypothalamus gland directs your body's other systems to make you really, really hungry. It also tells your body to make you too tired to move (thereby conserving energy) and to make your metabolic efficiency (the rate at which you burn calories) slow down so you'll regain weight. This hypothalamus, clever little gland that it is, can also trigger a barrage of hormones to make you crave higher-fat food (hence my teary-eyed yearning for peanut butter). When you diet too crazily, you slow the rate at which your body burns calories and increase your body's efficiency at sucking every possible calorie from food. You digest more quickly and get hungry again more quickly.

Yes, you can use willpower to tune out the wily hypothalamus's messages. But this strategy usually doesn't work forever. Sooner or later, that gland is going to beat you, and you'll eat a little more or exercise a little less, and then your weight inches back into your set-point range. That's what happened to me. The only way to win the war with your set point is not to play.

When you get way below your set point, the way I did, your hypothalamus gets more aggressive. No more Mr. Nice Gland. You may feel cold, which is a sign that your body is trying to conserve energy by sending less blood to your extremities, thereby reducing your metabolic rate. You may feel sluggish, depressed, apathetic, sexless.

The human metabolism, like Woody Allen's heart, wants what it wants. And what it wants is to keep your weight within that range. For most people that seems to be a ten-to-thirty-pound span. Staying within that range may require vigilance, but your body won't turn on you. Before I started dieting like a loon, I was fourteen years old and weighed about 165 pounds. Now I'm twenty-three and vary from 160 to 175. When I'm at the bottom of my range, I find myself getting hungrier than usual. When I'm at the top of my range, my body tells me it's time to eat less. Listening is much easier now that I've chosen to do so.

But Crystal, you may say to me, Americans have gotten so much fatter! It's unhealthy!

Here's my answer: Everyone loves to trumpet statistics about how much fatter Americans have gotten in recent years. About 65 percent of Americans are classified as overweight or obese. But almost no one points out that 29 million people became overweight *overnight* in 1998, when the government changed its body mass index's "overweight" category from 27 to 25. (Incidentally, seven of the nine members of the government's obesity task force were directors of weight-loss clinics—making thousands more people instantly "overweight" was great for them!) According to the new classification, many professional athletes are now considered overweight. Dwayne "The Rock" Johnson and Governor Arnold Schwarzenegger are both considered obese. Matt Damon and Kobe Bryant are overweight. Even former President Bush, who is considered one of the fittest presidents in history—the man biked up to 120 miles a week, and his doctors said he was in the top ninety-ninth percentile in fitness for men his age—was overweight, with a BMI of 26.

The thing is, for most people, being "overweight" doesn't seem to be a direct cause of health problems. In her book, Bacon beautifully lays out the big myths about weight, including this commonly cited statistic: More than four hundred thousand Americans die of overweight and obesity every year, which means that that fat may soon surpass smoking as the leading cause of preventable death in this country. That's what the U.S. government's Centers for Disease

Control and Prevention (CDC) announced in 2004, in the prestigious *Journal of the American Medical Association* (*JAMA*). There were press releases, news stories, a metric ton of attention.

The only problem: It's flat-out wrong. *JAMA* and the CDC both ran corrections in 2005. They'd gotten the numbers wrong; their analysis had serious computational errors. Using better methodology and newer data, the CDC's own epidemiologists reduced the estimate, saying that obesity and overweight are associated with an annual twenty-six thousand deaths, not four hundred thousand. That's a major, major difference; it reduces the estimate of excess deaths by a mind-blowing 94 percent. But somehow that statistic hasn't gotten the same play the original overblown one did.

The truth, Bacon shows, is that "overweight people" (those whose body mass index is between 25 and 30) actually live longer than normal-weight people. Not just skinny people: *normal-weight people*. There were eighty-six thousand fewer deaths per year in the overweight category than in the normal category. No one knows why. One theory is that having a little padding stimulates the body to make more muscle and bone, which helps us survive into old age.

But hey, can I repeat that? People like me, who are considered slightly overweight according to the BMI chart, have healthier outcomes than either underweight or "normal" people. And fully half of overweight adults and one third of obese adults have normal blood pressure, cholesterol, and blood sugar, which means they're not at increased risk for diabetes and heart disease, conditions usually blamed on fat. Suck on that, fat-haters.

That information doesn't come from a poorly designed study or anyone with a financial interest in weight loss. In 2006 researchers from the Mayo Clinic College of Medicine published a data analysis in *The Lancet,* a prestigious British medical journal, showing that patients with a higher BMI had better survival rates than patients with low *or* normal BMI. The data came from forty studies covering 250,000 people with heart disease—not a small sample! Another study involving fifty-two countries compared four different body measures: BMI, waist-to-hip ratio, waist measure, and hip measure. It found that waist-to-hip ratio, not weight, was the best predictor of heart-attack risk.

Among the obese people who do die in a given year, most are clustered at the extreme end of the range, with a BMI greater than 35. That's not where the majority of obese Americans are. Most have a BMI of 30 to 35. Not until you reach a BMI of 40 is there a statistically significant relationship between weight and mortality.

But the government hasn't communicated that. Instead, they've used misleading data to justify funding a war on obesity.

When news anchors trumpet the fact that obesity costs this country millions of dollars, how do they come by that statistic? "Millions of dollars" refers to the expenses associated with treating type 2 diabetes, heart disease, hypertension, gallbladder disease, and cancer. The underlying assumption was that all those diseases are caused by fat. But they aren't. What about genetics, activity levels, diet? What about the fact that there are plenty of thin people with those conditions? Again, correlation isn't causation. If you're sedentary, you might be predisposed to weight gain *and* more vulnerable to disease. You can't say with any certainty at all that the weight *caused* the disease.

No one has established a causal relationship between weight and ill health. Are people fat because they're unhealthy, or unhealthy because they're fat? Bacon shows the difference between the two with an example: Bald men have a higher incidence of heart disease than men with a full head of hair. However, this doesn't mean that baldness causes heart disease or that hair protects against heart disease. (And no one would suggest that bald men dig deep, show some damn discipline, and grow some hair.) No, what research shows is that high levels of testosterone may promote both baldness and heart disease.

See what I'm saying?

Yet the former surgeon general of the United States, Richard Carmona, called obesity "the terror within," a villain "every bit as threatening to us as is the terrorist threat we face today." Excuse me? Beth Ditto's thighs could destroy the World Trade Center?

Here's the part that may be hardest for people to accept: No one has ever proved that weight loss provides long-term health benefits. (In part, that's because so few people keep the weight off for over five years.) I'm not saying, "Yay, everybody go get fat!" High blood pressure is definitely two to three times more common in obese people than in lean people. But again, is it caused by fat? Research indicates it could be caused by weight cycling—losing and gaining weight repeatedly.

One thing that may be damaging to fat people's health, far more than fat itself, is the social stress of being fat. We know stress can kill. And the strain of being sneered at and picked on may be a huge cause of health problems. Then there's the fact that some overweight people are reluctant to seek health care out of fear of being discriminated against. Their fear is reasonable: There are doctors out there who do seriously stigmatize the overweight. Some heavy people wind up getting sick not because they're fat but because they haven't gotten regular checkups.

Bias has a snowball effect, too. Being fat can mean an inability to get health insurance. It can mean having to pay higher premiums than someone who may not be as healthy or may not exercise but is thinner. Of course we feel guilty when doctors order us to do something, because who ever heard of a doctor being wrong? (Thalidomide is safe! Have some fen-phen! Pour some hot oil in your ear to cure deafness!) A couple of years ago, I read a fun book about fashion and American culture called *A Perfect Fit: Clothes, Character, and the Promise of America* by Jenna Joselit, a professor at Princeton. She quotes Dr. Hoye E. Dearhold, the head of a Wisconsin sanatorium in the 1920s, saying confidently, "Scantiness in modern women's dress is partly responsible for the tuberculosis problem. Girls, between 15 and 25, striving for a boyish figure and wearing scanty clothing, have lowered their resistance to the point where they are easy prey of the disease." The notion that being curvy causes illness is no more scientifically proved than the notion that slutty clothes cause tuberculosis.

Bias is a fact. Obesity is more common among minority groups and poor people, and being a member of a minority group or a member of a lower socioeconomic class are both factors associated with higher disease risk. Would you tell a black person to become white so he or she would be less discriminated against?

Scientists have begun pinpointing the exact genes responsible for obesity. Some are hoping to sell genetic tests to predict fatness. What would we do with that information? I recently read and loved Jodi Picoult's novel *Handle with Care,* in which a mother debates testifying in court—in front of her daughter—that she would have aborted the little girl had she known she'd be born with a painful bone disease. If there were in real life a test that showed your baby would be fat, would you abort that baby?

As for the small number of people who have lost a ton of weight and kept it off for over five years, I salute you! I only hope your eating and exercise habits aren't as disordered as mine were. And please keep in mind that the whole "If I can do it, you can, too" exhortation doesn't work when someone is leaving behind a set-point range entirely.

For me, a weight loss of seventy pounds was unsustainable. I had every motivation to stay thin because it was my *job*. It was my dream. I told you how little I was eating. But my body simply rebelled. I can understand how that succession of anorexic models died in 2006—when you are eating almost nothing and you still can't lose weight, and you lose all perspective, the only thing left to eat is nothing.

What I find particularly disturbing is that body positivity has entered the cultural consciousness without being internalized. People talk about "health" when they mean weight loss. Marketers have mostly banished the word "diet," while continuing to pitch calorie-counting regimes and track poundage down to the nearest obsessive fraction.

I believe that good health, at all sizes, is correlated with joy. I think happiness is more life-enhancing and life-prolonging than any plate of steamed vegetables. I've learned that I feel best when I eat slowly and focus on what I'm eating.

Most Americans don't feel the way I do, though. A cross-cultural survey of French, Belgian, Japanese, and American citizens asked them what attributes they associated with food. Americans associated food with pleasure less than all the other countries' citizens did. When asked what came to mind when they heard the words "chocolate cake," Americans were most likely to say "guilt," while the French were most likely to say "celebration."

We Americans want our food to be all health and virtue, no fun. When we feel guilty, we're more likely to gorge instead of indulging in moderation. We need to find a happy middle ground.

All people are entitled to natural, healthy food that tastes good. It's a sin that organic, local food isn't available to everyone at every income level. I wish everyone could eat closer to the land, not because of concerns about weight or even health but because we're players in a bigger picture. We're members of a community and citizens of a planet we cherish. When we think about what's good for the earth—eating locally so we don't waste fossil fuels by shipping food across the country, choosing foods grown with fewer pesticides, buying more whole grains and less meat—we feel a sense of stewardship and responsibility. Knowing that our choices can help the planet is more empowering than thinking our choices matter only to our hips.

Back in 2002, my daily diet was lettuce with a side of batshit. Here's a typical day's diet now:

BREAKFAST: Two organic eggs, whole-wheat toast with a drizzle of olive oil and sea salt, an avocado, and a glass of organic orange juice

LUNCH: Salmon with brown rice and a big pile of sautéed vegetables

DINNER: Duck gnocchi, an arugula salad, crème brûlée

My favorite lunch spot is a health food restaurant in my neighborhood. The usual, for me, is a giant plate of salad, vegetables, rice, and organic chicken. I get sauce on the side (tahini, miso, carrotginger, black bean) and mix everything up. I'm as happy as a little kid making mud pies. I love getting a little bite of everything as I eat.

I can honestly say that food holds no terrors for me anymore. I wish I could say as much about exercise. I know that the relationship between activity and longevity is stronger than the relationship between weight and longevity. I know that for my long-term health, it's far more important that I exercise than that I be thin. But exercise is still a minefield for me. I get anxious when I enter a gym. Years of punishing workouts have taken their toll.

I used to have a habit of posing with my hip jutting way out, trying to show off the boniness there. Once in early 2003, I thrust my hip to the side, and a sharp, searing pain tore through the place where the ball met the socket. There was no way I would have gone to a doctor then—I didn't want a medical professional questioning me about my disordered eating and exercising behavior. I just gritted my teeth and ignored the pain, and gradually, it receded. I didn't change my workouts for even a day.

Now I can't exercise for longer than an hour without feeling intense pain. Did I pull a tendon back in 2003? Did I wear away the cartilage in my hip by grinding away for so many hours on the elliptical? I don't know. These days when I walk on the treadmill, I look like an old lady, moving slowly instead of race-walking fiercely. I used to adore walking around the city, but now I can't do it for longer than a couple of hours. I take more cabs than I'd like—from a fossil-fuels-burning perspective and from a fitness perspective. I recently went to the Metropolitan Museum of Art and couldn't get through the whole museum without sitting down to rest my hip a few times.

Yoga helps. A yoga studio has none of the frightening associations of a gym for me. I've been doing Bikram, a kind of yoga that's practiced in a very hot room; the heat helps my tight muscles loosen up and makes me sweat so much that I feel clearheaded and pure. I also meditate. I occasionally swim. I walk in the city as much as I can without overdoing it, and now and then I'll do my *Golden Girls* treadmill trot. The most frequent exercise, for me, is working on not freaking out that I'm doing too little.

Back in mid-2003, of course, I wasn't doing anything at all. I was focusing on feeding my brain and my body, on draping a layer of flesh over the skeleton. One night I took my bag of photos of myself from my skinny-modeling days, dumped them into the apartment bathtub, and burned them. I didn't want reminders of what I'd looked like when I was starving.

Meanwhile, unbeknownst to me, Carrie and Gary were battling it out over who would be my sole manager. Gary ultimately won out

("I outbitched her," he says modestly). As soon as I was feeling strong and healthy, we sat down to strategize about how to run my career.

I told Gary that I still wanted to do high fashion. "I want to be the same as a straight-size model," I said fervently. "I know I can make interesting pictures! I can make the clothes look beautiful!" The Agent had said the market wasn't there for plus girls in high fashion, but if she was right, I was determined to create the market. Franz Kafka said, "There are some things one can only achieve by a deliberate leap in the opposite direction." I simply chose to believe I could be more successful as a plus-size model than as a straight-size model. "Just let me prove myself," I begged Gary.

I was ready for him to push back and tell me I could be a really successful catalog model but no more than that. I was ready to dig in for a knock-down, drag-out fight.

"You're going to do it," Gary said.

Huh?

Gary told me he'd been waiting for a girl like me. He wanted the chance to prove that plus-size girls could break out of our little marketing niche and become mainstream icons of beauty and fashion. He knew I could be that emissary. He promptly started sending me out on all kinds of calls, not just calls for plus models. He'd call clients and say, "You have *got* to see this girl." He often didn't say I was plus-size.

"We'd send you to a casting, and two hours later, they'd call and say, 'I'm obsessed with her,' " Gary recalls. When I was straight-size, I'd be in and out of castings in five minutes. That didn't happen anymore. Now that I looked and behaved like a completely different girl, casting directors wanted to keep talking to me. I was confident and charismatic, animated, funny. I'd ask casting directors about themselves, which is unusual for models on calls. I was newly expansive. I'd express opinions. I was everything as a plus model that I hadn't been as a meek, spacey straight-size model.

Everyone who remembered me from my former life said I was completely different. Before, I'd been vacant, unable to think or function. Once I recovered, I had a spark.

It took me a while to get used to my newly filled-out face and body. I went back to the mirror to practice, the way I had in Clinton. I learned to work with my new attributes. By opening my mouth slightly, I could create a more defined face, as if I had more prominent cheekbones. Moving my elbows out from my sides made my arms look more graceful and expressive. When you're skinny, you don't have to think much about creating a flattering line with your body for a given shot. But if you're not skinny, there are no accidents. I had to learn to work new angles, new expressions. I couldn't clench my jaw—my old face-defining trick—because it made my cheeks pooch out. But by lifting an eyebrow, I could create a sophisticated, old-Hollywood look that had eluded me before. I was also learning how to read clients better, tailoring poses for different looks and moods. When you lift your shoulders and tighten, that's *Vogue*. When you drop your shoulders and relax, that's Lane Bryant. As a straight-size model, I hadn't had any range. I had one pose: deer in the headlights.

I started cracking up my friends by putting a piece of paper in front of my face, then slowly moving it away to reveal "model face." Eyebrows! Mouth! Icy glare! I'd cover my face with the paper again, then move it away to reveal regular Crystal. Cover, reveal. Cover, reveal. *Daaaarling!* Nine times out of ten, I could stop a wailing baby from crying with this trick.

Gary sent me out on everything, but he never overpromised. I was champing at the bit to get into *Vogue*—I was fiercely ambitious and utterly unapologetic about that fact. I was done being a delicate little flower. I'd faced down a beast and cut off its head. I wanted to roar. If anorexia couldn't beat me, there was no way the fear of casting directors or worries about being dismissed for being "big" would take me down.

But no one had seen anything like me before. I wasn't the typical plus model—a smiling, unthreatening girl-next-door type. I was working a smolder, a challenging stare. Casting directors said they adored me; they thought I was hot; they found me fascinating; but they didn't know what to do with me.

It was September 2003. I was eating normally. I was so full of competitive drive, it was as if I were on Red Bull all the time. Still, the work wasn't coming. My debt to Ford was growing. Gary said, "You need to get a job."

I understood. I got a waitressing gig at a little coffee shop. Wiping off tables and plopping down plates of pancakes didn't bother me. I knew it was temporary. I was determined to give this job, too, my full heart and attention. I refused to be the stereotype of the bored, annoyed model/waitress.

As my weight went up, I got a few modeling jobs; nothing major. The most satisfying was at *Modern Bride,* because the editors there remembered me from when I was skinny. They could not have been more enthusiastic and encouraging about my new size. "When I first met you, you looked a little like Brooke Shields in *Pretty Baby,*" remembers Fiorella Valdesolo. "You had these great strong brows, but you looked so frail—your head didn't look like it belonged on your body. The moment I saw you as a plus model, everything just fit, and it worked. You looked radiant." Fiorella's boss, Mary Clarke, didn't remember me as a straight-size model (which didn't bother me—I know I was pretty unmemorable) but was very taken with me as a plus model. When I talked to her recently about the first time I reentered *Modern Bride* as a size 14 or so, she said, "I thought, This girl is so comfortable with herself, and she's so young! It's rare to see a teenage model so at ease with who she is."

Mary and Fiorella hired me to do a beauty story—I wasn't specifically labeled as plus in it, which was unusual for an American magazine. The story went over really well. Fiorella kept saying she wanted to work with me again—and then she got a job at *Teen Vogue*.

Fiorella pitched me to her new boss, Kara Jesella. Kara was very enthusiastic. "The beauty section we wanted to create was modeled on *Sassy*," Kara says, "a teen magazine that showed different body types and didn't make girls feel bad about themselves." (Not coincidentally, Mary Clarke, who'd put me in *Modern Bride*, had been the beauty director at *Sassy*.) To Kara, my new size was a big plus, pun intended. Fiorella brought my book to Amy Astley, the editor in chief, who was excited, too.

Given my outsize ambitions, I was thrilled to be doing something with a magazine in *Vogue*'s stable. During the shoot in November 2003, I was vaguely aware of the stylist's sulky demeanor and eye-rolling vibe, but I blocked her out. Some fashion people are snotty drama queens; this is not news. Whatever was going on with her, I was determined to be positive and not get infected by her energy. Later, Fiorella told me that the entire time I was in makeup, the stylist had been clomping up and down the hall, sputtering into her cell phone, "I can't believe I have to style a FAT GIRL!"

Believe it, bitch.

The shoot in *Teen Vogue*, and the accompanying interview, was a huge hit. I wore a simple sleeveless hoodie and jeans and posed looking right into the camera, no artifice. I told my story in the press for the first time, and people responded. The issue sold well; news outlets picked up my story. Speaking out about my eating disorder and my decision to become plus-size was incredibly empowering.

A few days after *Teen Vogue* hit the stands, Gary called. "Are you sitting down?" he said.

"Uh-oh," I said, worried he was going to tell me Ford was dropping me.

"Anna wants you for *Vogue*! Steven Meisel is going to shoot you!"

I screamed like a beauty queen with a spider in her sash. I started jumping maniacally around the apartment, caroming off the furniture. Anna Wintour wanted to work with me! Steven Meisel, the pinnacle of American fashion photographers, wanted to work with me!

I'd been waitressing only a couple of months, but Gary said it was time to quit.

It was beginning. At long last, it was beginning. And this time it was happening on my terms.

7

INSIDE PLUSWORLD

I n my official coming out as a plus model in 2004, I told *Teen Vogue,* "When I walk through Times Square and see all these billboards, I think, 'Yes. I could be up there.' Hey, I changed. I have faith that other people in the fashion industry can change the way they think, too."

I still believe that. But the fashion industry, like most industries, can be slow to accept difference. Sometimes it needs a little push. In my case, that push came from Steven Meisel.

Steven is an icon. He's one of the most successful fashion photographers in history, famous for finding and championing new faces. His eye is so unerring, editors and advertisers wind up taking chances on girls they otherwise wouldn't. He's shot every cover of Italian *Vogue* since 1988. He took every photo in the magazine's controversial July 2008 "black issue," helping editor in chief Franca Sozzani craft a powerful statement on race and beauty and exclusion. He shot Madonna's art book, *Sex.* His work has been featured in a show at the Museum of Modern Art.

His pictures have a way of making girls look simultaneously

larger than life and very human. He's drawn to the attributes that make a girl special, not cookie-cutter. What others might view as a girl's flaw—a big nose, a neck like a giraffe, large thighs—becomes a source of undeniable power and beauty.

James Danziger, owner of the prominent New York City art gallery Danziger Projects, which represents the photos of artists such as Chuck Close, Annie Leibovitz, and Vik Muniz, has represented Steven. He says, "Meisel would be on anyone's list of the top ten tastemakers in fashion. He's as interested in pushing the envelope as any fashion photographer now working, but he does it effectively within the traditions of high-fashion photography, as opposed to simply for shock. He's interested in expanding the vocabulary of fashion photography. He could have done any number of books, but he isn't particularly interested in having a traditional gallery career. He cares only about the pictures he's taken and the next picture he's going to take."

Steven hired me to pose for the "Shape" issue of *Vogue*. Every April, *Vogue* devotes a number of pages to celebrating different body types. I represented "curvy." When I arrived at Milk Studios in the Meatpacking District of Manhattan on that cold February morning in 2004, I was so jumpy that I was worried I'd puke on my shoes. I was terrified of messing this up. I was so broke, I couldn't afford a manicure. I kept shoving my hands, with their bitten nails, into my pockets.

The studio was shaped like an L, with the buffet and styling sections on one leg of the L and the shooting area on the other leg. I walked in and spotted the rack of clothes, and my eyes bugged out of my head. I'd never seen so many gorgeous designer pieces in one place. This was most definitely a *Vogue* shoot. My gaze went right to an exquisite silver mesh hobo bag by Chloé. I told myself if I ever had money, I'd buy it for myself.

No one looked up as I entered. Trying to look cool, I sauntered over to the food table. There was shrimp, one of my favorites, but I was too anxious to eat. So I admired the shrimp. Pretty, pretty shrimp. Very pink.

Then I felt the presence of someone next to me. Out of the corner of my eye, I saw that it was Steven. I'd never met him, but I knew what he looked like from pictures in magazines. There was no mistaking the dark, beautiful, long, straight hair; the strong jawline; the piercing, nearly black, wide-set almond-shaped eyes; the cupid's-bow lips; the strong nose. (Later, reading the May 2009 issue of *Vogue,* I learned that Steven had been disparagingly called Pocahontas, just as I had. But in his case, the teasing came from the designer Halston.)

While Steven studied the buffet, I studied Steven. He'd tied a bandana around his head; I'd read that he often did that when he worked. He was dressed in black, wearing boots, looking brooding and stubbly and impossibly, intimidatingly handsome. My mind raced. Should I act blasé? What should I say? I finally decided to be myself, just as Mom had always told me. So I turned with a big smile and said, "Hi, I'm Crystal. Do you know where the bathroom is?"

"I'm Steven," he said. "Down the hall."

"Thanks!" I chirped brightly, and ran off. I semi-hyperventilated in a toilet stall for a while, got myself under control, and strolled back to the shoot, all lackadaisical, not a care in the world.

Another model arrived. She was "short." (For the chance to be in *Vogue,* any model in the universe would accept any adjective the magazine wanted to bestow on her. "Troll-like!" "Hirsute!" "Octagonal!" Call us whatever you want, just shoot us!) "Short" and I traded cigarettes as more girls arrived and the shoot got under way. Watching Steven work was fascinating. He was such a visual thinker. He'd tell a girl to move her pinkie, and when she did, her entire body would miraculously look different. He had a genius for giving tiny directions that resulted in more intriguing or pleasing poses.

I watched for almost five hours. Tonne Goodman, *Vogue*'s fashion director, came over to apologize to me. "Can you come back in a couple of hours?" she asked. "I'm sorry this is taking longer than we expected." I assured her it was no problem and left for a walk. An hour or so later, my phone rang. It was Gary, who said, "They're glad you're so patient! But they're still running late. They want you to come back tomorrow."

I was happy to. Having an extra day to watch Steven work and get used to the scope of a *Vogue* shoot was an advantage. The next morning, I felt calm. Which was lucky, because otherwise, when I saw the incredible electric-yellow, ruffled, strapless Carolina Herrera minidress I'd be wearing, I might have swooned.

Garren, the hairstylist, helped me ditch my remaining nervousness. He's like a scientist, very clean and precise and intellectual, a little bit reserved. He's a classic Libra, diplomatic and balanced. When he was through ministering to me, I sported big, wavy, cascading, sexy hair.

As I tried on the yellow dress, I saw an assistant staring at my hands. "You didn't get your nails done before you came?" she asked, eyebrows raised. I didn't see the point in saying that I'd had to choose between a manicure and subway fare.

For the first pose, Steven had me lie on my side. He directed me mostly with his hand, like a conductor, giving minimal instructions like "Teeth!" "Wonder!" "Eyes catching the light!" and "Just looking!" What he meant was perfectly clear, at least to me. We did only four or five shots. I looked right into the camera. Then he said, "Got it." It seemed to take only a few minutes, but that was all he needed. Some photographers are click-click-click-click all the time, but in my experience with Steven, he's more deliberative. He knows exactly what he wants and when he has it.

My next outfit was a white ruched Norma Kamali bathing suit and Pucci wrap, very old-fashioned pin-up girl. Everyone on-set was debating how I should pose. I thought, I'm feeling Marilyn. So as they were talking, I shook out the robe so that it billowed in the air, then let it fall by my side and pool around my ankles. I bent one knee and tilted my head upward, thinking about the way a woman who'd lived her whole life in front of cameras might pose. I imagined a character who perpetually and unconsciously turned her face to the light. I heard Steven say, "That's great." Everyone else stopped talking.

I focused on embodying a woman who was drawn to the camera but resented it at the same time. I could tell Steven liked what I was doing. But I was in a weird position, with my neck stretched and my head held slightly backward at an unnatural angle while my knees were slightly bent. I kept losing my bearings—I couldn't see the floor—so I had to stop every few seconds and reposition myself. I was grateful not to fall over in front of everyone, though even so, I could see that some people were giggling. (At least my physical discomfort was minimal compared to that of the girl who'd done a ballroom-dance-themed shoot with Steven a few years before. Katie Ford, the former CEO of Ford Models, told me that Steven had made that girl dance like mad for three days straight.)

Before I knew it, we were moving on to the third outfit: a red blouse, a wide black belt, and a black-and-white patterned skirt. I pretended I was a cool Upper East Side wealthy socialite, cocking my head to the side as if I were feeling judgmental. I could tell Steven liked that pose, too. "That's it; we've got it," he said. I thanked everyone and left, hoping that Steven liked working with me as much as I'd liked working with him.

I needn't have worried. Before I even got back to the apartment, Steven had called my agency and booked me for Italian *Vogue*.

The next week, I flew to Los Angeles for the shoot. I wore the same outfit I'd worn to the American *Vogue* shoot, a vintage cream-colored lace-trimmed cotton dress, black tights, and combat boots.

I'd spotted the dress in the window of a boutique called Mama JJ's on the Lower East Side. This was when I first moved to the Ford apartment and wasn't working and spent my time taking long walks around the city. I had absolutely no money, but I went inside and just stroked it. It was a hundred and fifty dollars—at the time, it might as well have been fifteen thousand. I said to the owner, "This sounds crazy, but I'm in love with this dress, and I can't pay. Is there anything I can do?" She saw how passionate I was. People who love clothes are like people with eating disorders; we can sense our own kind. She said, "You can pay me twenty dollars a week for it." I wore that dress a couple of times a week for months. I still cherish it. But in early 2004, it was the only nice dress I owned. I couldn't afford another one. I hoped no one would notice that I'd worn it to both shoots.

As soon as I got off the plane, I started to feel ill; over the two days of the shoot, I developed a fever and strep throat. But there was no way I was going to whine. I was working with Steven again!

The Italian *Vogue* shoot had a different vibe from the American *Vogue* shoot. The latter was vaguely '80s-feeling, a bit vampy and celebratory, shot in cool studio light. This shoot was outdoors, in punishingly bright sun. The set was a brutally modernist glass and cement house, all hard lines and angles.

When I got off the van from the airport, I spotted Pat McGrath, the most esteemed makeup artist in the business, standing by the catering table. I'd never met her, but I'd heard she was hilarious, unpretentious, and spontaneous. That was true, as I immediately found out. The moment she saw me, she shrieked, "Hooray! A girl I can *EAAAAT* with!" And she picked up a doughnut from the table and ripped it in half with her teeth.

The shoot produced one of my favorite pictures ever. I call it "Alien Jessica Rabbit." I'm lounging in a candy-red plastic chair in a black corset top and fishnets and cartoonishly high heels. One leg is at an impossible yet seductive angle; one arm is flung across a screamingly yellow table. The pose adds to the feeling of everything being off-kilter. The chair is resting on sun-scorched grass, with a forlorn little rosebush off to my right, and behind me, a black wall meets a white wall in the exact middle of the shot, bifurcating it in a vaguely ominous way. My hair, augmented with loads of extensions, is blown out big and straight. The makeup is harsh and gleaming. The overall effect is slightly robotic. Yet my face is completely peaceful and relaxed. The shot raises more questions than it answers. It's the kind of fashion photograph I love, because it's as much about composition and mood as about clothing.

It's funny that I managed to keep my face so serene, because a few minutes before the picture was taken, I'd nearly fallen in the pool.

I was teetering on those stratospheric stilletos, trying to walk across the damp lawn while getting accustomed to the giant, heavy wad of fake hair on my head, when suddenly, one heel sank into the mud and stayed there. The rest of me kept going. I started to tip over, and began pinwheeling my arms like Wile E. Coyote to regain my balance. I toppled into the photo assistant, who was holding the umbrella meant to keep shadows out of the picture, and the assistant started to stagger, nearly falling onto the other model in the shot, Jessica Stam. A scream went up from the assemblage as I bellowed *FUUUUUUCK ME!* I grabbed the umbrella to steady myself and almost knocked *that* over. But at the last minute, the umbrella, the photo assistant, Jessica, and I all managed to stay upright.

The comic relief proved to be the last laugh of the day. I'd been told I would get the magazine's cover, but when the time came to put on the designated dress—a lacy couture number—it didn't fit. The dress was supposed to be skintight, so there wasn't even a zipper. It had to be wriggled into, then laced up the back with corset ties. The seamstresses, who were amazingly talented, cut up the teeny seams all along the sides of the dress, hoping they could sew me into it, but it just wasn't happening. A humiliating team effort ensued, with everyone on-set trying to stuff me into that garment, but my boobs were hanging out, and it was clear that no amount of magic would get the dress to close. The stylist said, "He can't shoot that on you."

Another girl got the cover.

I excused myself and went into the trailer on-set. I held myself together until the door was closed, and then I burst into tears. I knew I might never get another chance at the cover of Italian *Vogue*. (Indeed, so far I haven't.) I dried my eyes and went back to the set.

At the end of the day's shooting, all the models piled into a van to go back to the hotel. I asked the producer, "Can I say goodbye?" The producer looked at me appraisingly and said, "Smart move." I crept back to the set, where Steven was studying a book of Helmut Newton photographs. I said, "Hey," and he looked up. "Thank you so much," I said hesitantly. "I had a wonderful time working with you." He said, "I'm glad. I'll see you soon." He rose to his feet and kissed me on both cheeks. I thought, I will never wash these cheeks again.

I ran back to the van, where the other models, annoyed, were waiting to get back to the hotel and jump in the pool.

After I got home, I felt as if I were biding my time. I couldn't wait for the March issue of Italian *Vogue* and the April issue of American *Vogue* to hit newsstands. I knew that back-to-back issues of two different editions of *Vogue* with the same plus-size model would capture people's attention. After what seemed like forever (but was really only two months), Gary called me. He had both magazines.

I raced to the Ford office on Fifth Avenue and grabbed the American *Vogue* from Gary's hands. When I saw my own image in the magazine, I screamed. (Years later, Kara Jesella at *Teen Vogue* told me that she and Fiorella had screamed, too. "Knowing we had something to do with that was thrilling," Kara said.) A two-page spread of me in the yellow dress opened the feature. They'd chosen the shot of me resting on my side, looking at the camera, lips parted. The pose emphasized the curve of my waist and hip. It celebrated my body instead of trying to minimize it. I stared at the picture, scarcely able to believe I was looking at myself. It was the culmination of so many dreams.

After I received the Steven Seal of Approval, work began to pour in. Now that my body was fueled and I was able to think again, I was a far better model. I wasn't vacant anymore. I had the confidence a girl needs to make interesting pictures. And I reveled in being a part of the world of high fashion, playing with fabrics as delicate and luxurious as butterfly wings, wearing makeup so wild I could look like a Monet water lily, a futuristic bot, or an early-sixties vinyl sex doll. I did better work as a plus-size model than I'd been able to do as a straight-size model, not only because my brain was more fully engaged in the act of creation but because I was more real. Knowing who I truly was made it that much easier to try on new guises for a shoot. The best models do not have the IQs of coat racks.

Getting to work with the top talents in fashion gave me the opportunity to develop my craft. Snotty people may say, "What craft? You just stand there!" That's not so. The way you pose changes according to the photographer's and the stylist's vision. Learning from the best helped me move more creatively and fluidly. Modeling means breaking your body down to its component parts, isolating elements and moving in ways that convey different moods. It's like narrative Pilates. When I first started, I had a hard time figuring out what to do with my hands, but now I tapped in to my martial arts training to pose in lyrical or powerful ways. I got braver in exploring the different ways my body worked in space, making myself look languorous or limp, full of bravado or genuinely strong. I took more risks in my posing. I was proud of my body and thrilled to be working with photographers who could help me learn to showcase it.

Now that I had breasts and softness, I felt more sexual and womanly. I also had more range; when I was skinny, my body looked sharp, but my poses weren't as crisp, because I didn't have assertiveness and strength. Now I could convey angularity and edge when I wanted to, but I could also offer mystery and poetry.

In rapid succession, I shot for Italian *Vanity Fair,* Italian *Elle, CosmoGirl,* Lane Bryant, and Nine West. In November 2004, when I was nineteen, I posed for French *Vogue* (aka *Vogue Paris*). The photographer was Craig McDean, a British-born New Yorker with a bold, technical, conceptual visual style. He's all about color and texture, and he treats fashion as architecture. Craig used to be an auto mechanic (he did an art book about drag racing), and like me, he studied martial arts. I immediately connected with him. He's very serious and respectful. Unlike Steven, he takes hundreds of frames; he edits afterward, not during the shoot. He likes his models to stay more still than other photographers do, because of all the work he does with light and graphic construction. In one shot, I posed with a giant white Galliano ballgown with a print of pears and swirls, a confection of ruffles and tiers. It wasn't made for someone my size, so I didn't zip it. I held it in front of my body, almost as if I were dancing with it. The curve of my back and the sides of my legs were bare, and I looked over my shoulder at the camera. I made that too-small dress work for me.

Then Craig said, "Do you mind if we show you naked?" This wasn't in the plan; some photographers are notorious for trying to undress models during shoots. But that wasn't Craig's rep. And this was the new me. I threw off my robe and lay down as if I were alone. I had complete trust in Craig. I knew the outcome would be stunning. I felt like a beautiful sexual being, because I was finally a sensual being. My brain and my body were in sync.

The image the magazine chose looked like a conscious statement to the dictatorial thinness-obsessed world: FUCK YOU. Check me out. I'm sitting up, head thrown back, looking through half-lidded, lavender-shadowed eyes at the viewer. I'm draped in gossamer black and dark green silk. One breast is hidden behind a swath of fabric; the other is bare. My legs and hip look fleshy; thanks to Craig's genius with light, my skin is glowing. In another shot, I stand tall, chin pointed to the ceiling, hair flowing down my back, swathed in masses of edgy, frayed, punk-rock ruffles, some voluminous and some tiny. My breasts peek from the fabric. Showing a plus-size girl in sexy, powerful poses challenged the fashion world—and magazine readers—to expand their perspective of beauty.

My next big shoot was also for *Vogue Paris*—an eight-page black-and-white layout inspired by Hollywood stars of the 1920s and East Village New Wave popsters of the 1980s. Called "La Belle Americaine," it was all about voluptuousness and texture: I wore a furry little beret, tons of chains around my neck, a studded belt. The clothes were dark and Gothic; in one shot, I have a fake snake around my neck; in another, there's a cigarette tucked behind my ear; in a third, I'm holding a square of dark chocolate. My eyes were smoky, lined in black, surrounded with gray shadows. The shoot was styled by Carine Roitfeld, *Vogue Paris*'s editor, an iconic figure in the fashion world. The look encapsulated her aesthetic—relaxed, challenging, rock and roll.

For me, the most fun part of that shoot was reconnecting with Didier Malige, the photographer from my first shoot for *Seventeen* in 2001, back when I was skinny. Didier is a hairstylist as well as photographer, and on Carine's shoot he was doing the hair. (He gave me a piecey updo that was brilliantly '20s-meets-'80s, flapper meets St. Marks Place—a sort of wavy, deconstructed bob.) He remembered me from the lifetimes-ago "Born to Ride" Harley shoot and very sweetly brought me a print from that story. He couldn't get over the way I looked now: at ease in my body and far better at my job.

The photographer on this shoot was Patrick Demarchelier, whose great gift is making women look gorgeous. He doesn't do *jolie-laide;* he's all *jolie.* He's famous for a host of images: Naomi Campbell in Masai warrior paint, Christy Turlington with a giant white rose partially obscuring her face, Keith Richards in all his craggy fabulousness. But he's perhaps best known for his exquisite, timeless photos of Princess Diana. After working with him once, Diana requested Patrick as her personal photographer, and he became the first non-British official photographer of the royal family. In 2008 his work was the subject of a thirty-year restrospective at the Petit Palais, the museum of fine arts in Paris.

I've worked with him a number of times now, and I know that every time he'll make me look lush and womanly, with incredible skin. His photos are clean and deceptively simple. Katie Ford says, "Patrick loves women, and you can see it in his photography. Whether he's shooting a model, a celebrity, or a political figure, he knows how to make her look incredibly beautiful."

Patrick is also *le plus français* person I have ever met in my life. It's mortifying to admit, but I cannot understand a word he says. His accent is so strong, and there's usually a fan blowing to tousle my hair, and he's yelling directions into the wind, and I'm constantly thinking, What? He might as well be Pepé Le Pew. I feel like such a déclassé American when I work with him. I usually ask a stylist to repeat everything he says, discreetly.

Patrick knows what he wants and is very directional; I have less leeway with him than I do with other photographers, but that's totally fine. I like having different experiences with different people behind the lens.

In October 2005 I achieved one of the highlights of my career: walking the runway for Jean Paul Gaultier, in his spring 2006 prêt-à-porter show. Gaultier is an iconic figure—not just because he designed Madonna's *Blonde Ambition* corsets but because his witty designs reflect his funny, warm, generous, curious spirit. He's not too cool for school, like some fashion people. He's full of enthusiasm and wildness, playful, and a little punk—once he supposedly mailed live turkeys to fashion editors he felt had insulted him. His career started when he was only seventeen, with no formal fashion training—he sent fashion sketches to Pierre Cardin, who made him a design assistant. Gaultier has had his own label since 1976, but his work never, ever looks tired. He's open to new ideas and to challenging the status quo—it's no wonder he's excited to work with plus-size girls.

I went to the fitting and saw the dress I was going to walk in and nearly fainted. It was otherworldly in its beauty. It was a tulle candy fantasy, an earthbound mermaid dress—skintight through the bodice and hips, then exploding in a burst of loose tulle below the knee with a train of cascading fabric trailing behind. He fitted it right to my body, like a second skin. Brilliantly colored silk flowers were hand-sewn onto it while Jean Paul and I chatted. The flowers—all different kinds and colors and shapes—covered my shoulders and then trailed down the middle of the dress in a sinuous, organic way. It was a little girl's fairy-princess fantasy gone utterly high-fashion.

The runway was covered in straw, and a lot of the dresses had straw in them—straw embroidery, a straw bustier. He told me that the look of the show was a riff on country people's Sunday best or a farm wedding. The show featured fabulous hats, Eastern European–inspired peasant blouses, and folkloric, rustic touches from different cultures all brought together in a happy mishmash. There were kids in the show, because what's a wedding without children?

I don't know why Monsieur Gaultier chose me—especially since

I'm not known as a runway girl—but I suspect it was because my lush body fit with his theme. The show's imagery was all about fertility and nature and happiness; it didn't have any of the hard edges of urban, minimalist fashion. With my messy, teased what-was-she-just-doing-in-the-straw hair and swinging hips, I looked fecund and sexy, like a postnuptual bride in a fairy tale.

Doing the show felt like jumping out of an airplane. It was a huge rush. The music, the audience on either side of the catwalk, the other girls, the madness backstage: Runway is all adrenaline, all the time. I have a fairly natural runway walk—it's not the stylized boom, boom, boom hip-swiveling Clydesdale strut of a Naomi Campbell—and I never know how the audience will react to me. You can often tell immediately what they think of an outfit. You hope for a strong reaction, not crickets. This time I felt their enthusiasm and shock the moment I hit the catwalk. Here I was in all my size-12 glory, covered with brilliant flowers. Get a load of me, black-clad hungry bitches!

My next major gig was a Dolce & Gabbana campaign, which I shot in February 2006. The following spring, it started running in every major fashion magazine; for a few months, my body—clad only in a leopard-print corset and panties—was inescapable. Steven was the photographer, and I was thrilled to work with him again. I even got to wear my favorite lipstick (NARS Jungle Red).

Steven and I have done several more international and American *Vogue* features together—and every experience has been wonderful. We have great chemistry. Sometimes he puts a mirror behind him as he shoots, so the model can see herself. I love this, because it keeps me in the moment and makes me feel like a true participant in his vision. I see myself as Steven sees me. I think I have a good sense of my body and where I am in space and how I move, but it's still helpful to check in with that mirror and feel that everyone in the room—Steven, the stylist, the editor or producer, the assistants, the lighting guy, the girl holding the fan—is in search of the same image. When you get into a groove, it's as if you're in a private yet self-aware dream, and the photographer is a voyeur. But you have power, because you know he's watching. It's a thrill and a dance.

Steven's style is characterized by the broadness of its references. He has an amazing sense of fashion and art history—Katie Ford told me he has a huge library of vintage magazines and art books, and he's studied fashion history since childhood. His work alludes to great images of the past, but he also has an ultra-modern, wide-ranging interpretation of beauty. To him, individuality is glorious. That's why his work has such an imprimatur; he shows other fashion people what beauty is. Steven has an air of mystery—his coolness and self-possession make fashion insiders trust him as an arbiter of taste. The fact that he's very private and almost never gives interviews adds to his mystery and allure.

Frequently, editors and advertisers need a push to show them that difference can be fabulous. Speaking about the fashion business's fear of the new, Steven told *The New York Times,* "They are looking around, over their shoulders, asking, 'Is that cool?' It can only be stated by a certain five people and then they go with it." Well, Steven is one of those five people. A paradigm shift always needs a paradigm shifter, and he's it. When he said I was cool, everyone else believed it.

Thanks to his influence, I was finally earning some money. That spring I bought myself a treat—the Chloé bag I'd coveted at my first American *Vogue* shoot. It had made its way to eBay, and I got it for a song. Good things, like an eBay bag or a plus-size modeling career, come to those who wait.

In May 2006 *Glamour*—a body-positive magazine that has embraced me and plus-size women in general—let me tell my story of recovery, accompanied by luscious black-and-white photos by Patrick Demarchelier. At the end of that year, I got my first mainstream fashion-magazine cover—*Harpers Bazaar*'s Russian edition, a first for any plus model. Shot by the very young and very talented Matt Jones, the cover featured me in tight close-up, with Medusa-like hair, deeply red lips, and an intense, hooded stare. It was formidable, not pretty-pretty.

But for all-out crazy fabulousness, you can't beat working with Ellen von Unwerth. Shooting with her is like a mad, decadent fever dream; it's what people imagine the fashion world is like all the time and rarely is. On-set, there's often champagne. Ellen is a divine mental case, dancing around with her camera, laughing and bellowing, "MORE, YA?" in her Lotte Lenya accent. Her work is louche, super-sexy, drenched with color. A story I shot with her for *Above* magazine in August 2006 took place in a bedroom with an ornate carved dark wood bed and red satin sheets. The pictures are sexually charged. In one shot, I'm pretending to kick a male model in the face. He's looking at me and another girl appraisingly; she's looking teasingly at him while clinging to me. Am I flirting or attacking? Does she want him or me? I love the ambiguity. In another shot, I'm straddling the corner of the bed, wearing a little Gaultier minidress and a bra with fishnet kneesocks—it's very Weimar cabaret. In another image, I'm wearing a men's suit by Sonia Rykiel Homme with a bra and no shirt, a cigar clenched between my teeth, lips parted and glossy, posing possessively with a girl in a virginal white (but very sheer) Betsey Johnson dress.

For another shoot with Ellen, I went to the beautiful countryside outside Paris, where we shot at a glamorous old château. Ellen had all us models rolling around in the mud—it had been raining off and on—in fabulous clothes. We were filthy. Mud was everywhere, and I do mean everywhere. Ellen went back to Paris for the night, and we models were supposed to return to our hotel in a nearby town to sleep. But just before we were scheduled to leave, a giant rainstorm rolled in. We were trapped at the château. We showered off the mud, but we had no fresh clothes. So we just gathered around the fireplace, all of us wrapped in towels. As the rain slashed against the stained-glass windows of the castle and lightning lit up the sky, the château's owner brought us a huge, antique platter of glorious French cheeses and grapes. I played *Für Elise* on the piano, and the other models lounged about, licking their fingers, the towels now abandoned on the two-hundred-year-old carpet. I thought, *This is a moment. Always remember this.*

Modeling is about drama. A photo is a performance. Some shooters (such as Ellen and Ruven Afanador) put the playacting and fantasy right in the viewer's face—it's apparent in every shot. But even in the most minimalist, subdued pictures, a good model needs to be performing. Her performance may last only as long as it takes the shutter to click, but it's there.

I look for a story in all the work I do, as I zigzag between commercial work and avant-garde work, catalog and high fashion, upscale and mass market. The variety keeps things interesting. For retail clients like Lane Bryant and the Barcelona-based retailer Mango, my priority is to show off the clothes; those shoots are less about mood and atmosphere. I like the challenge of *selling* while simultaneously trying to create an elegant photo.

Some of my most fulfilling retail work has been with Evans in the UK, because I adore their line. Everything is so on-trend; so many of the pieces have an interesting, progressive cut. Their wide-legged jeans and leather jackets have magical fit properties—somehow they're flattering on every shape. I love the company's message that you don't have to sacrifice style for size, and the fact that I believe in the brand makes it easy to sell. (I sing its virtues so incessantly, I've gotten a bunch of my American friends to buy the clothes online.)

I'm grateful to Lane Bryant for supporting my career from the beginning. I love that this company has such a wide reach—women can find a store almost anywhere and try on a huge variety of looks to see what works for them.

The one runway show I never miss is Elena Miro's in Milan. Doing live fashion shows is always heart-pounding, with quick changes and backstage chaos that evaporates the minute you turn the corner onto the runway. Then it's all theater, all serenity. Elena's collections vary widely from season to season, which keeps things interesting.

Being backstage at a fashion show is a crash course in media training. Usually, my interactions with the media are, well, mediated. I know what the ground rules are. I collaborate with a writer on a magazine or newspaper story and with TV interviewers who ask questions that I'm expecting. Backstage, in the adrenalized and sweaty atmosphere of a show, you never know who's going to ask you what. A microphone appears in your face, and someone's hurling unexpected questions at you like spitballs. In 2007 at Elena Miro, a journalist demanded, "Does Jean Paul Gaultier fart?"

My mouth hung slack. "What?"

"Fart! Does Gaultier fart? I hear he farts quite often!"

I stammered, "Everyone farts."

"Did he fart in the showroom? Did you smell it?"

I gathered my wits enough to say, "Excuse me, I need to get changed."

(Believe it or not, that interviewer was not Sasha Baron Cohen, playing Brüno. I have no idea who the person was, but I'm relieved I haven't run into him since.)

As my career gathered steam, more and more people got interested in the notion of a model who chose to be healthy. I told my story on the *Today* show, *The View, The Tyra Banks Show.* When I got the call from *The Oprah Winfrey Show,* I freaked. Oprah! I was scared out of my gourd. I had to cancel a major job at the last second, and the client was furious and I felt terrible, but: Oprah! I dressed conservatively, in a black Donna Karan skirt and pumps. I looked like I was going to a condo board meeting in 1987. Oprah was warm, a real pro, and it was scary-fun to be myself in front of an audience and feel waves of support from them.

One of the highlights of 2007 was the beginning of my association with Ruven Afanador (who, not coincidentally, shot the cover of this book). His sets are magical, sumptuous tableaux. Think of his shoots for the *New York Times,* Nordstrom's, countless editorials, and the famous breast cancer awareness campaign. Ruven plays lots of classical music while he's working—Chopin and Mozart and Debussy—to help make the shoot feel majestic, as if you're on a stage. He makes it easy to play a part. On his sets, the atmosphere is serene and focused. No one shrieks about their sex life or giggles into their cell phone about other jobs.

Ruven is a very tall man, reserved and quiet. He's a minimalist communicator, in a good way; I always feel encouraged to find my own poses when I work with him. I suspect he senses whether a model prefers more or less direction and shifts accordingly. On shoots with Ruven, I've worn couture gowns so big I couldn't fit through a door or into a bathroom stall. One Atelier Versace ball-room skirt was so vast I couldn't lift it—or, for that matter, walk in it. But clothes needn't be just utilitarian objects, functional items you wear to run to the corner to get milk. Clothes can be dreams.

For the December 2007 issue of Italian *Elle,* Ruven shot me in a coolly stylized setting of gray industrial carpeting, battered cement-looking walls, and deliberately unfinished-looking fabric backdrops. The austere setting offset the lushest, most ornate gowns you can imagine. I wore an insanely poofy lime-green silk Lacroix dress and strange curvy satyr heels; I was swathed in purple Dior feathers and silk flowers; my naked breast peeked from behind the silk of a Giorgio Armani black dress with a plunging sweetheart neckline reminiscent of the gown worn by John Singer Sargent's Madame X. My poses were super-stylized and expressive, as befitting the garments. Ruven is a master of juxtapositions and the use of color. I want to cry when I think about a particular Dior confection in the setting Ruven created for it—it looked like a pale peach peony surrounded by coils of industrial gray. In the photo, my skin has a Renaissance glow. The only bright color in the shot is one simple, faraway strip of electric-blue backdrop fabric. The composition—overlapping angles and squares with my curves in a profusion of silk waves in the middle, plus that one eye-popping slash of color—is astonishing.

Italian *Elle* has been good to me. In December 2008 I got the cover and a nineteen-page (huge!) editorial feature, both shot by Matt Jones. The magazine called me "*la bellissima* Crystal Renn." We took the pictures in a field behind Matt's house in upstate New York, and they're some of my favorite pictures ever. The clothes were hippie-inspired, and I felt like a peaceful flower child in them. As we lay in the grass, the stylist made a daisy headband for me. There was a shawl crocheted like an old tablecloth, a skirt shredded like newspaper. Matt's a very reserved Englishman—he's shy, I think. He's a bit skittish about eye contact, like me. He's kind. He likes folk music. Because he's such an intuitive, thoughtful person, working with him feels mellow and easy. This boho shoot was the perfect meeting of photographer, setting, styling, clothing, and mood.

I don't speak Italian, but I did have to laugh at the cover line on that issue. The word "*innocenti*" is poised next to a shot of me looking wide-eyed and naive—but inside, I'm showing off my naked breasts yet again. Not so *innocenti*.

A hallmark of my career has been my comfort in taking off my clothes. Showing my body has made people see that flesh is sexy, that super-thin is only one kind of beauty. I do try to make sure that whatever I do is in service to the vision for the editorial (I sound like an actress saying "I'll do nudity if it's integral to the story," right?).

A few years ago, I was scheduled to shoot for German *Vogue,* and I asked about the clothes only to hear "Oh, we don't have any clothes!" They'd wanted a nude shoot, but no one had told me. I did the job because I'm a professional. Once we started shooting, I got into it, as I always do. The pictures, which were black and white, came out stark and lovely. But I felt a bit blindsided. After that, I decided to pull back from being the all-boob-all-the-time channel. I'm happy to bare all if it's for charity, the way I did for Ruven, or if it's a creative shoot that's about the interplay between the body and the clothes, the way I did for Matt. But otherwise, I'd like to keep Bonnie and Clyde under wraps for a while, if you know what I mean, and I think you do.

All of my experiences with nudity have felt safe and professional. The one bad experience I had wasn't on a topless shoot. I was vamping, fully clothed, for a famous photographer when he passed the camera to an assistant and cupped my breasts with both hands. I couldn't believe it. I froze. I immediately started second-guessing myself. Had I done something to make him think this was okay? He saw my panic and backed off. I went home and cried. Then, as is my wont, I pushed the bad thoughts out of my head. I refused to turn on myself after all the work I'd done to stop hating my body. This creep had the problem, not me.

That was the only time I've felt victimized since becoming a plus model. (And it could have happened to me when I was thin. It could have happened if I'd never been a model at all.) The wonderful shoots have far outweighed the bad ones. I've gotten to travel the world much more as a plus model than when I was thinner. I've been all over Eastern and Western Europe, Asia, South America, the Caribbean. My favorite destination so far is Morocco. I loved the minarets and mosques, the crumbling palaces and glittering fabrics, the salmon-pink scarred walls and riotous patterns of Berber carpets draped over ropes in the souk. I loved the scent of saffron and the pounding beat of *Gnawa* drum music. I loved the Majorelle gardens of Yves Saint Laurent, with their bright blue accents and tiled fountains.

I'm on the road so often, I've become a dervish of efficiency when I pack. I travel in comfy layers—usually a pair of black harem pants, a long tank top, a drapey sweater, and a many-pocketed long weatherproof parka. I wear a wide, stretchy fabric headband that does convenient double duty as a sleep mask; I just pull it down over my eyes. I can get through security in the time it takes other people to take off their shoes—bag of toiletries in outer suitcase pocket, easy-to-slip-off studded shoe-boots, laptop kept accessible, *whoosh*. As much as I love the travel, it's hard on me. A few months ago, I was in my third time zone in six days, and I was so exhausted, I hallucinated that Flounder from *The Little Mermaid* was talking to me.

I've come a long way, but there are still doors I'm trying to break down. I'd like more covers. I'd like a cosmetics contract. I'd like to feel I'm helping other plus-size girls get a foot in the door. I've never wanted to be the only girl in high fashion who looks like me.

Modeling is invariably a mash-up of rejection and over-the-top praise. The trick is not taking either too seriously. In January 2009 *Elle Québec* wrote about me, "In person, the 22-year-old radiates the confident sensuality of a Rubens model and the healthy voluptuousness of an Italian Renaissance muse. Her hourglass curves, creamy skin, lush eyelashes and ebony hair—which she inherited from her Cherokee ancestors—work their juju, whether she's playing the femme fatale, the ingenue or the tease." *Wow, that girl sounds pretty hot!* Unlike the poor hideous girl who was described on a fashion web site as looking like a "beached whale." Well, guess what? Both girls are me. That's a perfect encapsulation of why looking for validation from external sources is a huge mistake. You don't have to be a model to understand that self-esteem and the projection of beauty come from within. (Exhibit A: My old junior high classmate, Madysson Middleton.)

I do radiate confidence because I'm happy. These days my weight is pretty steady. There's some fluctuation, maybe seven or eight pounds up and down. After I quit smoking for six months in 2008, I gained about ten pounds. When I started again (I know, I know), the weight came off. I fully intend to quit smoking for good, weight consequences be damned, but it's so hard. I've heard nicotine is more addictive than heroin, and I believe it. But I also know that smoking is a much bigger health threat than ten extra pounds.

I'm thrilled to live in PlusWorld, the universe of plus-size models. Here, it's not only the waist and hip measurements that differ from those of the straight-size world. The language, the mores, and the attitudes are different as well.

Most plus models fall into the overweight category on the BMI charts. (My set-point range usually puts me there, too, if barely.) When you look at us in real life, as opposed to in the pages of a magazine where emaciation is the norm, you're unlikely to think, Ooh, she's fat. As Kate Harding, founder of the wonderful body-acceptance blog Shapely Prose, wrote in *Salon* in January 2009, "Whenever you read an article about THE OBESITY EPIDEMIC BOOGA BOOGA BOOGA, you should know that they're talking mostly about people who look like me—and like your mom, your neighbor, your coworker, your kid's teacher . . . Only about 6 percent of the adult population is categorized as severely obese. The vast majority of people classified as obese are about as fat as I am, in the BMI 30–35 range. I am the face of the obesity crisis everyone's so worried about, and yet I constantly have people telling me I'm not fat. There's some, uh, food for thought."

Plus models, too, are constantly told we "don't look fat." This is meant as a compliment, but it gets tiresome. Most of us like the way we look. If you choose to believe the BMI charts, we're fat, yet we're fine with our size. It's simply bizarre that "normal" is the new overweight. We've seen that super-skinny women can be as unhappy as the fattest fat girl. We know how awful it is to obsess about every calorie. We've just opted not to make ourselves crazy.

That said, I'm not a typical plus model. Historically, plus models have been cute, happy, accessibly pretty girls. The industry has rewarded girls who look smiley and approachable, like the nonthreatening best-friend character in a movie. I'm generalizing, but not much. There are many plus models whose work I've admired, but overall, the look that gets plus jobs isn't the look that resonates with me.

I am not the best-friend character in the movie. I'm the hot girl. I don't tend to smile a lot in pictures (though I do in real life) because I'm wary of being pigeonholed as the girl next door. I want to play different characters, many of them sexual or challenging or tough. If I looked entirely open and inviting, I would have a harder time creating those looks. I'm more editorial than is usual in the plus world. My wild hair and big eyebrows are definitely not sweet and tame. When I go to castings, I dress more rock-and-roll than demure. I'm not proper, and I think my impropriety has helped me be seen as a model, not just as a *plus* model. Being true to myself has only helped. Now I compete against straight-size girls, auditioning for every fragrance and beauty campaign. I'm plus, but that's not all I am. I contain multitudes.

Only a handful of plus models have been successful in editorial. I want to join their ranks. But I want to model my career on that of Kate Moss. When Kate started out, she was "the waif," but she quickly became known for so much more than her size. People realized she had a very expressive face and body and an amazing personal style. She's managed her career brilliantly. Now she's designing for the retailer Topshop, using her styling skills to extend her career past the usual straight-size-model sell-by date. Her body has changed as she's gotten older (a British newspaper recently called her fat!), and she seems utterly comfortable in her own skin. She gives almost no interviews. She has developed a mystique. Her elusiveness makes her that much more enticing; what you don't know, you want. It's not surprising that she dated Johnny Depp, who also has that unknowable quality. Alas, I can't emulate how social she is. I am not good at the schmoozing part of my job. Kate seems to need to be with people; I always want to be home on my balcony, reading a book.

It's undeniably harder for plus girls to break through when so few editors and designers want to use them. I understand that some designers feel clothes look better on stick-thin girls. But customers don't always agree. I was interested in a 2008 study from an Australian Ph.D. candidate, Phillippa Diedrichs, showing that average-sized models in advertisements made consumers more favorably disposed toward the product. Diedrichs created a series of mock advertisements for a range of beauty products, clothing, and accessories, then showed them to over three hundred men and women, aged eighteen to twenty-five. Some featured models who were a U.S. size 4 to 6; others featured viewed models who were a U.S. size 10. The viewers rated how likely they were to buy the products in the ads and how they felt about their own bodies after seeing the ads. Men and women found both sets of ads equally effective, and women felt better about their own bodies after seeing the bigger models.

Artifice is a fact of life in the fashion business, whatever size you are. Some straight-size clients trim me down with Photoshop; some plus-size clients bulk me up with digital tricks. I've been given extra chins and belly pooch; I've seen my cheekbones enhanced and I've seen them taken away. I've worn padded gel shorts (akin to bike shorts with gelatinous inserts—they feel like ass, literally) and padded bras (making me a DD instead of the small C I am). I joke, "I don't care what you do to me, just book me!" Dolce & Gabbana ran two versions of my ad—my thighs look thinner in one than in the other. I'm not sure where each ran.

All of this does bother me a little. I want to promote health, and I know I'm the size that's normal and healthy for me. But pretense is everywhere in fashion, on both sides of the thinness divide. Sometimes fakeness is appealing, like a crazy robot girl in a hyper-green garden in a Steven Klein shot. But sometimes it pervades that which *should* be real. That kind of falsehood is more ominous.

Labels are strange things. What does "plus" even mean? What's a size? A 6 in one label can be a 10 in another label, a 4 in a third. I'm far from the smallest girl on the plus board. Some plus-size models are a size 8 today, the size of some straight-size supermodels in the eighties. Yes, it's insane and depressing to think of an 8 as plus-size. On the other hand, getting bogged down in the semiotics of it all doesn't help anyone. I prefer not to dwell on labels and simply to encourage the arbiters of fashion to book girls of all shapes and sizes.

I know I'm too fat for some *Vogue* readers and too skinny for some Lane Bryant customers. It's not my job to fulfill everyone's fantasies. That's why diversity is so important. We want to see ourselves reflected in the culture, whatever we look like.

When I model in Europe, I'm less likely to be labeled "plus" in the magazine. I'm just a girl, just Crystal. Those magazines don't expend type justifying my presence in their pages the way American magazines often do. Americans are more likely to scrabble desperately to point out the plus girl, soliciting applause for using her, differentiating her from all the *normal* girls. Ooh, let's title this story "Dangerous Curves" or "Larger Than Life!" "In the American fashion magazine market, everything has to be so compartmentalized," says Fiorella Valdesolo, who is now a freelance stylist. "Tall! Petite! Plus! Why can't a good model just be a good model? If someone has a connection to the camera and is graceful, her size just becomes one of her attributes." I agree.

When Steven Meisel photographed the black issue of Italian *Vogue* in 2008, he got a hundred pages to show black models. There was a huge range of looks in those pages: A hundred different moods were represented. So it should be with plus girls; we're all different, as different as straight-size models. Let a thousand flowers bloom!

"It's so crazy to live in such a narrow, narrow place," Steven told *The New York Times.* "Age, weight, sexuality, race—every kind of prejudice." I hope more people of influence will follow his lead in using nontypical models. Whenever I see seventy-eight year-old Carmen Dell'Orefice in an ad, I gasp. I want to buy the product, because she is so ravishing and I so respect a company that appreciates older women's beauty. She's worked for over half a century (she did her first shoot for *Vogue* in 1946), looking more magnificent every year. That's inspiring.

I think the industry is changing, slowly but surely. I think incremental change is good—that means it will have staying power. Showing one plus-size model is a trend; having us throughout the magazine is the future. And I hope that more high-end designers move into larger size ranges. Being a size 12 or bigger shouldn't mean you have to sacrifice chicness or quality.

Gary's favorite expression is "Everything is crawl-walk-run." He believes we'll get to the point where every shape and size will be represented on the runway, as long as we get there the right way. Plus-size models aren't interchangeable; that's insulting. You want the right girl for the right job. My sexy look wouldn't be right for every client. But the fact that I'm curvy, the fact that you can't immediately tell my age or nationality—well, I think that could have resonance in a changing America.

8

LOVE STORY

For most of my life, my only love affairs were with books. That's not such a bad thing. Books fulfilled my need for romance— when I read an explicit sex scene, I felt an erotic charge. No teenage boy could compare with Mr. Darcy or Rhett Butler. I've read that reading engages the visual sense as well as the verbal sense, so it taps in to both sides of the brain. That's true for me. When I read, I'm transported. Books are a vacation between endpapers. When I fall in love with a man on the page, it's a perfect little compressed relationship, with all the attendant emotions, pounding heartbeat, and arousal. Not bad for the cost of a paperback.

I've always had a weakness for romance novels. They're pure escapism. I get a kick out of their predictable arc: Headstrong woman and imperious man start off loathing each other, then come to respect each other while fighting off their growing attraction before succumbing in a white-hot explosion of sex-scene sparks. The men in those books don't leave their dirty tighty-whities on the floor. They don't ignore you because they're hollering at the TV as Ole Miss gets its ass handed to it. You don't catch them standing in front of an open fridge, drinking orange juice out of the carton. Oh, sure, they may take over your family's ancestral plantation, subvert your plan to marry the local gentry, and deflower you by the sugar mill, but hey, they're blameless on OJ spillage.

My very favorite romance novel has always been *Ain't She Sweet* by Susan Elizabeth Phillips. She's a writer I adore in general. She's funny, for one thing (you don't read a lot of romances that are both genuinely hilarious and genuinely hot) and her heroes are strong and old-school and kind of dickish; I like that in my escapism. I don't want a sensitive New Age guy in my fantasies. But Phillips's men are also deep and layered and fundamentally decent. I admire her gift for writing sweep-her-off-her-feet scenes that aren't rape but have a whiff of genuine danger.

In *Ain't She Sweet,* the hero is a writer named Colin Byrne. I don't think it's an accident that his name recalls both Gabriel Byrne and Lord Byron. He's the heroine's former high school English teacher. The heroine, Sugar Beth (I'm a southerner; how could I not love a book whose heroine is named Sugar Beth?), returns to her small Mississippi town to search for a mysterious painting she believes is hidden in her family's old house. Colin now owns that house. Hot shenanigans ensue. I love that both characters are proud and self-sufficient, flawed and stubborn. They have hate-sex that turns into something more. Every sex scene is hotter than the one before.

I vowed to my friends and Mom, "One day I'm going to marry a man like Colin Byrne." Everyone dismissed my little fantasy. But sometimes life is better than any romance novel.

It took a long time for my books to give way to actual flesh-and-blood romance. I was celibate the whole time I was a straight-size model. Becoming larger—specifically, becoming a larger model who brought sexiness to a formerly rather staid industry—coincided with my own sexual awakening. It wasn't until I was no longer starving, no longer full of scorn for my own body, that I felt open to a relationship for the first time. I couldn't embrace my sexuality until I stopped being a control freak. I had to learn to appreciate taste and sensation. I had to loosen up. People with anorexia don't do a lot of laughing.

The first step in my sexual maturation was learning to listen to my body again. Developing a healthy attitude toward exercise helped me see my body as a friend, not an enemy. Walking (instead of running so hard on a treadmill I looked like I was being chased), swimming for meditation as well as exercise, and doing hot yoga all have helped me get in touch with my body. I stopped associating workouts with weakness and lack of control. There's something very sexy about Bikram yoga in particular; not so much doing it—which involves sweat dripping stingingly into your eyes as a guy next to you smells increasingly like a kennel, and you get hypnotized by his armpit hair during downward dog, and the room starts to feel like the seventh circle of hell—but afterward, when you're drenched and limber and thirstily gulping water. It's visceral. I feel hyperpresent and a little light-headed and very free and very good.

In *Health at Every Size,* Linda Bacon writes, "Your body is your physical connection to the world. Becoming active can help you chip away at any bad feelings you may have had for your body, enabling you to appreciate its functionality, de-emphasize its looks, and revel in your strength and capabilities." That's true for me. My prescription for a healthy sex life involves having lots of physical movement in my day; eating real food that's not stuffed full of chemicals, hormones, antibiotics, and preservatives; enjoying and being present with the food I do eat; eating a variety of plants and whole grains; and managing stress by taking time for myself, reading, meditating, window-shopping, chatting with friends, playing with my pets. If you're wound tighter than a drum, it's hard to let go enough to enjoy sex.

One study found that two thirds of American women have some degree of sexual dysfunction related to body image. I believe it. One manifestation of that dysfunction is fixating on your flaws during sex: Is he looking at my belly rolls? He's looking at my belly rolls! No, wait, he's touching my cellulite! He's wondering how he ended up in bed with a cow! You get so wound up in your own self-critique, you can't be in the moment. There's no way you can become aroused, let alone have an orgasm. The famous sex therapists Masters and Johnson suggested that "spectatoring"—focusing on yourself from a third-person perspective during sex rather than tuning in to your own sensation or the erotic arousal of your partner— can whip up performance fears and have a disastrous effect on enjoyment. That resonates with me. You needn't be anorexic to find your sexuality stifled by body hatred.

I didn't spring into immediate, curvy, healthy sexual selfhood, like Athena leaping fully formed from Zeus's head. Just as it took a while for me to get physically healthy, it took time for me to get sexually healthy. I'm grateful to Nick, the first boyfriend I had after I started gaining weight, for helping me get there. I met him at the gym in 2003—I'm aware of the irony there—when I was trying to develop healthy, nonobsessive workout habits. I was on the treadmill and felt his energy from across the room. I looked up, and there he was by the weight machines, smiling at me. There was something so sweet about his face—I instantly felt a connection. It didn't hurt that his body looked like a marble statue.

Objectively, he and I weren't the greatest match. He was twenty-eight; I was seventeen. He probably shouldn't have been dating someone so much younger. But he was a little immature, and I was a funny combination of worldly (from having worked in the business for a year and deciding to remake my career and not die) and innocent (from refraining from partying or dating for so many years). Nick was quiet and let me take the lead in every aspect of our relationship. That made him the perfect person to be with when I was healing. I was way too fragile for bad-boy drama, and he was nothing like the jerky popular boys of Clinton, Mississippi.

We should have continued to take things slowly. But circumstances forced our hand. We'd been dating only a few months when I was invited to Katie Ford's birthday party in 2003. Once upon a time, I would have been hugging the wall at a fancy shindig like that, but I was no longer so shy and self-conscious. I sauntered up to the bar and ordered a screwdriver. It was delicious—it tasted like orange juice, not vodka. So I ordered another.

I was the furthest thing from a drinker. Once, in eighth grade, Tina and I liberated a bottle of tequila from her dad's liquor cabinet and took one swig each. I coughed and gagged and choked so hard, I thought I was going to breathe flames. Another time, a girl at Ford and I shared a bottle of wine at the apartment, and I got so wasted I wound up horking into the toilet. That was the full extent of my partying. But at Katie's party, pounding screwdrivers made me feel relaxed and funny and happy. I loved screwdrivers! Whoo!

I vaguely remember the fourth one, but apparently, I had two more after that. I don't remember anything between the fourth screwdriver and the moment I woke up in my bottom bunk in my underwear. My *wet* underwear. There was a garbage can full of puke by my head. I started screaming.

A couple of other models came running out of their rooms. A girl I barely knew told me, "The chaperone brought you back here. You vomited all over her Marc Jacobs shoes and ruined them! She had to drag you out of the party and throw you in a cab." I stared at her, dumbfounded. She told me I'd spent the whole cab ride hanging my head out the window, hollering. The chaperone had to hold onto a fistful of my hair to keep me from heaving my entire upper body out of the cab. When we got to the apartment, she'd called upstairs, and the rest of the girls had half dragged, half carried me up two flights. I spattered the bathroom wall with puke. "It totally looked like *CSI* in there," the girl told me. She continued, "I took off your disgusting, puke-covered dress, threw you in the shower, and dumped you on your bed."

So that's why my underwear was wet. I stared at the girl, wide-eyed.

She shook her head. "You *so* owe me one."

What had I done?

After my two previous drinking experiences, I should have known better. My Mom had always warned me that with out family history, alcohol was dangerous—we seem to have lower tolerance than anyone else on the planet. Nowadays, when I do drink, I almost never have more than one glass. But hindsight is always 20-20.

The chaperone was still asleep. I knew she loathed me. She'd loathed me even before this happened. Her predecessor in the model apartment, an older woman, had been asked to move out for being too lenient with the girls. This chaperone was twenty-three and de-termined to be a hard-ass, and I was having none of it. I never sneaked out, I never went clubbing, but I liked having my freedom to walk around the city and go out to dinner with Nick without hav-ing to rush back for a nine P.M. curfew. She knew I had an attitude about her power-tripping and rulesiness.

Coming out of so many years of repression and denial, I think I got drunk because I wanted to act out and explore new sensations. I wanted to *feel*. Other models smoked pot on the roof or stayed out all night, but they knew enough to be secretive. Not me. I was right out there, too clueless or reckless to hide my illicit behavior. I was in big trouble, and I knew it.

Sure enough, the chaperone told Ford that I was an alcoholic and she could no longer live with me. I was still pretty new at the agency; no one yet knew how boringly reliable, professional, and controlled I was. I was asked to move out.

Ford set me up with a woman in accounting at the agency who was looking for a roommate. The accountant was perfectly nice, but I felt like an intruder in her tiny studio. I slept on her chintz-covered couch on her floral sheets. The traditional, girly decor and heavy furniture were oppressive. I was still waitressing at the time, coming home exhausted. One night I brought home Tofutti ice cream, forgot it in the bag, and fell asleep on the couch. The chocolate ice cream melted all over the accountant's flowery sheets. She told Ford she wanted me to move out.

Now what? I didn't have enough money for my own place. I was freaking out. I'd completely betrayed Ford's trust. Since the 1940s, the agency had been known for insisting on upright behavior from its girls, and I'd blown it.

I cried on Nick's shoulder. He took my chin in his hand. "Move in with me," he said.

I didn't want to live with a man before marriage. We'd been dating only three or four months. But I felt I had no choice. He was a sweet, caring person. And it was live with him or live under a bridge.

I still hadn't slept with him at this point. He was infinitely patient, willing to wait until I was ready, but it was definitely the elephant in the room. The other elephant was his entire family. He lived with them in the Bronx. It was as if I were moving in with a whole herd of elephants. Though Nick had his own room, I don't think he asked permission for me to live there. His family was very close-knit, and they were clearly suspicious of me and my motives. Once I smoked a cigarette on the stoop in front of his mother, and she said it was not ladylike. Nick and his family were Asian, and his parents spoke little English, so we also had a language and a cultural barrier. If his parents and sisters were talking when I entered the room, they'd fall silent and look at me. It wasn't as if I'd have understood what they were saying, but it wasn't fun to feel that they were talking about me.

Within a few weeks, when Nick's family saw that I wasn't an opportunist or a slut, and when they realized how deeply their son cared for me, they warmed up a bit. But the cultural gulf between us was huge. Nick's mom cleaned that apartment for hours a day, scrubbing on her hands and knees with a rag. It was backbreaking work. The men in the family never helped with housework, not even washing one dish. I felt terrible for her. Plus, the entire family living under one roof was more intimacy than I was accustomed to.

I understood how different Nick's and my backgrounds were the day we went to visit his ancestors' graves. On one hand, I was moved by his family's respect for the elderly and their determination to remember relatives who'd passed away. On the other hand, I felt awkward as we picnicked on the gravesite, drinking beer and eating pork ribs by the headstones. Nick explained that the pig was a symbol of wealth. By offering pork to the ancestors, the surviving relatives were asking for prosperity and continuation of the family. As he and his parents and siblings burned paper money over the grave, I sneaked off to huddle behind the van. Hidden by the spare tire, I smoked a cigarette. I felt very left out, very lost.

Still, I didn't want to break up with Nick. He made me feel safe, even though we weren't intimate. I didn't feel he was my soul mate, more like a dear friend. I'd experienced so much transition so quickly, and he felt like a constant. We stayed together for over a year, from mid-2003 to the beginning of 2005. When I started to make a little money, we were able to move out of his parents' place and get an apartment together in Queens.

Something held me back from consummating our relationship.

He stepped up the pressure, but I continued to resist. I didn't begrudge him for wanting what he wanted, but I wasn't ready. In my soul, I knew he wasn't someone I wanted to spend my life with. I'm a small-town Southern girl at heart, and I wanted to save myself for marriage. He was a bookmark, a placeholder. I realize that sounds brutal, but it's true. I don't know how conscious I was of that at the time. I'm full of self-awareness, but all too often it's only in retrospect.

What predicated our breakup was Nick's admission that he loved me more when I was a size 8. (In 2005 I was a 12, the same size I am today.) Like a lot of personal trainers, he had very strong feelings about what people should and shouldn't eat, and his opinions weren't always grounded in science. He'd order me to eat more protein and less fruit. He'd be furious if I combined certain foods in the same meal. If I wanted ice cream, he acted as if I were craving human blood. Nick's increasing attempts to control my food intake hit any number of my triggers. I got up the courage to move out.

I moved to Brooklyn Heights. Alone. I was nineteen. No boyfriend, no family, no model apartment, no chaperones. I missed Mom desperately. I was scared to be completely on my own. But I was thrilled, too. I cherished my solitude. There's a scene in *Lost in Translation* in which Scarlett Johanson and Bill Murray are looking out over the silent, glittering expanse of Tokyo—it's a perfect, crystalline moment in a hectic city. That's how Brooklyn felt to me. I could stand in the window of my very own space, overlooking the city, and feel at peace.

I realized I'd stayed with Nick too long out of fear of being alone. Now I understood that reacting out of fear is no way to live. How could I have forgotten that I enjoyed my own company? Nick was a good-hearted person, but he wasn't the right person for me.

Once I was ensconced in my new place, I got a dog. Sophie is a

Maltese, a little cotton-ball puff of cuteness. Her love is uncondi-
tional. She doesn't glare at me if I eat ice cream. (She gives me more
of a forlorn stare.)

We often have to find out what we don't want in order to figure
out what we *do* want. When I met Greg eight months or so after
Nick and I broke up, I knew he was the one. I was a wide-awake
Sleeping Beauty, and Greg was the handsome prince who kissed me
on my own terms. I didn't need rescue. I'd already rescued myself.

It was a sweltering night in August 2005. I went out to a bar in the
West Village with my friend Jon, a booker at Ford, and a few of his
other friends. We were all sitting on a banquette, drinking icy-cold
Stellas. I turned to my left and was faced with a tall, broad-shouldered
guy who looked exactly like the image of Colin Byrne I'd seen in my
dreams. I felt my heart leap. He also looked like Nick Cave, the post-
punk rock star. He had pale skin, black hair, dark eyebrows like mine.
He was thin but well built, with sharp cheekbones and a wry, hooded
gaze. I kept my composure. But when our forearms accidentally
touched, I felt an electric charge shoot up my arm.

Another model friend of Jon's ordered me rather imperiously to
get another round of drinks. "Get your own drink," I told her. Mr.
Nick Cave Manqué shot me a look, clearly thinking me rude, and I
asked him, "What are you looking at?" He looked away. The girl
got her own drink. I decided Mr. Nick Cave Manqué was a
schmuck.

Later, we all wound up back at a friend's apartment. It was quieter, so we could talk. I found myself standing near Mr. Cave again
and thought, Hmph. *That* guy. It turned out he had gone to college
with Jon at the State University of New York at Binghamton. To be
polite, during a lull in our conversations with other people, I asked
him what he did for a living. I expected him to say he was in investment banking. Instead, he said, "I'm an English teacher." I thought,
Oh, reeeeeeally. Just like Colin Byrne.

Greg told me he taught English in an underperforming (that's educationese for "lousy") outer-borough high school. He'd gotten a master's in education at Brooklyn College. He loved working with at-risk kids. As we chatted, I thought how different he was from the modelizing hedge fund trolls and hairdo musicians who usually hit on me when I went out.

I loved listening to Greg talk about his job, his passion for literature and for teaching. He was idealistic but realistic, too—he didn't glamorize his work or pretend that these tough kids could be saved with a simple dose of teacherly devotion and a little Shakespeare.

There's nothing more attractive to me in a person than loving what you do for a living. Perhaps thanks to my grandmother's background in education and emphasis on its importance, I'm utterly wooed by teachers and those who've read widely and have a strong point of view. As Greg shared stories about the gang kids in his classes, his additional job coaching a youth baseball team, and his big, warm, loud Catholic family, I was smitten. I liked that he was liberal and open and intelligent. I liked that he was thoughtful about his religion. Though he felt very identified with it, he still had theological questions and reservations.

I was so attracted to this guy, I felt like I was radiating energy. The hairs on my arms were standing straight up. Every cell in my body was singing. However, I knew this time to take things slowly.

I went to the bathroom to splash cold water on my face. As I came out, a friend of mine (also a model, also a friend of Jon's) grabbed my arm and told me she thought the guy I was talking to was cute. She confessed in a giggly whisper that she was going to invite him to go home with her. I gave her the Death Glare and turned into the sassy, finger-wagging, Press-On-Nailed girlfriend in a sitcom: *"Girl, step away from my man!"* She backed off immediately, presumably terrified because I had channeled Mo'Nique.

Greg and I spent that entire night on the couch. We talked for eight hours straight and dozed off in each other's arms. I woke up at around six A.M. as he gently extricated himself. "I have to go," he whispered. "I'm coaching a game in a couple of hours, and I have to change."

You are a good person, I thought.

He asked, "Can I give you my number?" I loved that he didn't ask for mine. It seemed so courteous, giving me the choice to call him or not. After having felt micromanaged in my last relationship, I was impressed that he was being careful not to invade my space.

I called him that night. I knew I wanted him and wasn't interested in playing games. We made a dinner date for the following week. And we've been together ever since.

I love Greg's values. He's not one of the sycophants and hangers-on whom the fashion industry seems to attract. He never dated a model before me. We share a love of reading and of real estate. We pore over the Sunday *New York Times* apartment listings every week—we love going to open houses, talking about where we'd like to buy property one day, what would be a good investment, how we'd flip a building. What constantly impresses me is how generous he is with his attention and with his affection; I'm touched by how close he is to his family and how up-front they are when they're in conflict about something. Since being with him, I've learned that there are different ways people communicate. He comes from yellers, high-decibel big-gesture stock. Because of my childhood experiences with Lana, I grew up terrified of conflict. Now I see that you can yell at people and still love them.

I fell in love with Greg right away, but that didn't mean I didn't need to do a little tinkering. Gary says he used to look like a frat boy. He always wore half a suit: a dressy blazer, a button-down shirt, a tie, and jeans. That was his going-out look. He had a short, tidy, little-boy haircut. (Predictably, Mom loved this look the minute she met him. It's a very Mom-friendly look.) I told him, "You wanna turn me on? Grow your hair out." Now it's down to his shoulders. He pushes it back off his forehead and looks more like Nick Cave than ever. He's so hot it slays me. I knew long hair would look good on him, but I had no idea how good.

For me, though, the attraction is more about his intellect and values as it is about his smokin' looks. Yes, I love his height (he's six-four), his gorgeous wavy locks, his soulful dark eyes. But in my line of work, I'm around male models all the time. Greg's looks may have drawn me in, but his conversation kept me there. And I love how positive he is. When I go to the dark place, when I hate a picture or lose a job or feel sad about my sisters, he can pull me back from the brink without condescension or bullying. He gives me perspective. I'm in a business of air kisses and hyperbole. A model can start believing her own hype when she's told all day long how beautiful she is. A bigger compliment, for me, is to be told I'm intelligent. Greg does that.

I couldn't be with someone in the fashion business. I don't want to talk about where my picture appeared or who's walking in whose collections. I want to know about the wider world. Because I dropped out of high school and haven't been to college (yet), there's a lot I hope to learn. Greg explains political and historical references I don't get. (And I recommend novels to him.) I always crave more knowledge. My career could disappear like *that*. Anyone who makes a living off her looks needs to be cognizant that she's on the clock. I want a relationship that lasts beyond my youth, even if my career doesn't.

In February 2006 I left New York City to do Elena Miro's show in Milan. The night before I got on the plane, Greg and I had a huge fight. We always seem to fight about nothing right before I go away on a job. I think it's our way of expressing our distress at being apart.

I was miserable, and being fitted for the show didn't make me any happier. One woman working at the fitting was critical of my body, eyeballing me with a look of—was that loathing? She was eyeing my thighs the way you might look at roadkill. I thought maybe I was being paranoid until I heard her bark at another girl, "Don't you dare order pasta at dinner!" I knew I wasn't being paranoid when she ordered a third girl: "Lift up your shirt. I want to see how fat you are." It was brutal and atypical for the plus-size business—certainly atypical for Elena Miro, a designer who loves curves.

I crept away to call Greg. I wept into the phone, "I'm sorry we fought. I miss you so much. I wish I were home." He told me he loved me. "We'll see each other before you know it," he said.

The next morning, February 26, 2006, I put on my fierce face and metaphorical stylist-protection armor and did the show. When I came backstage after the final outfit, there was Greg, beaming. I screamed. He said, "When you called yesterday, I was actually in the airport. I was covering the phone, hoping you wouldn't hear the intercom!" I leaped into his arms, giggling and crying.

We went to the Duomo, Milan's gorgeous fourteenth-century cathedral. If stone and lace got married and had a baby, that baby would be the Duomo. It's the most intricate filigreed spun-sugar structure, with dazzling marble spires and pinnacles and buttresses. Greg and I held hands and gaped. Heading from ancient to modern beauty, we next went to Prada, where I bought a four-hundred-and-fifty-dollar headband—I presume I'll never spend so much on my head again unless it's for emergency brain surgery. But this is a very special headband; it's covered in metal pieces and beads and bits of crystal and beaded fabric. I've never seen anything like it anywhere else, and it seemed the perfect treasure with which to remember a treasure of a morning.

"Let's go across the street," Greg said. We crossed Corso Vittorio Emanuele and sat in a little café and ordered glasses of red wine. We sat on the same side of the table, watching the Milanese world stroll by.

Greg said, "You know, that was the first time I've seen you on a runway. You were amazing."

I leaned over to give him a hug and felt something in his pocket. "What's that?" I said.

"Oh, nothing," he replied.

Seeing the confused look on my face, he relented. He pulled out a velvet box and set it on the table. I just let it sit there, radiating energy.

"Is that what I think it is?" I asked.

"Absolutely," he said. "Will you marry me?"

"Absolutely," I answered.

We kissed, and laughed, and I cried. Finally, I opened the box. It was a 1920s-style ring from Doyle & Doyle, one of my favorite boutiques on the Lower East Side of New York City. It's owned by two cool sisters who track down one-of-a-kind, vintage and antique-looking jewelry. Greg, wisely, had asked our friend Jon for help with picking out the ring. The two of them did well—I adored it instantly.

I was getting fucking married!

I called Mom and shrieked, "*I'm getting fucking married!*"

There was a pause. "You said 'fuck'!" Mom gasped. Then she laughed. "I'm so happy for you, Crysti."

Mom had met Greg when she'd visited in September 2005. She'd been enchanted by his voice. "That is a Brooklyn accent!" she kept saying. "I cannot believe it!" To her, he sounded like Phil Rizzuto or Jackie Gleason. "He's so smart and gracious, such a neat guy," she'd told me that day. We'd all gone to New Jersey to meet his parents for dinner. It was one big lovefest.

After we called Mom from the Milanese café, we ran to the budget hotel I was staying in and checked out. We moved my stuff to the posh hotel Greg had picked out. We spent the night there and flew back to New York City the next day. I couldn't stop looking at my sparkly, sparkly hand.

On June 30, 2007, Greg and I got married in New York. I wore a dress called Papillon by the British designer Jenny Packham. It wasn't officially a wedding gown, but it was spectacular: an off-white floor-sweeping empire-waist gown with exquisite beading and embroidery, a sheer, shimmering overlay draped atop a silk spaghetti-strapped column with a delicate yet ornately beaded low-cut bodice. The overlay and beading are reminiscent of butterfly wings, hence the name. It was as beautiful a garment as I'd ever worn, and I've worn a lot of beautiful garments. I also wore amazing, jeweled Prada high-heeled sandals. They were like little chandeliers on my feet. ("Who are they?" my friend Ashley gasped as soon as she saw them, in the parlance of the industry. It's like an existential question. Yes, who are they? Who are any of us?)

I agonized about whether to invite Lana to the wedding. I wanted my sisters, then twelve and sixteen, there. The last time I'd been to Clinton was in the summer of 2002, when I was still in the midst of my craziness. Mom and I had an awkward dinner with Lana and my sisters. We didn't talk about the violent rupture in our relationship. I talked about modeling (and picked at my lettuce), the girls talked about school, and Lana sat in stony silence. The next day, Mom and I had gone back to Miami, and a few days after that, I was back in New York City.

I tried to find out whether Lana would let the girls come, but she was cryptic and withholding. The tension was so thick it crackled across the telephone wires. Finally, I called Clinton and said, "Never mind. Don't come. I'll see you guys another time."

It was a smallish wedding—only one hundred people. Mom looked incredible in a long, pale green gown with a little matching jacket. My Uncle Donnie, Aunt Tracy, and Aunt Kathy came, too. We all carried the memory of Grandma with us. Greg's big, raucous, loving family made up for the absence of mine—mostly.

The reception was at the swanky Hotel Gansevoort. We had

mojitos and sushi, a culinary mixed metaphor, but those were our favorite treats. Instead of a wedding cake, we had red velvet cupcakes from Billy's Bakery, the crème de la cupcake in a city that reveres and fetishizes the cupcake. Ashley and Rachel were my bridesmaids.

Gary walked me down the aisle. He'd gone from being my agent to being the most trustworthy man in my life—the only father figure I'd ever had. Greg had called him to ask for my hand. "If it had been anyone but Greg, I would have said no," Gary told me later. "I would not have signed off on this young charge of mine for anyone but Greg." (Sometimes Gary sounds like a Victorian governess.) Gary's endorsement of Greg meant the world to me. At the wedding, I told him, "I really do look at you as my father." He gulped, and his eyes filled with tears. In a strangled voice, he said, "Really, now, with all the cameras?" He couldn't get through his toast. He was too overcome.

I love looking at my wedding pictures. To be completely surrounded by people I love, all of them wishing me well—life has so few moments like that. I was torn about Lana and my sisters' absence. On the one hand, there was a hole in my life. (That hollow space is always there, always in the back of my awareness, a low-level ache.) On the other hand, I was grateful that I didn't have to walk on eggshells, half expecting a scene to erupt at any time.

The one off note at the event came via my old friend Hope from The Agency's model apartment. I remembered her steady stream of tiny digs at other people. I was happy and optimistic, and I could see that she wasn't. I realized our friendship now consisted only of fumes—all we'd had in common was our secret and shared dysfunction. The photographer caught a telling candid of her. She was holding one of the red velvet cupcakes, looking at it with disgust and longing.

I haven't seen her since that day. She's a chapter of my past now.

Greg is the present. Mom adores him. "You were blessed to meet him," she tells me. She thinks we balance each other. "You're emotional, reactive, exuberant, and he's intellectual, steady, reserved," she says. But Mom also finds him hilarious, a combination of professor and longshoreman. "It's like he came from an Ivy League preppy atmosphere, with the way he talks and the things he knows, but his accent is off the wall!" She laughs. I think she's still amazed that he can put up with me. I know why he does: because I'm the circus. I'm the trapeze and the cotton candy. Other girls always bored him to death, but with me, he's flying without a net.

Greg and I call each other Stumps and Stems, because when we lie side by side, my gams are so short compared to his. He looks like a daddy longlegs. We even have a tuneless little ditty: "Stumps and Stems, together again!" We say it every time I come back from a trip. He's graceful, long and lean, always stretching and lounging like a cat from *The Jungle Book*. I have a million mortifying nicknames for him, but I promised I wouldn't put them in this book. Suffice to say I call him many diverse goopy endearments in a cooing, wheedling baby voice. He looks at me and says, "You cut my balls off every day." His sense of humor is as dry as a martini; mine is edgy. He's Noël Coward; I'm Janeane Garofalo. And yet it works.

In 2008 we got a place of our own in Williamsburg, Brooklyn. We love it here, out of the epicenter of fashion madness. On my days off I like to be *really* off: no makeup, one of Greg's shirts thrown over leggings. Greg and I both have intense jobs, in different ways. We need a refuge to come home to. We're still decorating—we have a comfy leather couch, a bed piled high with cream-colored linens and satin pillows, a ton of bookcases, and my vintage juicer that looks like a medieval torture device but makes the most delicious, healthy concoctions. We got another Maltese, a friend for Sophie named Dave. (The notion of a white fluffy girly dog named Dave just cracks us up.)

I wish I were home more often. My incessant travel (sometimes I'm away three weeks out of the month) is hard on us. Greg gets surly when I come home exhausted; he wants to be catered to a little more. I get upset when he wants to spend time with his friends right after I get home; I want him all to myself. We're still working out the logistics of balancing our life with my crazy career.

When I'm home, Greg and I like to walk around Williamsburg. We go out for brunch, go to Goodwill to hunt for vintage treasures, sit in a coffee shop for hours. He reads. I write in a beautiful notebook I got at an indie bookstore on Bedford Avenue. We take Sophie and Dave to McCarren Park, which is beautiful, even though it's radioactive from various toxic spills back in the day. (You can't have everything.) The creativity and diversity of our neighborhood keep us inspired.

At night we don't go to clubs or hot restaurants. We watch the show *Taboo* on the National Geographic Channel. It's about weird subcultures and shocking ritual practices around the world. Nothing gives me more joy than seeing someone screaming as he's being branded while an academic expert drones on about how burning human flesh smells like meat. I love the episodes devoted to tribal coming-of-age ceremonies, like the one in which a young man in Papua New Guinea had his back covered in tiny slices made with a bamboo sliver, making his flesh resemble crocodile teeth. Among the Sepik people, crocodiles are believed to give birth to humans. But would our own culture seem any less strange to an outsider? Are our initiation ceremonies any less brutal? Mine involved starvation. Other teenage girls slice at their arms with the blades of scissors and kitchen knives. Coming of age in America today, for girls especially, commonly involves turning on your own body.

In another, lighter example of being drawn to the taboo, Greg and I never miss the HBO show *True Blood,* a bloody-funny-sexy southern Gothic meditation on vampires. I've always loved vampire stories, which are celebrations of forbidden, simmering passion. (Edward wants to bite, but he can't! Because he's nice! Except he isn't! Because he's a vampire!) Those *Twilight* books and other vampire movies and stories are thrilling because they're about deferred and delayed sexual gratification. It's no wonder almost every culture has its vampire fetishism (there's even an episode of *Taboo* about modern-day Americans who want to be vampires). The notion of fangs sinking into a proffered neck is inescapably erotic; the act is intimate, sexual, shocking. You could hardly be more vulnerable than when you offer a creature of the night that soft, unprotected part of your body. The notion of a more-than-human, less-than-monster timeless hottie who combines sex appeal with self-control is so alluring. Greg and I are both into the way *True Blood* spins the timeless story in a super-sexy way. As we watch, I lounge across his body and Greg runs his nails across my back, exactly as Mom used to do when I was a child. Like Mom, Greg makes me feel that I'm home.

Like Mom (and unlike Nick), Greg loves to see me eat. I jokingly accuse him of being a feeder, someone who gets off sexually by encouraging someone else to consume mass quantities of food. In reality, he just loves to see me enjoy myself. He didn't know me when I was so damaged, when food held so much horror for me. He knows only that he wants me to savor meals, sex, life.

Our relationship isn't perfect. We fight about two things, money and time—the two things working couples never have enough of. I've always been hungry for security: security in my own body, having a secure sense of family, financial security. Mom always told me, "When you can, buy a house. You'll always have a place to stay." She gave up her home, and she wanted to be sure I didn't make the same mistake. I was Scarlett O'Hara, and she was Gerald O'Hara, fiercely swearing to his daughter in his brogue, "Land is the only thing in the world worth workin' for, worth fightin' for, worth dyin' for, because it's the only thing that lasts!" I arrived in New York City at an insecure time: It was insecure for me personally, because I was sick and clinging to an impossible vision for my body; it was insecure for the city, still suffering after 9/11. Owning my own little bit of the city helped me feel grounded and safe. When I bought an apartment in Brooklyn, I felt I was exactly where I was supposed to be.

I do think about one day buying a house to have kids in. When I'm ready to breed, I'll go all in. I want two or three kids, and so does Greg. But we're not ready yet. I'm still too young. I did a shoot for Nordstrom not long ago in which I was cradling a baby, and I felt as if I were holding ten pounds of nitroglycerine. It was a jewelry shoot—they wanted me to enfold the baby while gracefully showing off the bracelets and rings I was wearing. The baby was perfectly pleasant about the entire procedure, yet all I could think was: Get this thing away from me! It was hard to pose gracefully when all I wanted to do was hand the infant off like a football.

For now Greg and I are satisfied with Sophie and Dave. Since Dave is still only marginally housebroken, he's not so dissimilar from having a baby. It's just a different species of poop.

As I get older, I find myself becoming more motherly toward up-and-coming models. Perhaps that's preparation for parenthood. I always stick up for the girls who are a little off. On shoots, I'm drawn to the girls who talk about how horrid high school was for them. Once, a girl chimed in, "Are you kidding? High school was the best time of my entire life!" Everyone at the shoot just looked at one another. Most of us artsy types—the string beans, the gay makeup artists, the dykey hairstylists, the spaced-out photographers—were picked on or invisible in high school. We couldn't wait to get out.

I also make it a point to eat on shoots. I want the other girls to see that you can have a healthy relationship with food and still work.

As I look to the future, I find that the person I most want to emulate is Nigella Lawson. To me, she's everything that is womanly and appealing. She has a multifaceted career, writing and cooking and doing TV. She has overcome tragedy—the loss of her mother, sister, and husband to cancer—and seems to come at life with a sense of joy. She's found love again. She conveys that food is about community and ease, sharing an experience with others. Eating, for her, is sensual and emotional. But the British public has been merciless in mocking her for her recent weight gain. I think she looks incredible. If she has gained weight, maybe it's because she's getting older. That's common. It's natural. It's what I did. Or maybe she's gained weight because she's happy. Does it really matter? She's still beautiful and sexy and sane. I love her response to the snark about her body. "Everyone is so critical," she told the *Times* of London. "All must be sacrificed to the great god of skinny. You must say no to everything. Life has to be pretty fabulous, surely, if you can afford to turn down occasions of pleasure?"

I've had too much sorrow to be able to turn down pleasure. Haven't we all? Life's too short to say no to everything. I've lost only one family member to cancer, but I have experienced other losses. I know how easy it can be to close yourself off. But I know that when I started saying yes—to food, to sex, to my authentic self—that was when I became upbeat and self-confident enough to let love into my life. My career took off when I trusted myself enough to reinvent what it could be. Accepting my true shape made me happy. As Linda Bacon writes in *Health at Every Size,* "Don't change your body to fit your mind's perception of what it should look like. Change your mind to appreciate your actual body."

When I did that, love—in its many manifestations—followed.

9

REAL IS THE NEW BLACK

The underlying promise of dieting—a promise as powerful as any industrial-strength foundation garment—is that once we reach our goal weight, our lives will be perfect. That's the fairy-tale ending glimmering after the credits of a weight-loss reality show. It's the story written in invisible ink in the margins of the exercise stories in too many women's magazines. Eating well isn't about offering our bodies nourishing food—it's about getting skinnier. Exercise isn't about becoming strong, managing stress, or supporting heart health—it's about getting skinnier. Getting skinnier means that life will start playing in Technicolor to the accompaniment of a glorious orchestra.

The problem is that real life doesn't work that way. Even if it were possible for everyone to be thin—and we've already proven that it isn't—thinness does not confer insta-happiness. It's hard for so many of us (including me, for years) to wrap our brains around the fact. We postpone living—taking beach vacations, buying the foxy dress that shows off our upper arms, asking out the cute guy—because we think that being daring is the province of the thin, and only after we've been "good" enough to get thin do we deserve life's prizes.

Weight is the most egregious example of "If only I achieve this one thing, my life will truly begin," but it's not the only example. Maybe you've thought if you only were more popular, if you only had a boyfriend, if your boyfriend would only marry you, if you only had more money, if you only had a better job, if your parents were only nicer people, your life would be perfect.

Guess what? It wouldn't be. I look back at pictures of myself in the spiral of my anorexia, when my eyes were sunk in my face and tendons stood out in my neck, and I think about where I was mentally back then. I was thinking, If only I were a little thinner, my life would be perfect. The only thinner I could have been was dead. Whatever our size, whatever our history, and whatever our burdens— if we choose not to be happy, we won't be. So many women spend their entire lives thinking they're too heavy, and then they look back at pictures of themselves when they were younger and realize they were beautiful. It's so sad that they didn't know it at the time.

In his 1938 ditty "Curl Up and Diet," Ogden Nash wrote,

To the world she may appear slinky and feline,
But she inspects herself in the mirror and cries, Oh, I look like a sea lion.

As the poem says, we are invariably our own worst enemy. So many of us think we look like a sea lion (or a manatee or a narwhal) no matter what size we are. Such self-loathing is a huge waste of energy—energy we could be using to enjoy the beach vacation, the foxy dress, the cute guy.

If you're worried that the guy might reject you on the basis of your weight, remember another couplet from Nash's poem:

So I think it is very nice for ladies to be lithe and lissome.
But not so much so that you cut yourself if you happen to embrace
or kissome.

There's evidence that men prefer slightly heavier women. A passel of research also shows that in tough economic times, men like women to be a little fleshy. One scientist studied forty years of *Playboy* centerfolds from 1960 to 2000 and found that in years with difficult social and economic conditions, the Playmates of the Year were heavier and had larger waists. Another researcher found that men who felt financially insecure preferred women who were an average of two pounds heavier than did men who felt financially comfortable. So you could argue that it's a good time to have a little pudge. (I shouldn't assume that all the readers of this book are straight; if you're a woman attracted to women, you may find even more body acceptance in the LGBT community.)

But let's be honest here: The culture—and the body preference research I just cited—is still about relatively thin women. A difference of five pounds isn't the difference between a size 2 and a size 22. The size 22 is still going to have a harder time in the world. We don't live in a culture that embraces truly fat women. But that's one more reason to look within for self-acceptance. When we value ourselves as kind, funny, lovely persons, we're less dependent on validity from external forces. If we live rich, full lives, we're more likely to find and spend time with individuals who see our beauty and appreciate who we are.

When it comes to romantic prospects, a guy who usually dates thin girls may find himself attracted to a heavier girl if she's the right heavier girl. Likewise, a guy who tends to like heavier girls may not like you for reasons that have nothing to do with weight. Body size is not always correlated with individual chemistry. Romance is not an exact science. What makes two people fall in love is hard to quantify.

One fact is a constant: Self-acceptance is a choice. You live in your body every day, and I live in mine. Some days it's difficult to live in my body, as I imagine it's difficult for you to live in yours. I used to hear a voice in my head every day telling me to obsess about my thighs. That voice is still there, but now it whispers instead of screams. I told the voice I wouldn't listen to it anymore. I told the voice, *I refuse to let you win.* Sometimes I wake up and I feel ugly, or I don't like the way I look in a picture, or I have a fight with my husband, and the whisper of self-hate gets a little louder.

What I've learned is that if you give in to the whisper a little, thinking that will make it shut up, the voice gets louder. It starts telling you that you really are ugly, you really are useless, and by the way, do you know how many calories are in that gum?

We carry our memories in our bodies. When I get on the treadmill for a reasonable workout, I hear the whisper deep inside me: You could run harder. You could stay on this machine for another hour. But now I growl back at the voice: *If I did that, my hip would hurt, and there'd be no further health benefit. Mindfuck self-torture is not a benefit.*

The voice inside me backs down.

I recognize that for some people, fashion and media fuel the inner voice in a bad way. Magazine images make them feel bad. Clothing brings them no joy. My response is nuanced: Fashion can be a delightful friend or a taunting frenemy.

An outfit can tell the world that you're a force to be reckoned with, that you're playful, that you're sexy. Fashion is semaphore. It's fun, but it's also a form of communication. I don't agree when people say, "Fashion's unimportant." You may not care about it, which is your prerogative, but your clothes are still sending a message about your values and beliefs, whether you choose to take control of the message or not. I love social history books that look into how fashion reveals a culture or historic period. People of all sizes, in all eras, have adorned themselves. Wearing clothes we love can make us feel great about our bodies. Is fashion frivolous, especially in a time of hardship, when there are so many huge problems in the world? That depends. Spending a zillion dollars on status items seems self-absorbed and wrongheaded right now. On the other hand, we've been covering our nakedness since biblical times. The question remains: What do we cover it with?

I hate fashion "rules," and I hate the term "problem areas." Can we ban it? I detest the tired old yadda yadda yadda insisting that apple-shaped women should wear this and pear-shaped women should wear that. Wear what you love, and you'll look comfortable and appealing. But your clothes should fit. I don't think anyone is flattered by fabric that's so shapeless it hangs, or by clothing that's so tight it cuts off the circulation (yet the wearer refuses to go up a size because that would hurt his or her self-esteem). Being able to move without splitting a seam is good for self-esteem.

Finding great clothes at any price point can be more of a challenge if you're larger than a size 10, no question. But it can be done. In April 2007 my plus-model friend Ashley did a great piece with *Vogue* about how she shops. She's educated herself about which designers cut generously and which don't. She doesn't pick endlessly through racks of tiny clothes, hoping for something in her size—she goes to the Web for sizes and brands she know will fit. She goes to bricks-and-mortar stores that have plenty of options in her size, such as Marina Rinaldi and Lane Bryant. Like me, she loves high-impact shoes and bags that make us feel great whatever size we are. When I first started making money, I bought three things: the silver Chloé bag I coveted on my first shoot with Steven; a decadent, commodious Balenciaga Le Dix bag that I carry almost every day, even to the gym; and a pair of kick-butt Ann Demeulemeester combat boots that I will wear forever.

Here's what I love about fashion: It's art we can all be a part of. Not many of us can own a Picasso, but we can all treat ourselves to clothing that turns the human body into a work of art. And this absolutely does not have to cost a ton of money. I love vintage and cast-off finds as well as designer stuff. Someone can spend three thousand dollars on an outfit and look silly, and someone else can put together a masterpiece at Goodwill.

Inspiration is everywhere. Once I had to restrain myself from running after an Eastern Orthodox priest on the street—I wanted to scream, "Dude, where did you get that robe?" In Williamsburg, I saw a Hasid in his *streimel* hat and formal capris, and I went nuts. I love unusual juxtapositions and uncommon shapes.

I've recently started styling some shoots, choosing the clothes and directing the poses. Getting to serve as both model and stylist has helped me understand fashion better. (I'm also learning about lighting and set direction, a far more productive way to channel my control-freak tendencies than my old strategy of not eating.) Seeing each potential outfit and shot as a blank slate has helped me be more creative and more daring with my personal fashion choices.

I want to look good, but I prefer that it not take much of an effort. So I have a uniform, as many other women do. Mine is black leggings, a long, soft tank or tee, a long sweater, and black combat or studded shoe-boots. I have an entire room of fabulous things—gifts from designers, thrift-store finds, and occasional splurges—but I rarely wear them. I treat them like art. (Or pets, since I often find myself stroking them.)

One of my favorite treasures is a sparkly little vintage '40s hat, a gift from plus-size designer Anna Scholz. She's one of my heroes—

she's a Valkyrie, 6'1" and plus-sized and blond and imposing-looking. But she's one of the warmest, funniest people I know. She did her thesis at Central St. Martin's (she's German by birth, but studied at the famous art school in London) on the tyranny of thinness. She's incredibly thoughtful about the beauty of plus-size women—I've learned so much from her. And when I look at that hat she gave me, I think about our history and friendship, and I brim with love for that little hat. Clothes are repositories of memories. Even when you never wear them!

One item I do wear constantly is a ribbed viscose and silk tank top by Rick Owens. You can wear it layered or alone; it's the ultimate base piece. The cut is amazing, with rounded almost-unfinished-looking hems and the perfect amount of sheerness. It's modern but with a Marlon Brando–like vintage broken-inness. I get so gushy about Rick Owens's work. He's an independent designer with a grunge bent, dark and dramatic and asymmetrical and slouchy. People call his work Gothic, but I think it's too structural to be truly Goth. The store Kirna Zabete's website (always a fun read) says of Rick, "His aesthetic is shaped by black and white Hollywood movies and the rawness of a decayed end of Hollywood Boulevard, where he started his label in the early nineties after dropping out of art school . . . There is definitely a Rick Owens cult. Watch out—buying one piece is the gateway drug." Indeed: a very expensive designer drug, which is the only reason I haven't become a raving, huffing, snuffing, sniffing Rick Owens addict.

Rick's palette is heavy on the black, which works for me. I still love black not because it's slimming but because it's easy. Everything matches. And black serves as a great backdrop for my jewelry collection. I troll souks and silver markets on my travels; I visit dusty old thrift stores and pawnshops in small towns. Jewelry can completely change a simple outfit.

When I feel like dressing up, my favorite item is a dramatic bell-shaped Ivan Grundahl skirt. It's shot through with wire, so you can scrunch it up or stretch it out to create any silhouette or length. I often wear it with a Victorian jacket I picked up in some long-forgotten European thrift store. I don't dress very "Look at me!" in my daily life, but I can dress pretty flashily when I go out. My attitude is "EVERYBODY LOOK! Look, so I can go the hell home!" I just got a pair of printed Pucci moon boots on eBay that I intend to wear with a sparkly evening dress. Dressy outfits, in my opinion, should make you look twice: Is she fabulous, or does she look like she should be pushing a shopping cart filled with discarded electronics down the Bowery?

Thrifting fills the void in my life left by the loss of the Easter-egg hunts of my childhood. It's about the thrill of the chase and the joy of finding treasures no one else has. At the fusty old shop down the street from my apartment, I picked up a black velvet jacket with gold Edwardian-looking passementiere embroidery. It cost maybe fifteen bucks. It dresses up anything I wear with it. The designer is Morton Myles, whose name I didn't know until I Googled him and learned that he became instantly famous in February 1961, when Jackie Kennedy wore his light blue sleeveless linen shift dress on the cover of *Look* magazine. (She was holding newborn John-John in one of his very first cover outings.) I love learning about the provenance and history of my clothes. Now, when I wear the jacket, I think about Morton Myles's and the United States fashion industry's past. Clothes are stories.

I want to look like myself, not like anyone else. That's why I'm uncomfortable standing in for every plus-size girl in America. I'm not a symbol; I'm Crystal. I need to be me, and you need to be you. There are websites that keep insisting that I would look better if I were heavier, that I was much prettier when I was a size 16. I was a size 16 for a short time when I was in recovery, learning what weight was most comfortable and easy for me to maintain. Then I discovered that the right size for me is a 12. It doesn't take effort for me to remain a size 12. Size 12 is not only the average American size, it is my personal set-point destiny. Saying that I betray womanhood by not being fatter (which is something that's been written about me) is just as reductive and harmful as insisting that every model maintain a dictatorial standard of thinness.

In one month in 2009, Australian *Harper's Bazaar* and American *Glamour* featured me in editorial layouts. Because of the lighting, the fit of the clothing, and the poses the photographer encouraged me to make, I looked a lot heavier in *Bazaar* than I did in *Glamour*. The public response was pretty funny. There were all kinds of dark murmurings about how much weight I'd gained or lost, how many months apart the photos must have been taken (they were taken within two weeks of each other), how much I'd been Photoshopped in the pictures I supposedly looked thinner in. (I had to steel myself not to look at comments on the *Bazaar* shoot. One person succinctly posted "Barf" on a website that republished the pictures.) The truth is, neither shoot involved a ton of retouching. But the *Glamour* shoot was by Patrick Demarchelier, whose goal is always pure beauty, and the *Bazaar* shoot was by Luis Sanchis, who I think was making a challenging, in-your-face point about largeness. The watery effect he created with light also made me look more dappled with cellulite than I am.

I understand the point Luis was trying to make, and I know sensationalism sells. But I'm still a girl with normal vanity, and I thought the pictures promoted the abstract idea of "fat girl!" rather than showcasing the real model. I'm always wary of the fetishization of fat. When designers and editors choose one fat girl to salivate over, and revel in her avoirdupois, I'm not sure how much it advances the cause of using girls of all sizes in a magazine. That one girl becomes a token. The magazine can congratulate itself on being tolerant and revel in the attention-getting debate, and readers can jabber in joy (or say "Barf"), and everyone gets worked up into a froth about obesity and health, but no meaningful progress on inclusion is made. I don't want the one big girl—whether that girl is me or someone else—to be an outlier. Celebrating a single fat girl who is blessed with huge confidence and a great body image doesn't mean you're truly tolerant. What I want is to see diverse portrayals of beauty—in size, race, and age—in every magazine. I don't want either Augustus Gloop–like crazed devotion to rolls and rolls of flesh as shock for shock's sake or attempts to minimize the fat girl so you can't even tell what size she is. Let's normalize difference and be inclusive.

To some degree, fashion is play, and that's fine. Photographs aren't a mirror reflection of real life. Editorial and advertising images are usually about selling ideals, dreams, fantasies. I realize this may not be a popular point of view, but I'm fine with a degree of retouching. Removing zits, stray hairs, veins, and capillaries is part of the process. We're not creating a documentary. This isn't hard news. That said, the trick is walking the fine line between glamour and full-on falsehood.

Like the crazy platform shoe I mentioned earlier, Photoshopping has tipped too far into excess. Eyes are widened, noses are straightened, teeth are whitened, arms and legs are slimmed, skin is shined up like a shoe, heads and bodies are removed, rejiggered, and rematched like ripped-up paper dolls. Perfect is the new normal. And that's a problem.

There's a trickle-down effect in action here: For a small additional fee, parents at most schools can have their kids' school pictures digitally retouched to erase freckles, remove braces, or fix errant curls. If your kid's school is one of the few that doesn't offer this service—or perhaps your kid is only sixteen months old—you can still get in on the action. Online retouchers will, for a fee, take your e-mailed photo of a toddler and make her look like Jon-Benet

Ramsey. Why can't we embrace children as children, in all their chubby, gap-toothed imperfection?

The tide is turning. People are getting tired of excess artifice. They're wary of being lied to. They're sick of dictatorial top-down fashion editors. And they're hyper-alert to evidence that they're being played. That's part of why the paparazzi business has exploded; consumers are sick of perfection being shoved in their faces. They're salivating for cellulite and zits.

Blogs and websites, the new truth squads, keep track of Photoshopping gone wild. Magazine readers institute letter-writing campaigns when publications bat their lashes at readers about the extent of their retouching practices. Celebrities like Kate Winslet (who tuttutted at being digitally slimmed for a *GQ* cover) and Andy Roddick (who openly mocked the digital overinflating of his already pneumatic arms on the cover of *Men's Fitness*) have openly protested the "perfectification" of their images.

On the one hand, I'm pro-honesty, pro-openness. On the other hand, someone once uploaded a picture of my naked ass in horrid lighting onto the Web. It was taken with a camera phone while I was changing backstage at a show. All the commenters discussed my cellulite. I have some right to privacy, and civility should still reign. People don't think models and celebrities are real, and they talk about us as if we're not human beings.

I have a sweet gig. I am aware that modeling is not working in a salt mine. I even understand why someone put my ripply, naked butt on the Internet. People crave authenticity. That's why Dove's "Campaign for Real Beauty" tapped such a nerve. That's why Jennifer Love Hewitt received more acclaim for defending her own dimpled butt, splashed across the tabloids in paparazzi photos, than she ever received as an actress. That's even why younger people get their news from Jon Stewart instead of the mainstream media. We are demanding that our world get real. The backlash against blank perfection has started, and in the age of Twitter and Facebook, it's hard to suppress a mass movement. For fashion editors, perfect may be the new normal, but for the rest of the country, real is the new black.

Women are clamoring to see bodies like their own represented and celebrated. The average American woman is five feet four inches and weighs 155 pounds. There are plenty of beautiful women who are bigger than that. Blogs like Shapely Prose, Manolo for the Big Girl, Too Fat for Fashion, Curvy Fashionista, Pretty Pear, The Rotund, and dozens more seek out and cheer plus-size beauty. If people don't find what they're looking for in the mainstream media, they'll go to the Internet.

As far as I'm concerned, the next frontier in fashion is having plus girls posing in meaningful numbers among the straight-size models across brands and jobs. That means we need more diversity within the plus world. Bring on the big girls with quirky features! *Vive la difference!*

It's essential to see that size is only one of the battlefronts. Those of us who want to see more plus-size women represented in fashion should also be supporting the use of more women of color and age. There's strength and solidarity in numbers. Diversity helps us all. And thin people are not the enemy. When we gripe at other women for being too thin ("Eat a sandwich!") as well as too fat, we allow ourselves to be distracted from the real issue. We have to change the culture by rewarding and applauding diversity in all its forms, not by vilifying individual women. We women are a lot more powerful if we see ourselves as fighters on the same side. But it's easier to judge others—their choices and their bodies—than to think about the struggles we share.

Things are starting to change. There are a few more size 2 and size 4 girls on runways. No, there are no 16s or even 6s. But we're taking baby steps in the right direction. It may be that cosmetics, hair products, and skin care will come further, faster, in employing women with curves, because there's no sample-size problem when you're selling those items. It may also be that the entertainment industry will continue to make gains faster than the modeling world, since fitting the clothes isn't a job requirement.

Promoters of broadening notions of beauty in modeling can take heart from the gains made by models of color. According to the fabulous Tatiana the Anonymous Model, an occasional inside-baseball modeling blogger for the women's website Jezebel, there was a serious leap in diversity on New York City's runways during February 2009's fashion week. In an amazing fit of number-crunching—and proof that not all models are stupid—she calculated that just over 18 percent of the girls in shows that week were nonwhite, which may not sound like much, but it's 6 percent better than in 2008. In 2007 *Women's Wear Daily* reported that one third of the New York shows employed no models of color at all. Perhaps all this is interesting only to people who follow modeling the way *Star Trek* fans follow Tribble mentions in the media, but I think it's significant. Italian *Vogue*'s 2008 black issue succeeded in getting people talking about how lily-white the industry had become since the eighties. That discussion led not just to more editorial and runway jobs for black models but to more work for other nonwhite models—notably Latinas and Southeast Asians—as well. Now we must push for even broader demonstrations of acceptance. When people who are marginalized realize they share goals of inclusion, they gain strength by supporting one another.

The messages about how we're supposed to look are inherently contradictory. It's impossible for any one human to meet them all. Most people see Beyoncé as perfect and luscious; some are horrified by an L.A. face with an Oakland booty. No one human body or, for that matter, no one human being will please all the people all the time. Two different magazines sometimes print the same picture of a celebrity, one calling her a do and another calling her a don't. Every year, when the Oscar-dress pictures come out, any star who dresses daringly triggers squeals of horror along with a few pats of praise for trying something different. We wonder why celebrities are styled to within an inch of their lives and why most red-carpet looks are so darn boring. The risk and realness get beaten out of them!

The solution is to accept that the only person you have to please is yourself. Indulge your instincts, wear what you love, and embrace your own natural size. As tired as it sounds, self-acceptance has to come from within. You simply cannot look to the wider world for a perpetual stream of affirmation. It won't be there. And life is too short to hate yourself.

Confidence is what ultimately makes us attractive, no matter what we look like. In *Ain't She Sweet,* Susan Elizabeth Phillips has her heroine Sugar Beth realize that she's responsible for her own happiness. But more than that, she understands that part of embracing one's own strength is making sure other people don't experience prejudice and disenfranchisement. "People will always try to steal your power," she tells a teenage girl in the book. "They might tell you not to feel bad about screwing up a math test because math's hard for girls. Or they'll say you shouldn't worry so much about injustice in the world because you're only one person. And even though they mean well, they'll be making you less than what you can be."

When we tell ourselves we're failures for weighing more than a chart tells us to, we're relinquishing our own power. Girls who value things about themselves other than the way they look—their intelligence, athleticism, musical ability, capacity for friendship—aren't nearly as affected by media ideals about beauty. Study after study has shown that. My most important advice, which may sound ironic coming from a model, is this: Stop obsessing about being looked at. Do stuff. *Be.* Don't wait to be thin to start living. As the fat-blogger Joy Nash says, "Life begins now."

After I did *Teen Vogue* and American *Vogue* in 2004, a TV show about teenagers called me. They wanted me to audition for a costarring role. How flattering! Despite having no training as an actress, I agreed to try out. To my shock, the scene I read at my audition involved wailing, "You don't like me because I'm fat!" What on earth made those people think I was the right person to play a girl like that? How ironic that I came to the producers' attention because someone saw a magazine in which I talked about my healthy body image. Yet here they wanted me to be a mouthpiece for typical fat-girls-must-hate-themselves attitudes. What kind of message does that send to impressionable teenagers?

You will be shocked to learn I was not offered the part. When I saw the show on TV, I discovered that not only was the character an insecure fat girl, she was entitled, mean, and manipulative. Great.

Adults owe it to kids not to transmit self-loathing attitudes. I think parents have a much more important role than the media. According to a 2006 Stanford University study, there's a direct link between parental weight criticism and bad body image. Of the girls in the study with body-related anxieties (such as eating disorders and preoccupation with their appearance), 80 percent reported being teased or criticized by their parents about their weight during adolescence. Parents' negative comments can turn teenage self-consciousness into permanent unhappiness with one's body.

Parents have power. It's power they can start tapping in to when their kids are very young. For a start, they can refrain from reading their kids books with hateful portrayals of fat characters. A friend of mine who's a mom told me that when she read her daughter the *Little House on the Prairie* books, she carefully edited or explained the stereotypes and slurs about Native Americans, and when she read *Dr. Doolittle,* she skipped the descriptions of black people as savages and childlike idiots. But it never would have occurred to her not to share the fat slurs in so many kids' books. Kids pick up on those messages. And when you slap your own ass and talk about how "bad" you've been because you ate a piece of peach pie, or you wail about the size of your thighs, or you dish about a friend who "let herself go," your daughter is getting a clear message about your values.

Many parents today couch their fear of overweight in the language of nutrition and health. They discuss anxieties about letting their kids have trans fat and white sugar, but I'm convinced that what they're really obsessed with is the horrid possibility of having a fat child. Micromanaging children's food intake is a fast track to crazytown.

My view is this: Celebrate your children. Tell them they're amazing. Try not to harangue them about their eating. Praise them for painting a great picture, being a kind friend, doing their best in school. Go to their games and dance recitals. That's how real self-esteem takes root, not from being told how thin and pretty they are.

I was fortunate to have a mom who conveyed over and over that she treasured me, and not because of the way I looked. If you're a teenage girl reading this, and you're not so lucky to have a relative who makes you feel truly loved and accepted, whatever your size, I recommend surrounding yourself with other people who can help you feel good: friends, teachers, a friend's mom. Please know that the bad stuff in your life won't last forever. Learn to trust yourself and tune out the noise of the naysayers. Inside, there's a place that's *you,* separate from anything that's ever happened to you. Don't be afraid to change the world.

Today I'm sorry I burned so many of my old photographs, because I wish I could look back at how far I've come. I'm discovering that I don't have to turn my back on everything that came before I was happy. There's a lot I can learn from what made me miserable.

I still get mired in philosophical and theological questions. I've started occasionally attending a church near my home, one that isn't all about judging others. I try to remember the sentiment in a quotation that's been ascribed to both Plato and Philo of Alexandria: "Be kind, for everyone you meet is fighting a hard battle."

Reading *How to Practice: The Way to a Meaningful Life* by the Dalai Lama has helped me create a vision for how to live a spiritual life. I do see the mockability of a model quoting the Dalai Lama (OMG, I could equate bitchy hairstylists with the takeover of Tibet!), but Buddhist thinking helps me live in a world that believes the body is everything. Again, modeling is a microcosm of the wider culture. We live in a society that treats the body as if it's more important than the soul it houses. Reading the Dalai Lama reminds me that the body is a temporary vehicle. "Some people may be quite fat, others thin, some handsome, yet if I look at them with an X-ray machine, I see a room full of skeletons with huge eye sockets," The Dalai Lama says. "Such is the real nature of our body."

The Dalai Lama's distillation of the Buddha's teachings is this:

If possible, you should help others.
If that is not possible, at least you should do no harm.

Those are the guiding principles for how I try to live. And when I get too caught up in my own career, I look to my husband's for inspiration. Here he is teaching disadvantaged kids in a public school system that doesn't always support its teachers and in a culture that undervalues the vital work educators do. My job is not very important compared to that.

As I get older, I'm not entirely sure where my life's headed. I'd love to do more freelance styling for magazines, then design my own plus-size line. I adore clothes, and I understand fit. The challenges are different when you're not straight up and down, and two different size 16s could carry weight in entirely different places. It's an exciting challenge, figuring out what looks great in a range of sizes and on a variety of body types. One day I'd love to design accessories, too, and have a cosmetics line. I'd like to travel for at least a year, *Eat Pray Love*–style, before settling down to have a family. I definitely know I want to stay involved in the fashion world, because I really love what I do.

I wrote this book not only to tell my truth but also to encourage other women to embrace who they are. I want all girls to know this one fact above all: You can escape your own private Mississippi. Look at what happened to me in the nine years between Picture A and Picture B. My appearance in that breast cancer awareness campaign, and the notion that someone as sick as I used to be can now represent a realistic ideal of female beauty and health, is a little bit miraculous. Women should be able to look to me and think: She's beautiful. But also: I can look like that.

AUTHOR'S NOTE

In the preface to *A Moveable Feast,* Ernest Hemingway wrote, "For reasons **sufficient** to the writer, many places, people, observations and impressions have been left out of this book."

To which I say, "What he said."

Some names and identifying characteristics have been changed. Nonetheless, it's my true story.

ACKNOWLEDGMENTS

Endless thanks to Gary Dakin, without whom *none* of this would be possible. Father figure, agent, friend—you saw the big picture when no one else did. Thank you for believing in me and fighting for my dream. Thanks also to everyone at Ford, especially Jon Ilani, Jaclyn Sarka, Michele Pryor, Cathy Quinn, Caroline Poznanski, and of course, Katie Ford. Thanks also to John Caplan.

Thanks, too, to Carine Roitfeld, one of the chicest and strongest women I know; Kate Armenta, the former casting director at American *Vogue*; and Cynthia Xanthipi Joannides at *Glamour*, who booked me for one of my last jobs as a straight-size model. Cynthia expressed concern for my health, encouraged me to gain weight, and could not have been more supportive when I became a plus model. And she and her husband, Constantine, are my role models in marriage—thanks for showing me it's possible to have a normal life and work in fashion!

Jay Dunn, Robert Vega, and Kathy Quickert from Lane Bryant have been wonderful, and Lane Bryant as a whole has been there for me from the beginning. Thanks to Rachel at Evans for letting me pour my heart out, for listening like the wonderful mother you are, and for pushing plus-size style to the next level.

Steven Meisel changed my life with his vision and confidence in me. I can't thank him enough. Thanks, too, to Craig McDean, Ellen von Unwerth, Patrick Demarchelier, Matt Jones, Max Abadian, and all the other wonderful photographers I've learned so much from. Delois Ursini (who introduced me to Steven and is flat-out awesome), Raul Martinez (an innovative thinker who hired me for Dolce & Gabbana), Pat McGrath, Caroline Noseworthy, Lara Bonomo, Laurel Wells, Jennifer Venditti, and Stefanie Stein— thank you. Rachel Alexander and Ashley Graham have been tried-and-true friends and the most beautiful bridesmaids a girl could have.

Thank you to my Aunt Tracy, for acting as my chauffeur instead of watching Dr. Phil.

And of course, shout-out to my literary agent, Mark Reiter; as well as to my editor, Kerri Kolen; her assistant editor, Kate Ankofski; and everyone else at Simon & Schuster, especially David Rosenthal. You guys have been incredible. A million thanks to Ruven Afanador, who shot the perfect images for this book, creates a beautiful ambiance on every shoot, and has been consistently amazing to work with—Ruven, you are truly a master.

Marjorie, you and I had the ultimate adventure writing this book. Every emotion, memory, and thought were filtered through you. With all the garbled mess, you and I created my life story. You know me in a way most people never have, and I thank you for our partnership and most of all our friendship. This is just the beginning.

And to Greg: Thank you for everything.

Crystal Renn, June 2009

•   •   •

WILDLY effusive thanks to the never-thanked-with-sufficiently-wild-effusiveness Mark Reiter, as well as to Kerri Kolen and everyone at S&S. Thank you to Gayle Forman for editorial cheerleading. Thanks and love to Josie and Maxine, for being patient with my absence, and thanks to Jonathan picking up the parenting slack and keeping all those damn plates in the air. And thanks most of all to Crystal, for being a hilarious, sweet model of ambition and physical confidence. May my daughters grow up to be as comfortable in their bodies as you are.

Marjorie Ingall, June 2009

BIBLIOGRAPHY

Bacon, Linda, Ph.D. *Health at Every Size.* Dallas: BenBella, 2008.

Brumberg, Joan Jacobs. *The Body Project.* New York: Vintage, 1998.

Dalai Lama. *How to Practice: The Way to a Meaningful Life,* translated and edited by Jeffrey Hopkins, Ph.D. New York: Atria, 2002.

Gross, Michael. *Model: The Ugly Business of Beautiful Women.* New York: Harper, 2003.

Harding, Kate, and Marianne Kirby. *Lessons from the Fat-o-Sphere: Quit Dieting and Declare a Truce with Your Body.* New York: Perigee, 2009.

Kolata, Gina. *Rethinking Thin: The New Science of Weight Loss—and the Myths and Realities of Dieting.* New York: Picador, 2008.

Martin, Courtney E. *Perfect Girls, Starving Daughters: How the Quest for Perfection Is Harming Young Women.* New York: Berkley, 2008.

Pollan, Michael. *In Defense of Food: An Eater's Manifesto.* New York: Penguin, 2008.

PHOTO CREDITS

ABOUT THE AUTHORS

Crystal Renn is the leading plus-size model in America. At twenty-two years of age, she has appeared in four international editions of *Vogue*; starred in a Dolce & Gabbana ad campaign; served as the final model in Jean Paul Gaultier's Spring 2006 prêt-à-porter show in a gown that Gaultier designed specifically for her curvaceous figure; was the cover girl on an international edition of *Harper's Bazaar;* and has been photographed by Steven Meisel, Ellen von Unwerth, Ruven Afanador, and Patrick Demarchelier. She lives in Brooklyn.

Marjorie Ingall is a contributing writer at *Self* magazine and a columnist for *Tablet*. She has written for many other publications, including *The New York Times, Glamour, Redbook, Seventeen, Ms., Food & Wine, Wired, The Forward,* and the late, lamented *Sassy,* where she was the senior writer and health editor. At *Sassy,* she won several awards for health and social issues coverage. She is the author of *The Field Guild to North American Males;* the co-author of a sex-ed book for teenagers, *Smart Sex;* and a former writer/producer at the Oxygen TV network.